VIZ GRAPHIC NOVEL

Di Gi Charat ™

VOL. 1

Di Gi Charat ™
Volume 1

English Adaptation by
Gerard Jones

Translation/Mari Morimoto
Touch-up & Lettering/Andy Ristaino
Cover & Graphic Design/Yuki Shimotoku
Editor/Eric Searleman

Managing Editor/Annette Roman
VP of Sales & Marketing/Rick Bauer
VP of Editorial/Hyoe Narita
Publisher/Seiji Horibuchi

Published by Viz, LLC.
P.O. Box 77064
San Francisco, CA 94107

10 9 8 7 6 5 4 3 2 1
First printing, January 2003

  store.viz.com
www.viz.com

CONTENTS

Di Gi Charat

1ST PARTY

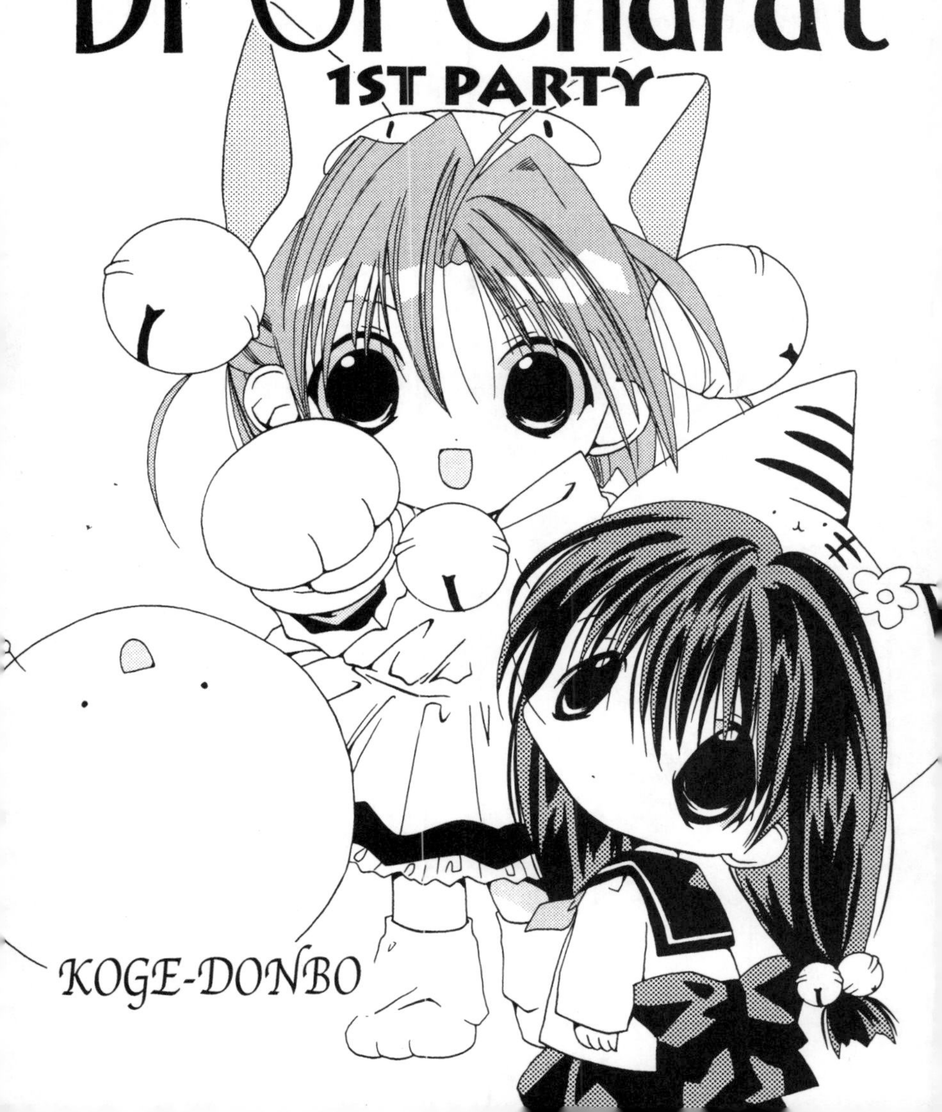

KOGE-DONBO

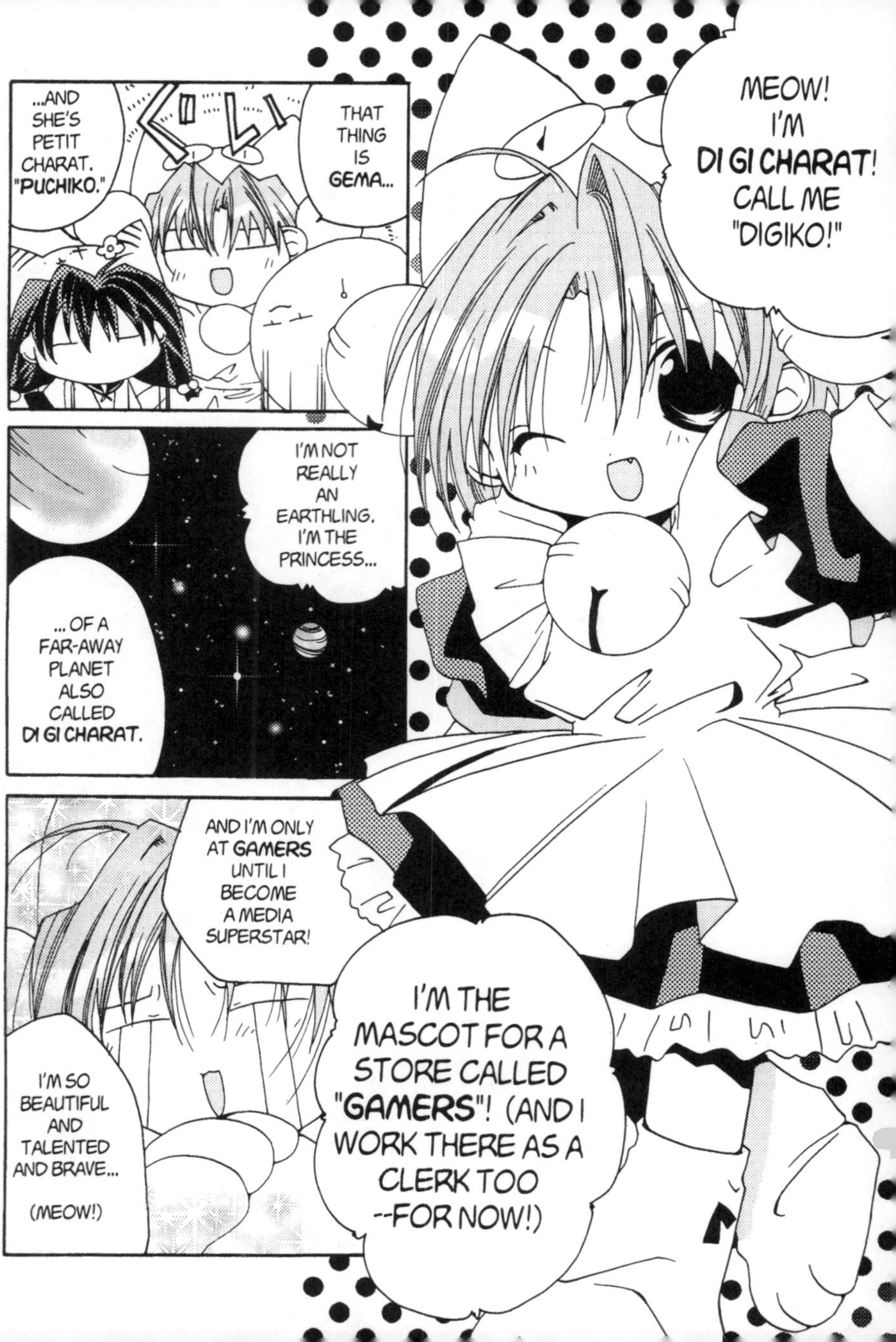
MEOW! I'M DI GI CHARAT! CALL ME "DIGIKO!"
I'M THE MASCOT FOR A STORE CALLED "GAMERS"! (AND I WORK THERE AS A CLERK TOO --FOR NOW!)
THAT THING IS GEMA...
...AND SHE'S PETIT CHARAT. "PUCHIKO."
I'M NOT REALLY AN EARTHLING. I'M THE PRINCESS...
... OF A FAR-AWAY PLANET ALSO CALLED DI GI CHARAT.
AND I'M ONLY AT GAMERS UNTIL I BECOME A MEDIA SUPERSTAR!
I'M SO BEAUTIFUL AND TALENTED AND BRAVE...
(MEOW!)

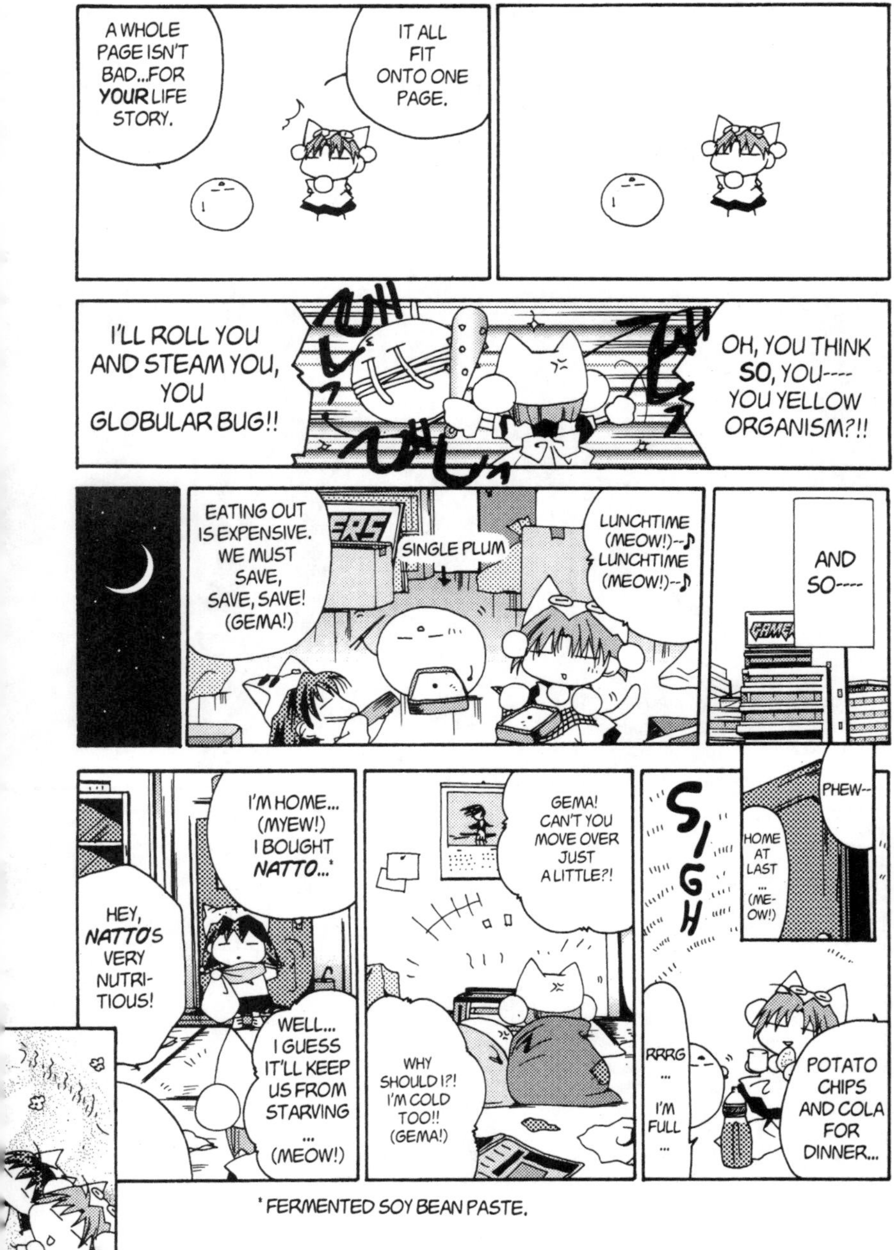
IT ALL FIT ONTO ONE PAGE.
A WHOLE PAGE ISN'T BAD...FOR **YOUR** LIFE STORY.
OH, YOU THINK **SO**, YOU---- YOU YELLOW ORGANISM?!!
I'LL ROLL YOU AND STEAM YOU, YOU GLOBULAR BUG!!
AND SO----
LUNCHTIME (MEOW!)--♪ LUNCHTIME (MEOW!)--♪
SINGLE PLUM
EATING OUT IS EXPENSIVE. WE MUST SAVE, SAVE, SAVE! (GEMA!)
PHEW--
HOME AT LAST ... (ME-OW!)
SIGH
POTATO CHIPS AND COLA FOR DINNER...
RRRG ... I'M FULL ...
GEMA! CAN'T YOU MOVE OVER JUST A LITTLE?!
WHY SHOULD I?! I'M COLD TOO!! (GEMA!)
I'M HOME... (MYEW!) I BOUGHT ***NATTO***...*
HEY, ***NATTO***'S VERY NUTRITIOUS!
WELL... I GUESS IT'LL KEEP US FROM STARVING ... (MEOW!)

* FERMENTED SOY BEAN PASTE.

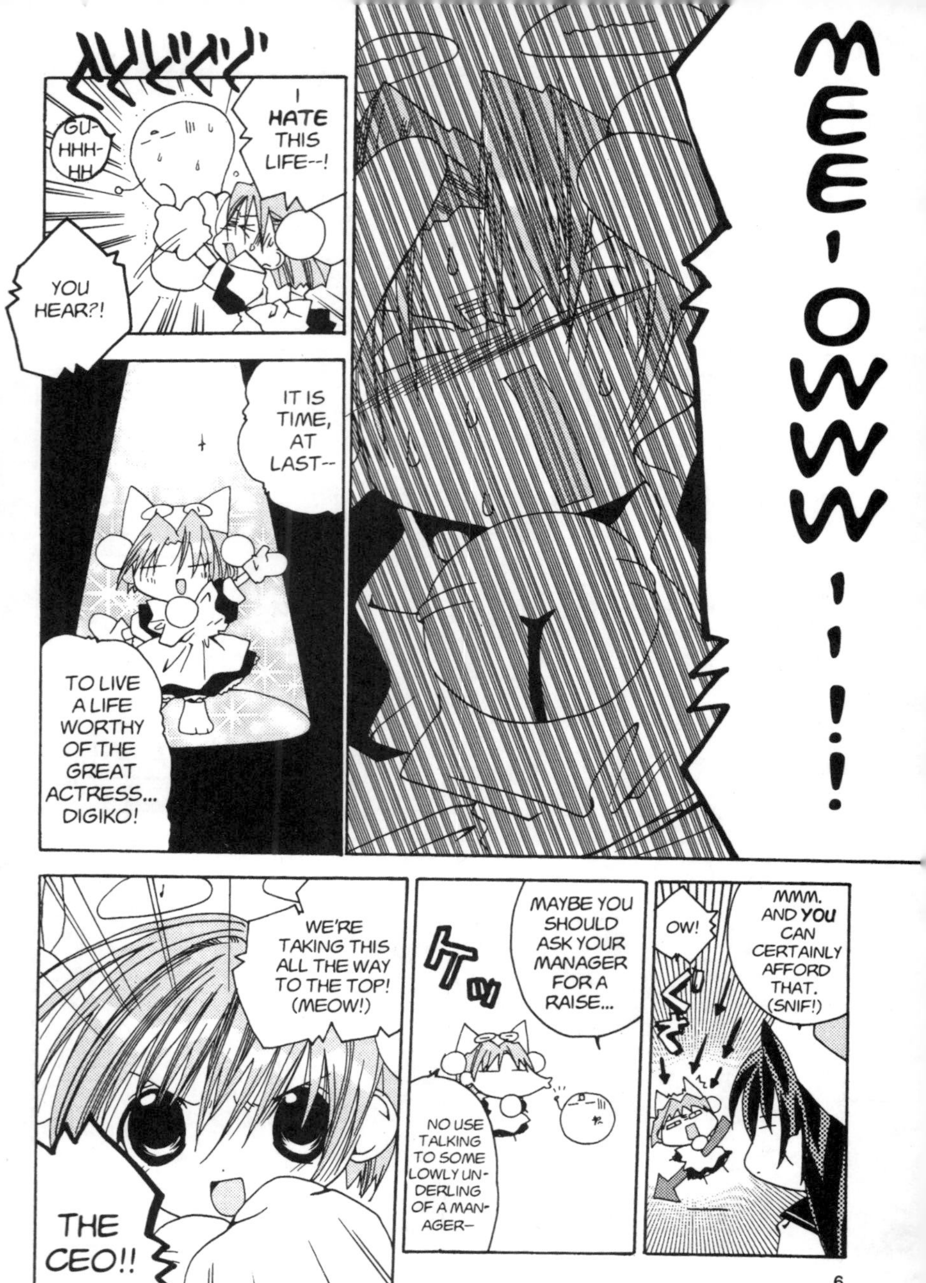
MEE-OWWW!!!
I HATE THIS LIFE--!
GU-HHH-HH
YOU HEAR?!
IT IS TIME, AT LAST--
TO LIVE A LIFE WORTHY OF THE GREAT ACTRESS... DIGIKO!
MMM. AND YOU CAN CERTAINLY AFFORD THAT. (SNIF!)
OW!
MAYBE YOU SHOULD ASK YOUR MANAGER FOR A RAISE...
NO USE TALKING TO SOME LOWLY UNDERLING OF A MANAGER–
WE'RE TAKING THIS ALL THE WAY TO THE TOP! (MEOW!)
THE CEO!!

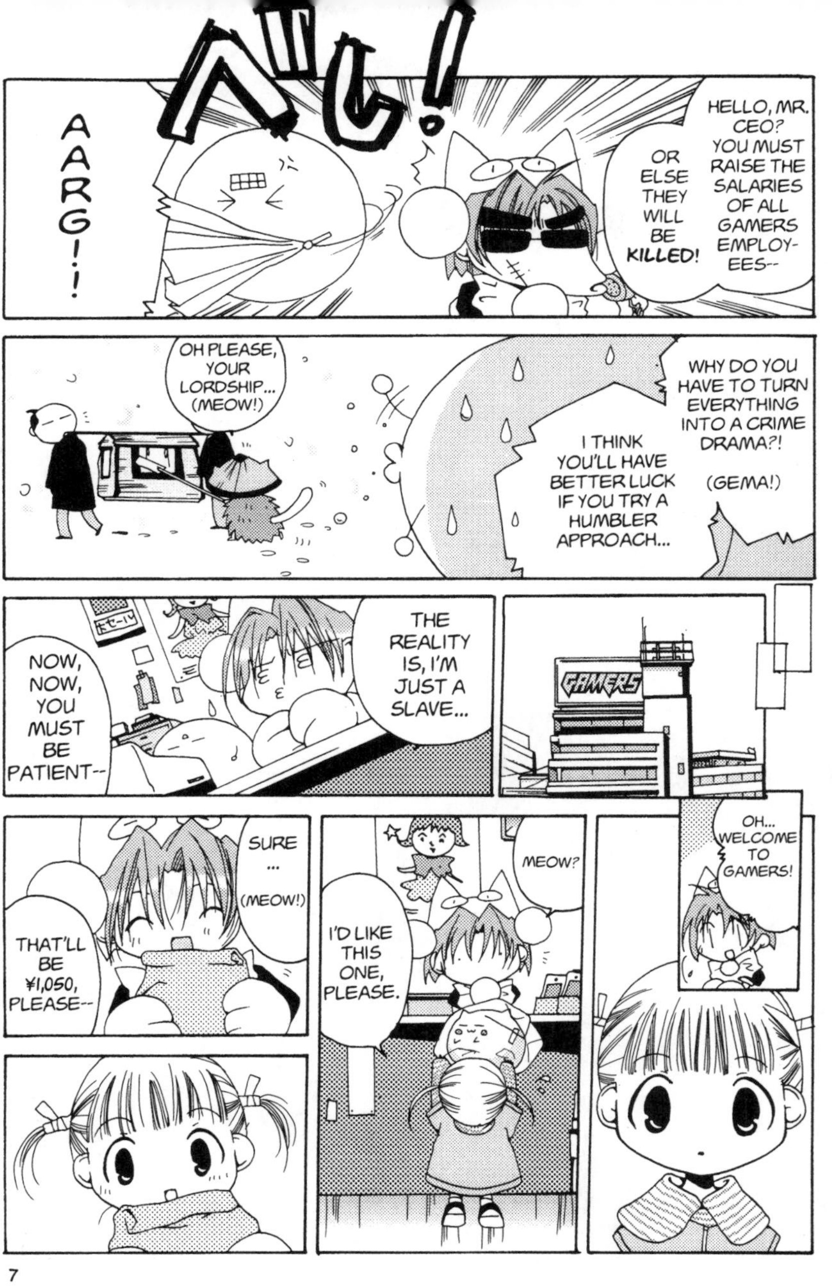

べし!
HELLO, MR. CEO? YOU MUST RAISE THE SALARIES OF ALL GAMERS EMPLOYEES--
OR ELSE THEY WILL BE KILLED!
AARG!!
WHY DO YOU HAVE TO TURN EVERYTHING INTO A CRIME DRAMA?!
(GEMA!)
I THINK YOU'LL HAVE BETTER LUCK IF YOU TRY A HUMBLER APPROACH...
OH PLEASE, YOUR LORDSHIP... (MEOW!)
GAMERS
THE REALITY IS, I'M JUST A SLAVE...
NOW, NOW, YOU MUST BE PATIENT--
OH... WELCOME TO GAMERS!
MEOW?
I'D LIKE THIS ONE, PLEASE.
SURE ... (MEOW!)
THAT'LL BE ¥1,050, PLEASE--

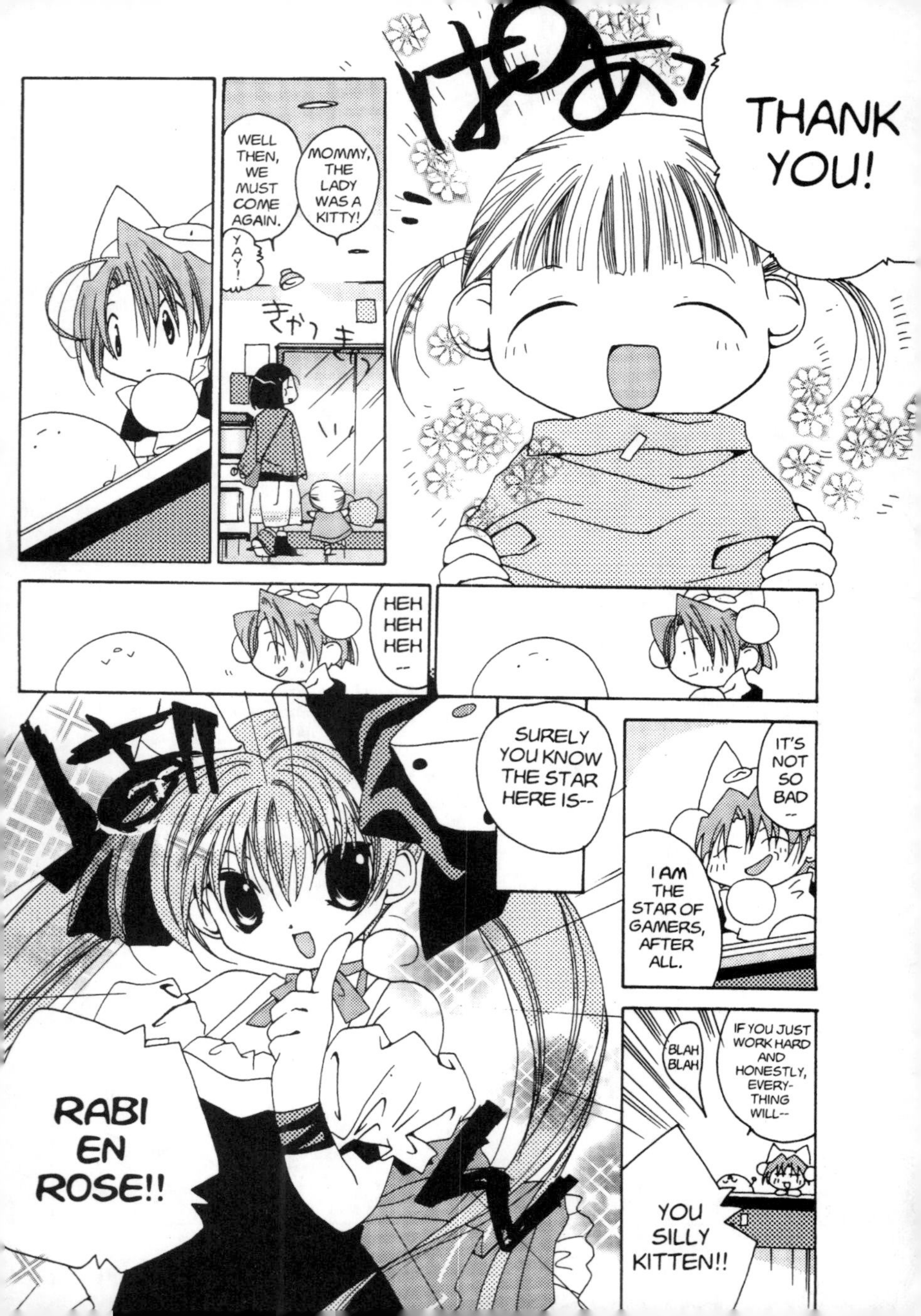
はあっ
THANK YOU!
MOMMY, THE LADY WAS A KITTY!
WELL THEN, WE MUST COME AGAIN.
YAY!
きゃっ きゃっ
HEH HEH HEH --
IT'S NOT SO BAD --
I AM THE STAR OF GAMERS, AFTER ALL.
IF YOU JUST WORK HARD AND HONESTLY, EVERY-THING WILL--
BLAH BLAH
YOU SILLY KITTEN!!
SURELY YOU KNOW THE STAR HERE IS--
RABI EN ROSE!!

2ND PARTY

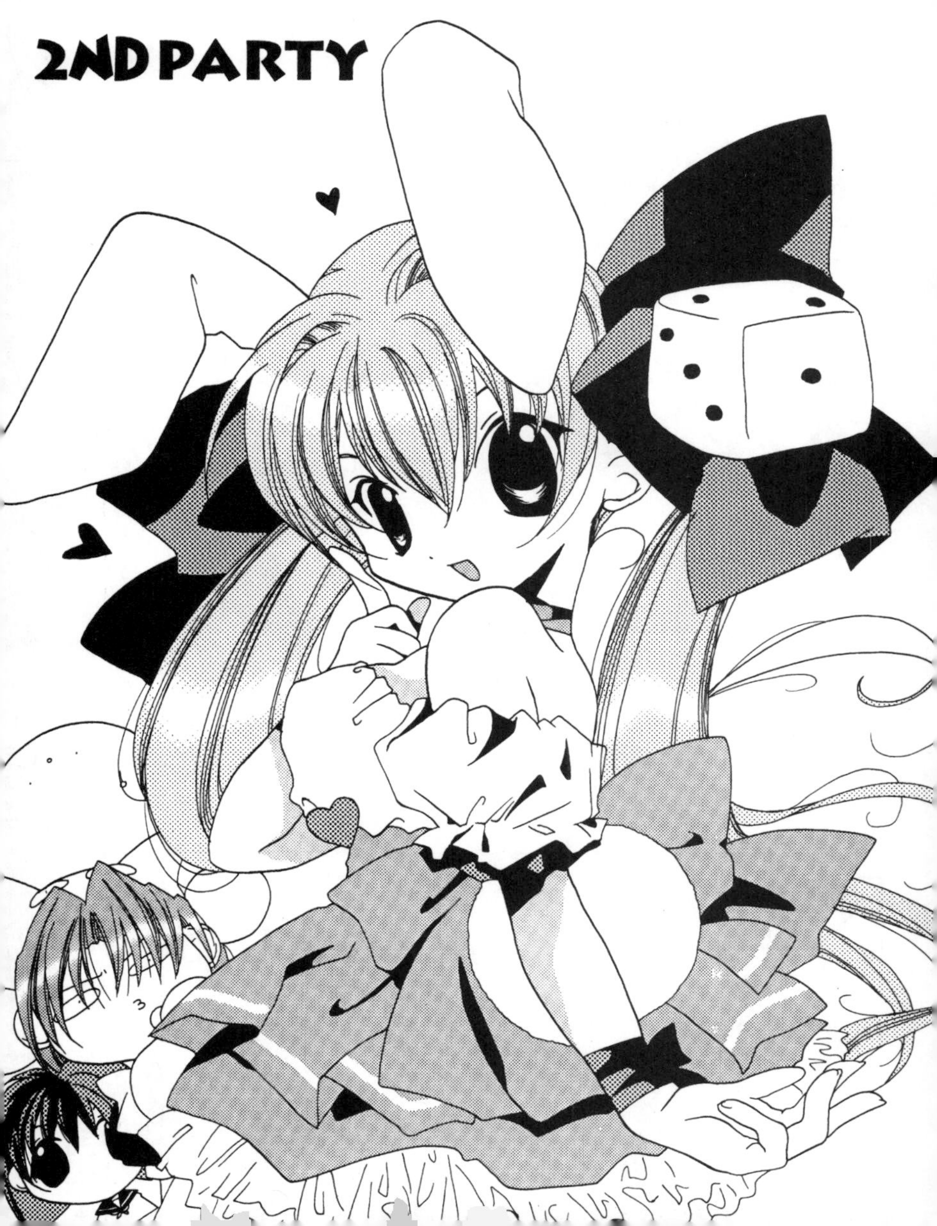

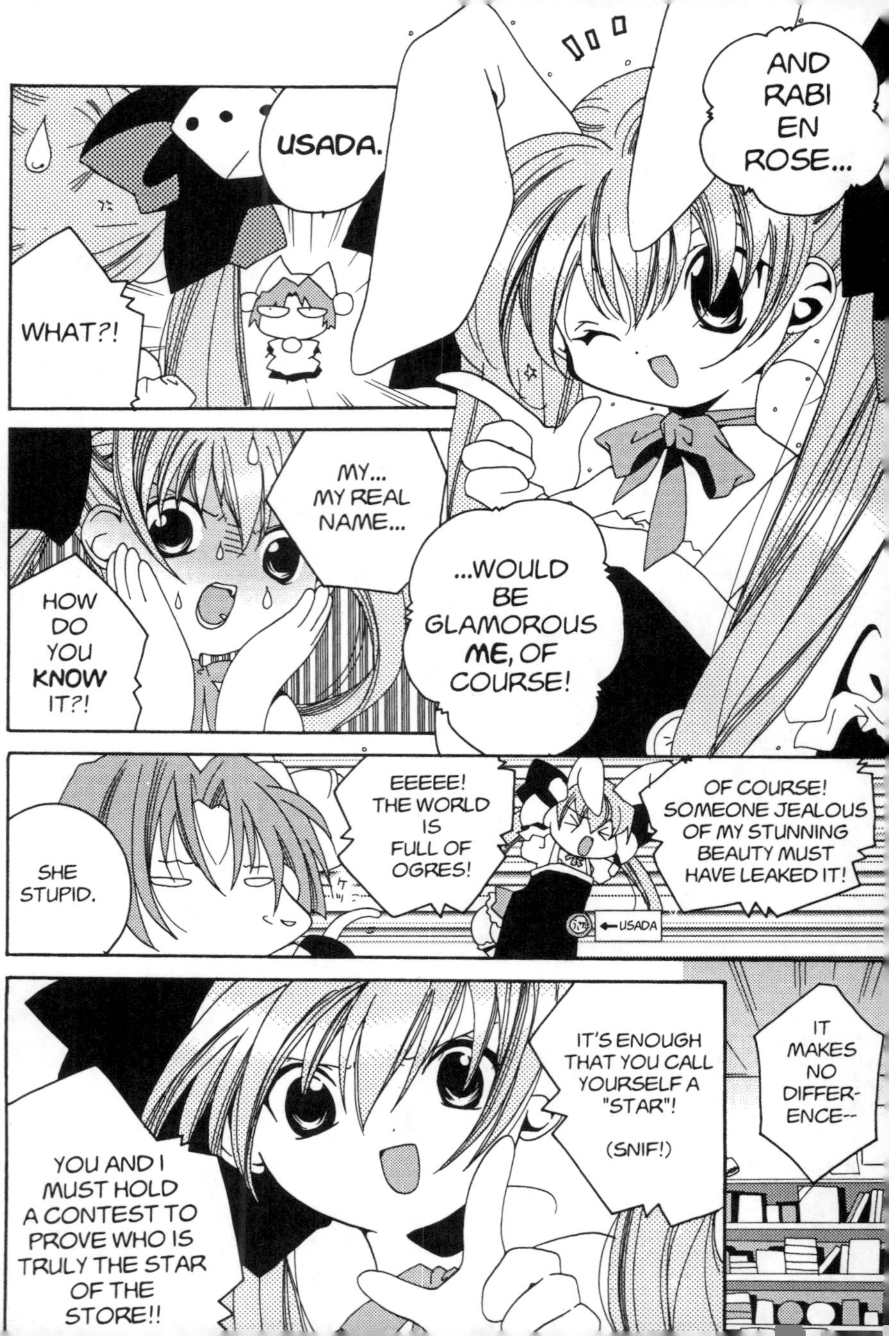
AND RABI EN ROSE...
USADA.
WHAT?!
MY... MY REAL NAME...
HOW DO YOU **KNOW** IT?!
...WOULD BE GLAMOROUS **ME**, OF COURSE!
OF COURSE! SOMEONE JEALOUS OF MY STUNNING BEAUTY MUST HAVE LEAKED IT!
EEEEE! THE WORLD IS FULL OF OGRES!
USADA
SHE STUPID.
IT MAKES NO DIFFERENCE--
IT'S ENOUGH THAT YOU CALL YOURSELF A "STAR"!
(SNIF!)
YOU AND I MUST HOLD A CONTEST TO PROVE WHO IS TRULY THE STAR OF THE STORE!!

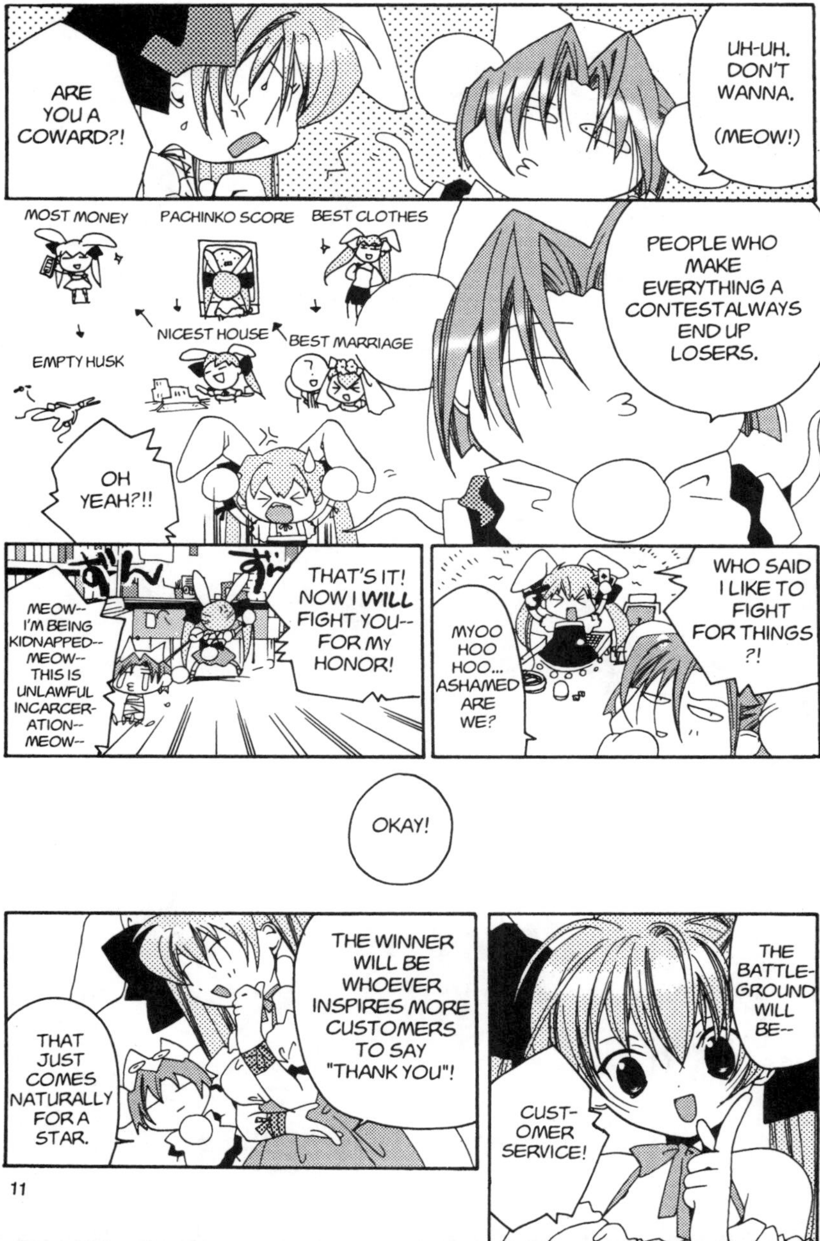
UH-UH. DON'T WANNA. (MEOW!)
ARE YOU A COWARD?!
PEOPLE WHO MAKE EVERYTHING A CONTESTALWAYS END UP LOSERS.
BEST CLOTHES
PACHINKO SCORE
MOST MONEY
BEST MARRIAGE
NICEST HOUSE
EMPTY HUSK
OH YEAH?!!
WHO SAID I LIKE TO FIGHT FOR THINGS ?!
MYOO HOO HOO... ASHAMED ARE WE?
ずん ずん
THAT'S IT! NOW I **WILL** FIGHT YOU-- FOR MY HONOR!
MEOW-- I'M BEING KIDNAPPED-- MEOW-- THIS IS UNLAWFUL INCARCER-ATION-- MEOW--
OKAY!
THE BATTLE-GROUND WILL BE--
CUST-OMER SERVICE!
THE WINNER WILL BE WHOEVER INSPIRES MORE CUSTOMERS TO SAY "THANK YOU"!
THAT JUST COMES NATURALLY FOR A STAR.

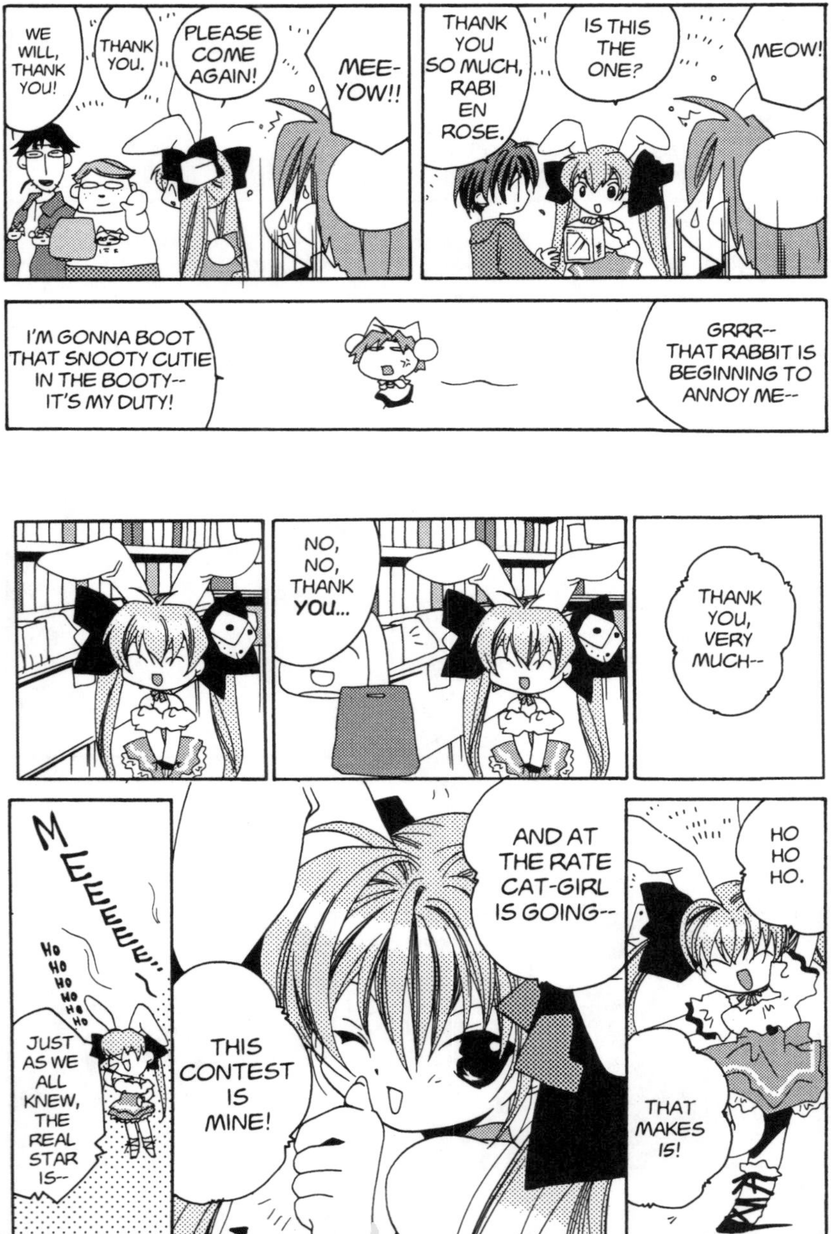
MEOW!
IS THIS THE ONE?
THANK YOU SO MUCH, RABI EN ROSE.
MEE-YOW!!
PLEASE COME AGAIN!
THANK YOU.
WE WILL, THANK YOU!
GRRR-- THAT RABBIT IS BEGINNING TO ANNOY ME--
I'M GONNA BOOT THAT SNOOTY CUTIE IN THE BOOTY-- IT'S MY DUTY!
THANK YOU, VERY MUCH--
NO, NO, THANK **YOU**...
HO HO HO.
THAT MAKES 15!
AND AT THE RATE CAT-GIRL IS GOING--
THIS CONTEST IS MINE!
MEEEEEEE...
HO HO HO HO HO HO HO
JUST AS WE ALL KNEW, THE REAL STAR IS--

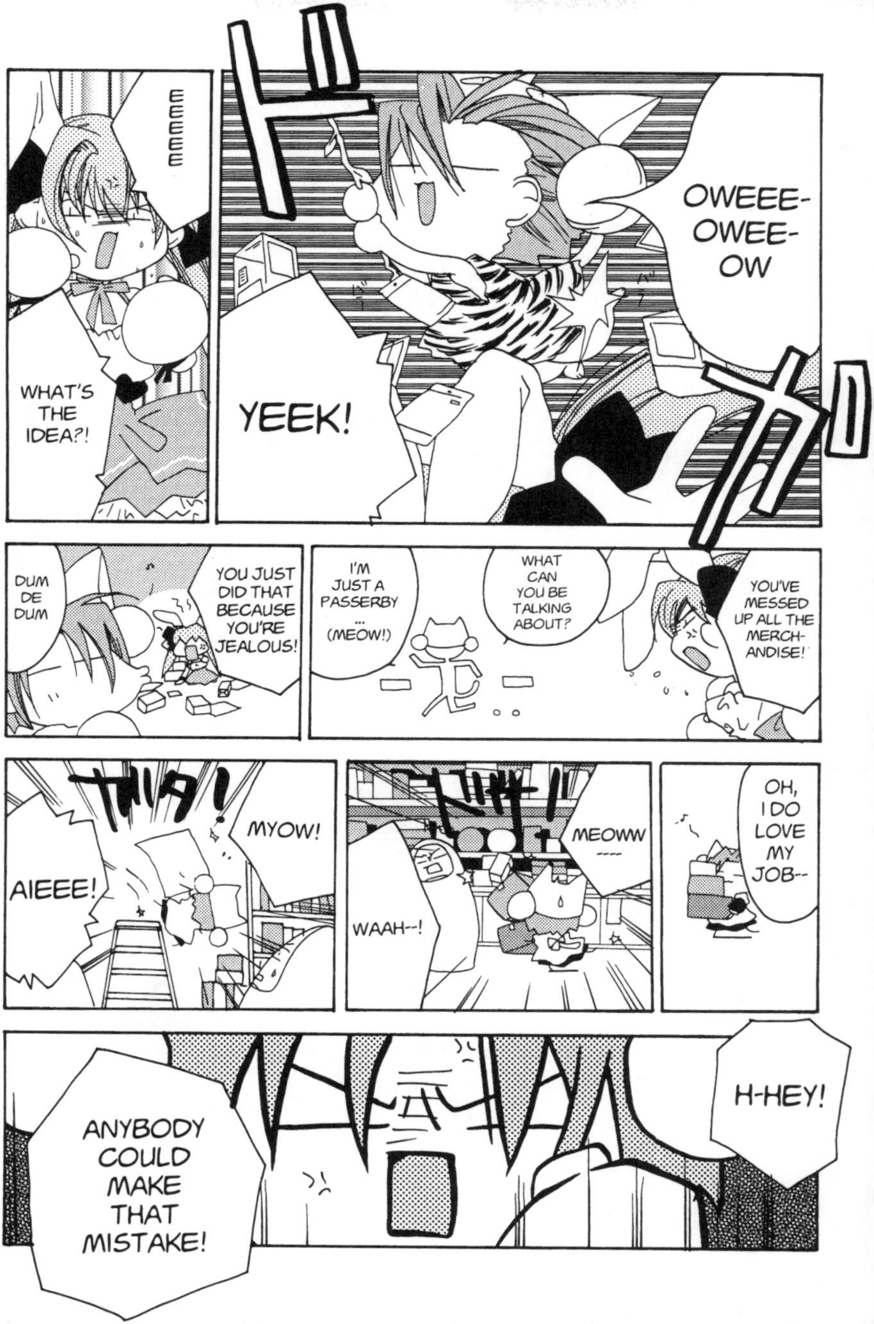
OWEEE-OWEEE-OW
YEEK!
EEEEEE
WHAT'S THE IDEA?!
YOU'VE MESSED UP ALL THE MERCHANDISE!
WHAT CAN YOU BE TALKING ABOUT?
I'M JUST A PASSERBY ... (MEOW!)
YOU JUST DID THAT BECAUSE YOU'RE JEALOUS!
DUM DE DUM
OH, I DO LOVE MY JOB--
MEOWW ----
WAAH--!
THWAP!
MYOW!
AIEEE!
H-HEY!
ANYBODY COULD MAKE THAT MISTAKE!

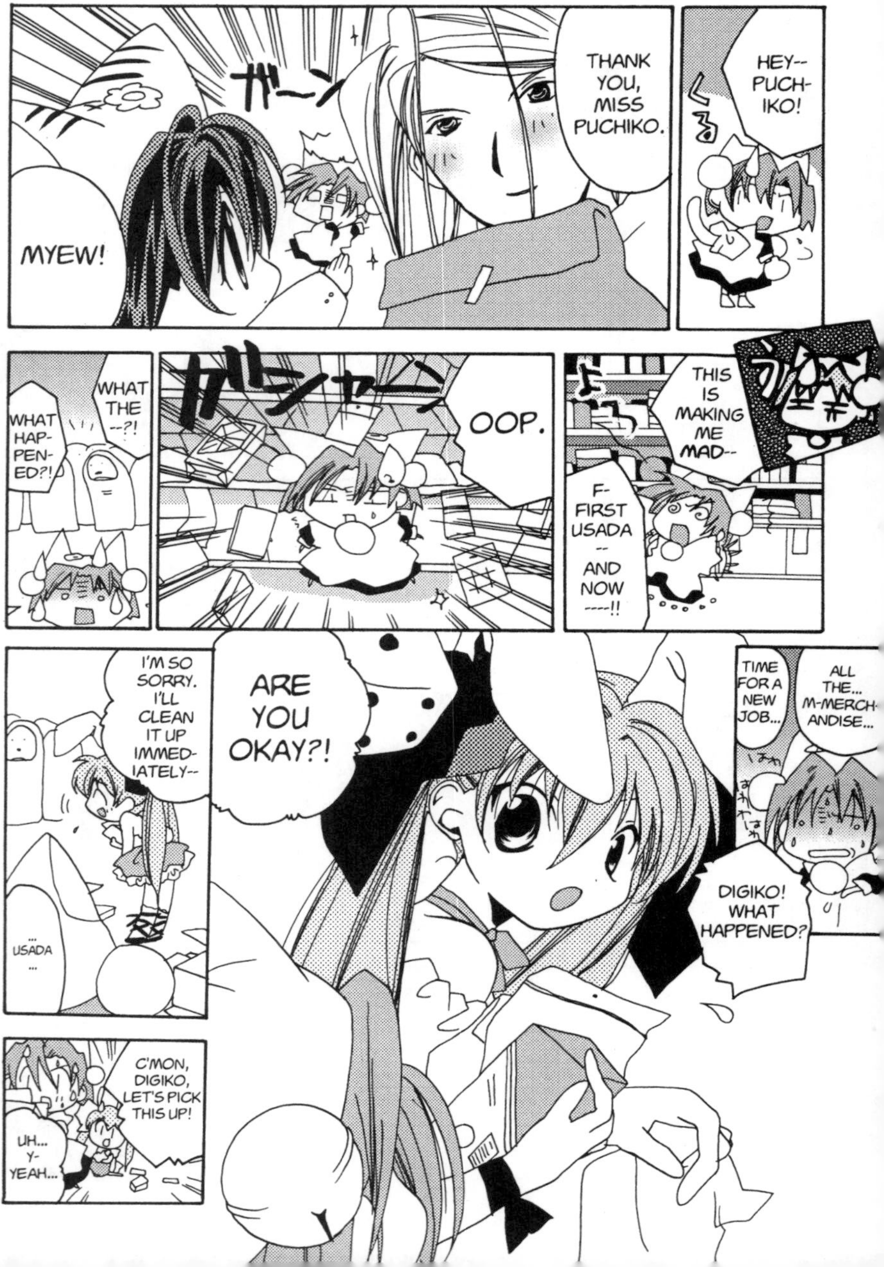
HEY-- PUCHIKO!
THANK YOU, MISS PUCHIKO.
MYEW!
THIS IS MAKING ME MAD--
F-FIRST USADA -- AND NOW ----!!
OOP.
WHAT THE --?!
WHAT HAPPENED?!
ALL THE... M-MERCHANDISE...
TIME FOR A NEW JOB...
DIGIKO! WHAT HAPPENED?
ARE YOU OKAY?!
I'M SO SORRY. I'LL CLEAN IT UP IMMEDIATELY--
... USADA ...
C'MON, DIGIKO, LET'S PICK THIS UP!
UH... Y-YEAH...

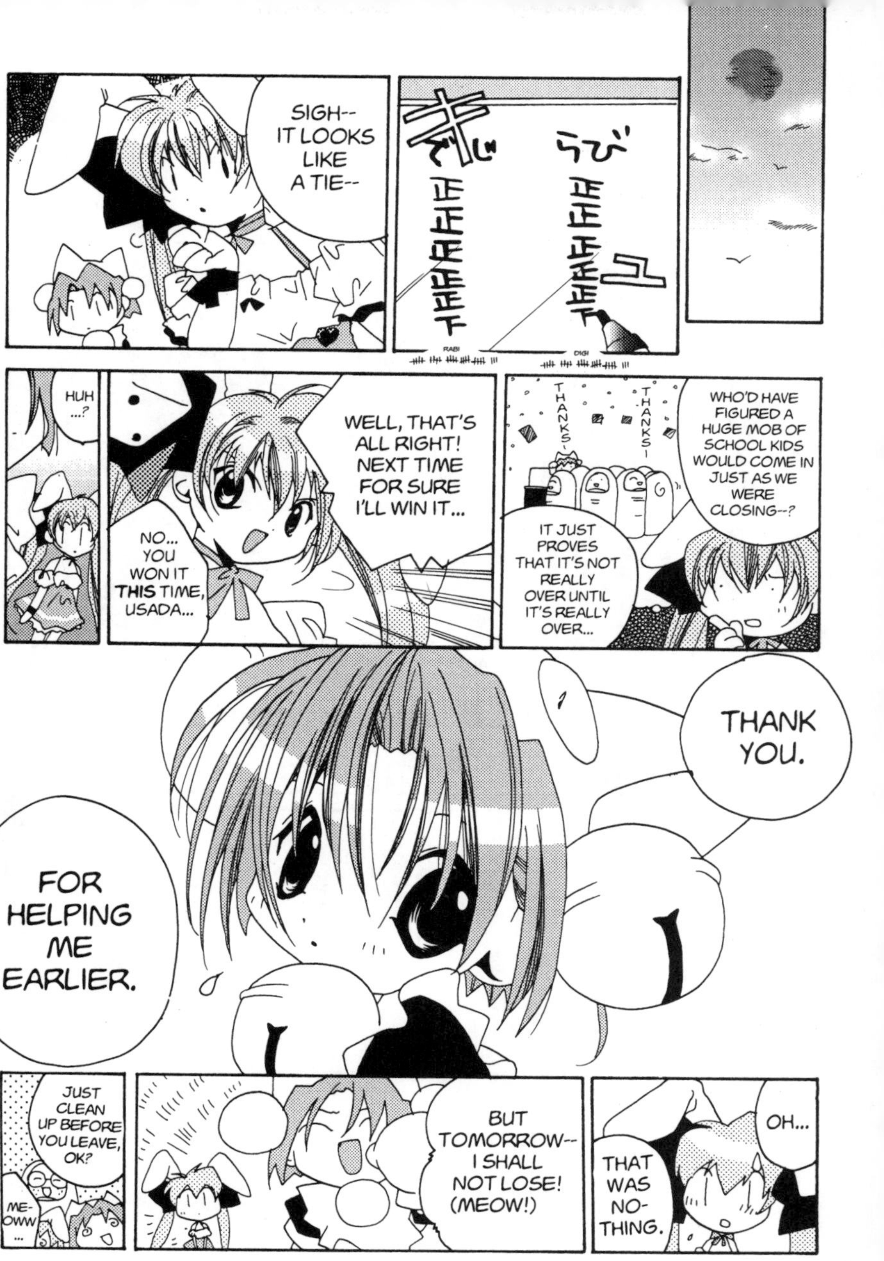
RABI
DIGI
SIGH-- IT LOOKS LIKE A TIE--
WHO'D HAVE FIGURED A HUGE MOB OF SCHOOL KIDS WOULD COME IN JUST AS WE WERE CLOSING--?
THANKS!
THANKS!
IT JUST PROVES THAT IT'S NOT REALLY OVER UNTIL IT'S REALLY OVER...
WELL, THAT'S ALL RIGHT! NEXT TIME FOR SURE I'LL WIN IT...
NO... YOU WON IT THIS TIME, USADA...
HUH ...?
THANK YOU.
FOR HELPING ME EARLIER.
OH...
THAT WAS NO-THING.
BUT TOMORROW-- I SHALL NOT LOSE! (MEOW!)
JUST CLEAN UP BEFORE YOU LEAVE, OK?
ME-OWW ...

THIS RAN ORIGINALLY IN **DENGEKI COMIC GAO** IN JAPAN. SORRY, BUT THEY ARE NO LONGER ACCEPTING ORDERS. (AND YOU MIGHT HAVE TROUBLE BUYING A ¥300 MONEY ORDER AT YOUR LOCAL POST OFFICE ANYWAY!)

LAST PARTY

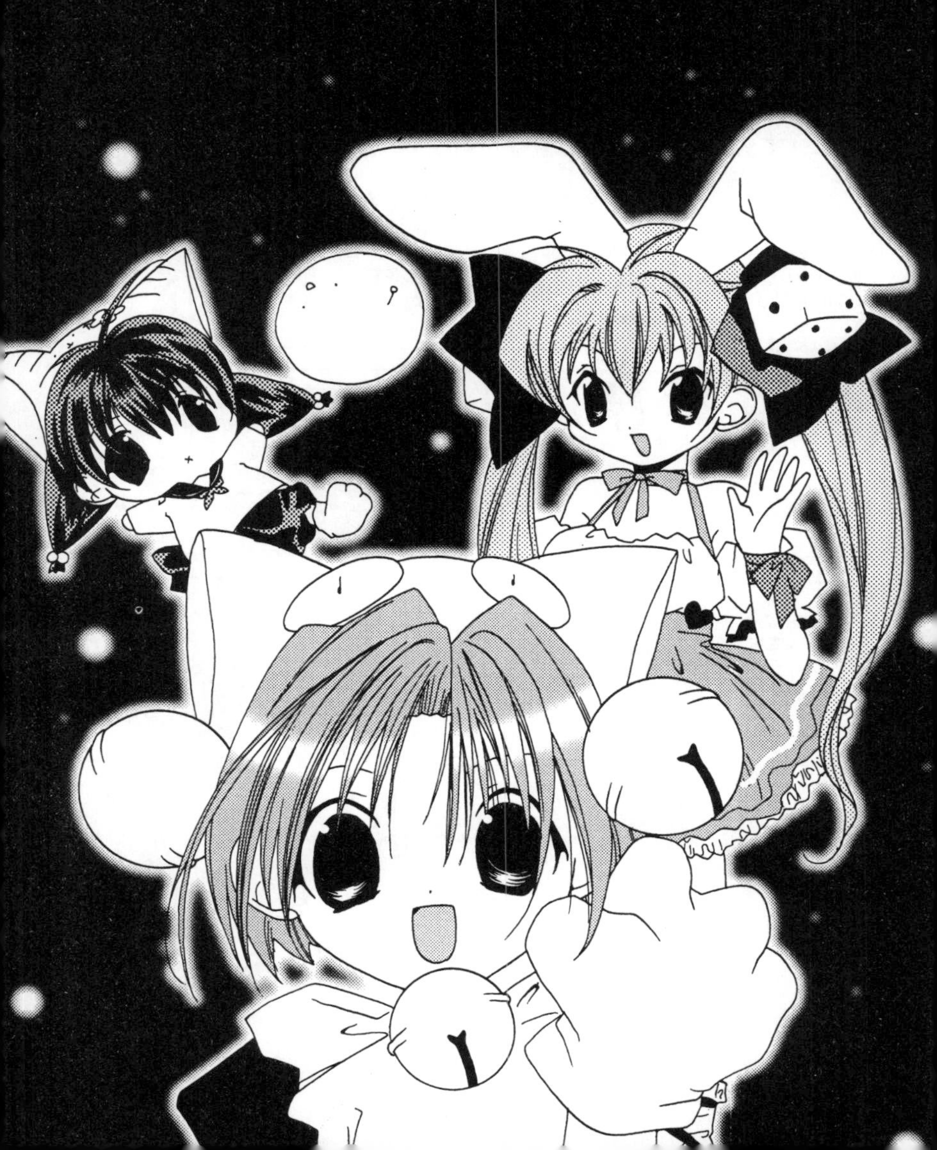

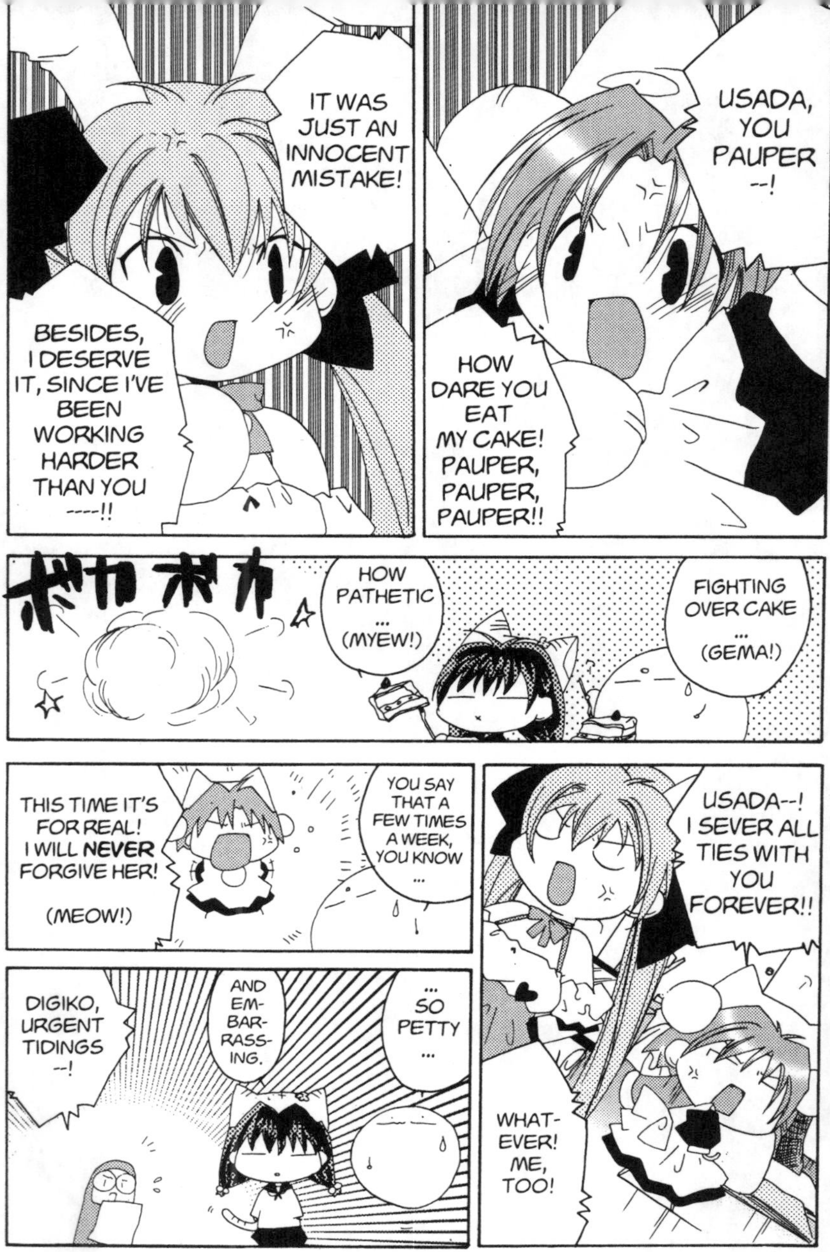
USADA, YOU PAUPER --!
HOW DARE YOU EAT MY CAKE! PAUPER, PAUPER, PAUPER!!
IT WAS JUST AN INNOCENT MISTAKE!
BESIDES, I DESERVE IT, SINCE I'VE BEEN WORKING HARDER THAN YOU ----!!
FIGHTING OVER CAKE ... (GEMA!)
HOW PATHETIC ... (MYEW!)
ポカポカ
USADA--! I SEVER ALL TIES WITH YOU FOREVER!!
WHAT-EVER! ME, TOO!
YOU SAY THAT A FEW TIMES A WEEK, YOU KNOW ...
THIS TIME IT'S FOR REAL! I WILL **NEVER** FORGIVE HER! (MEOW!)
... SO PETTY ...
AND EM-BAR-RASS-ING.
DIGIKO, URGENT TIDINGS --!

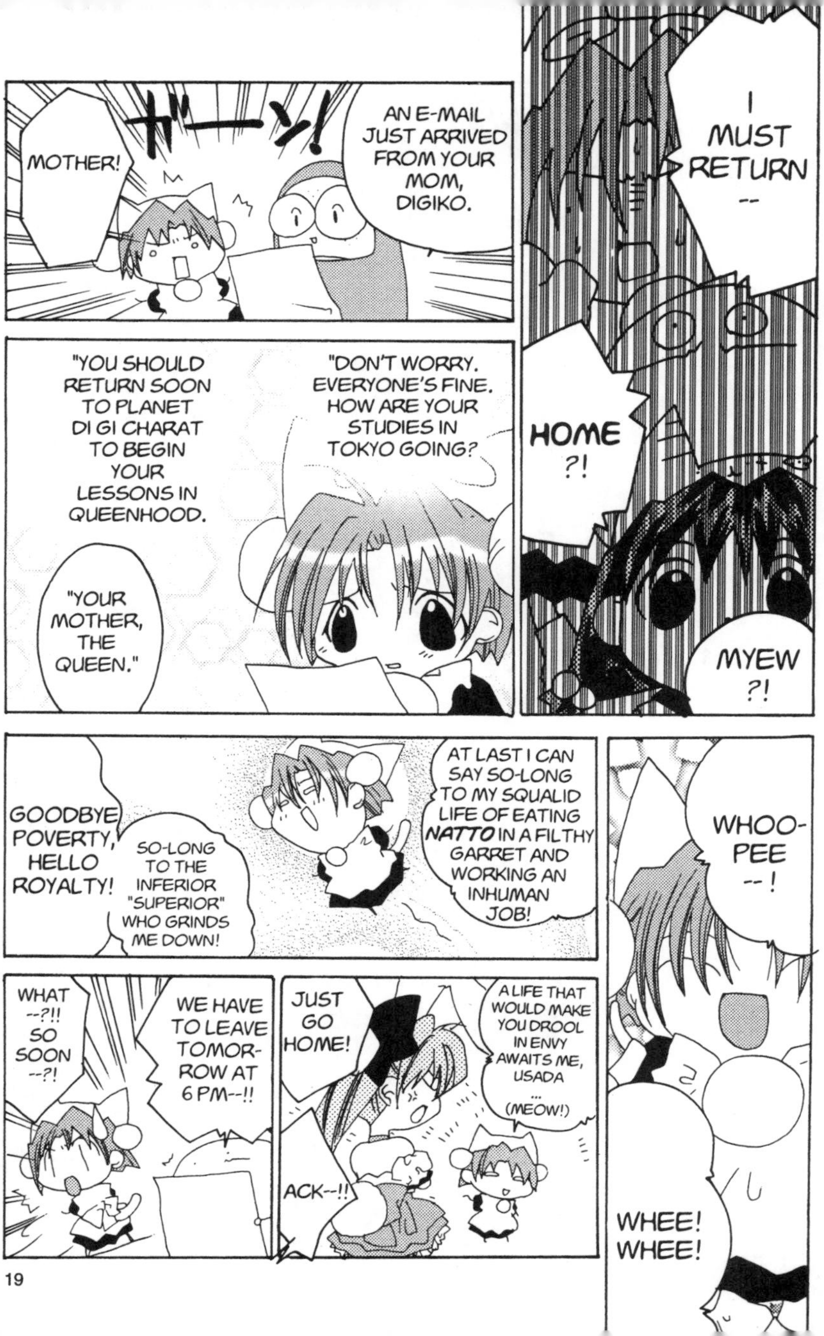

I MUST RETURN --
HOME ?!
MYEW ?!
AN E-MAIL JUST ARRIVED FROM YOUR MOM, DIGIKO.
MOTHER!
"DON'T WORRY. EVERYONE'S FINE. HOW ARE YOUR STUDIES IN TOKYO GOING?
"YOU SHOULD RETURN SOON TO PLANET DI GI CHARAT TO BEGIN YOUR LESSONS IN QUEENHOOD.
"YOUR MOTHER, THE QUEEN."
WHOO-PEE --!
WHEE! WHEE!
AT LAST I CAN SAY SO-LONG TO MY SQUALID LIFE OF EATING *NATTO* IN A FILTHY GARRET AND WORKING AN INHUMAN JOB!
SO-LONG TO THE INFERIOR "SUPERIOR" WHO GRINDS ME DOWN!
GOODBYE POVERTY, HELLO ROYALTY!
A LIFE THAT WOULD MAKE YOU DROOL IN ENVY AWAITS ME, USADA ... (MEOW!)
JUST GO HOME!
ACK--!!
WE HAVE TO LEAVE TOMOR-ROW AT 6 PM--!!
WHAT --?!! SO SOON --?!

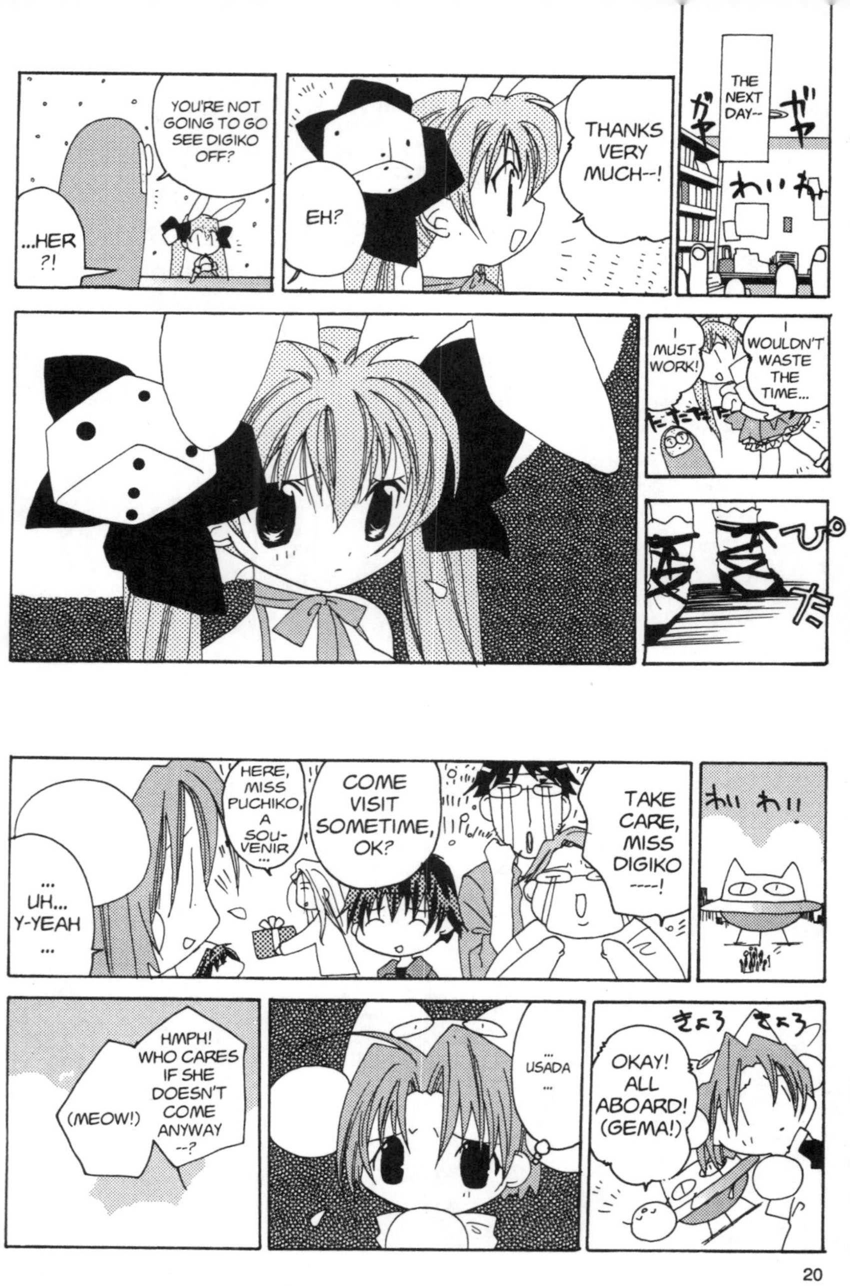
THE NEXT DAY--
ガヤガヤ
わいわい
THANKS VERY MUCH--!
EH?
YOU'RE NOT GOING TO GO SEE DIGIKO OFF?
...HER ?!
I WOULDN'T WASTE THE TIME...
I MUST WORK!
だだだだ
わいわい!!
TAKE CARE, MISS DIGIKO ----!
COME VISIT SOMETIME, OK?
HERE, MISS PUCHIKO, A SOU- VENIR ...
... UH... Y-YEAH ...
きょろ きょろ
OKAY! ALL ABOARD! (GEMA!)
... USADA ...
HMPH! WHO CARES IF SHE DOESN'T COME ANYWAY --?
(MEOW!)

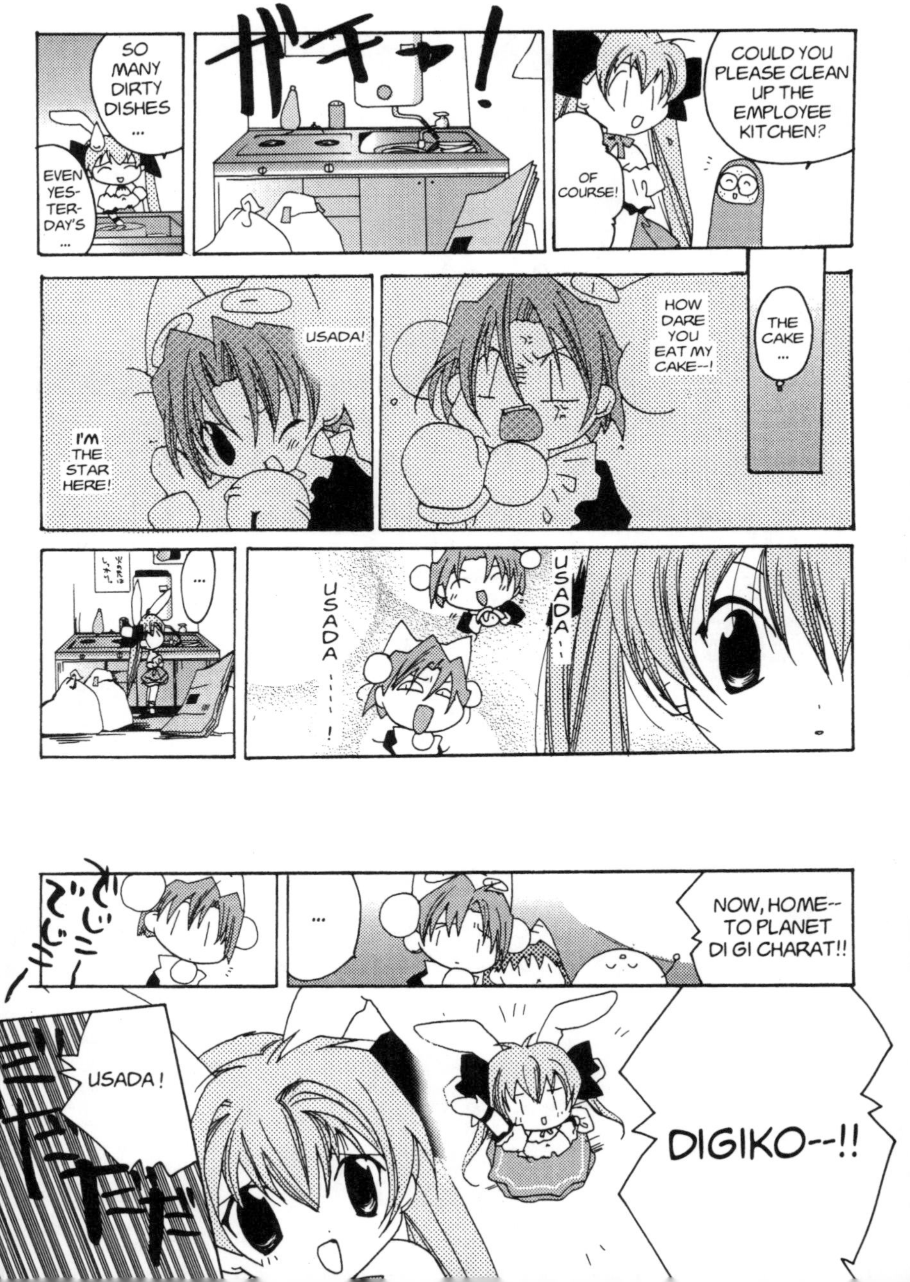
COULD YOU PLEASE CLEAN UP THE EMPLOYEE KITCHEN?
OF COURSE!
ガチャ!
SO MANY DIRTY DISHES ...
EVEN YES-TER-DAY'S ...
THE CAKE ...
HOW DARE YOU EAT MY CAKE--!
USADA!
I'M THE STAR HERE!
USADA ...!
USADA ....!
...
NOW, HOME-- TO PLANET DI GI CHARAT!!
...
DIGIKO--!!
USADA!

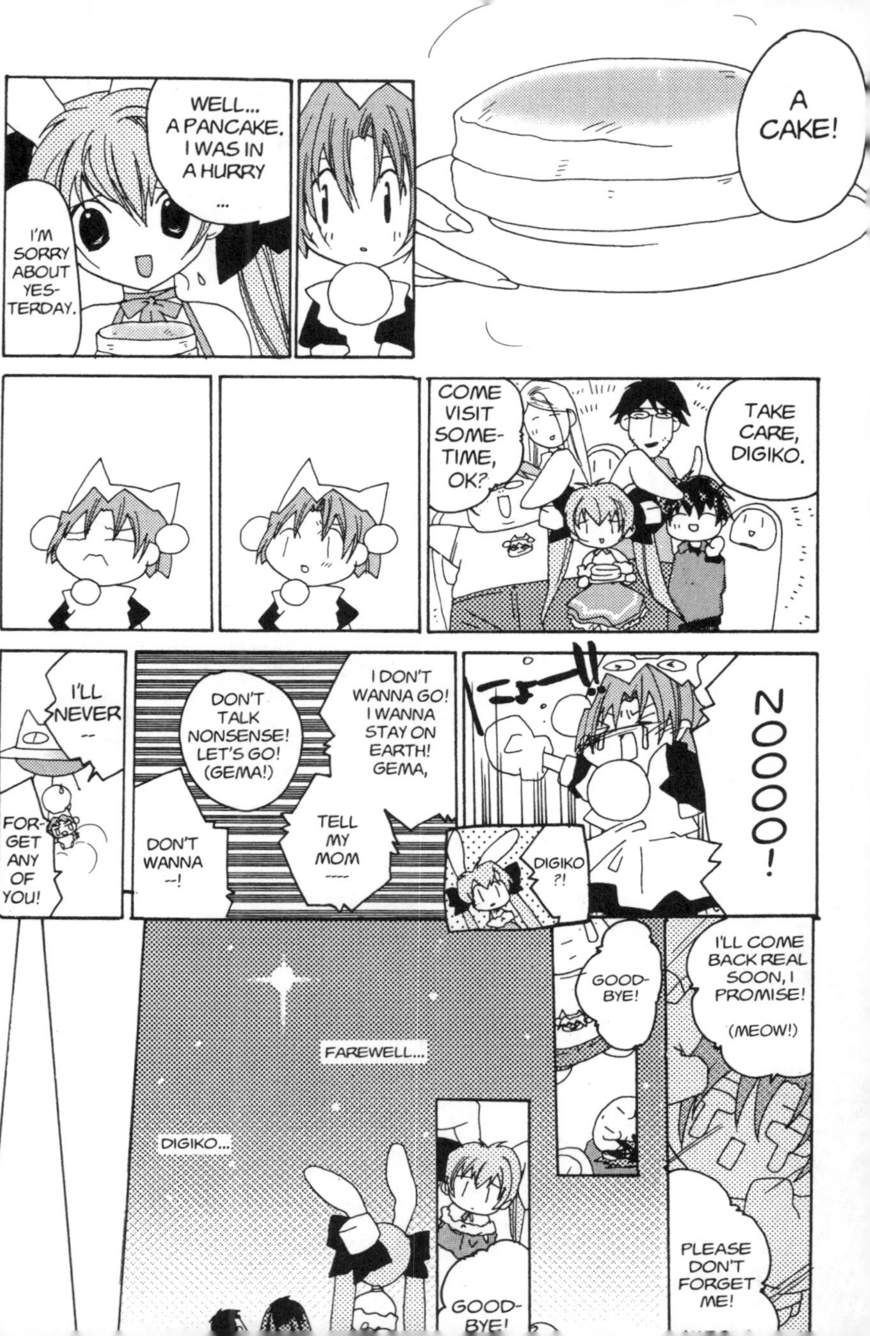
A CAKE!
WELL... A PANCAKE. I WAS IN A HURRY ...
I'M SORRY ABOUT YES-TERDAY.
TAKE CARE, DIGIKO.
COME VISIT SOME-TIME, OK?
NOOOOO!
DIGIKO ?!
I DON'T WANNA GO! I WANNA STAY ON EARTH! GEMA,
DON'T TALK NONSENSE! LET'S GO! (GEMA!)
TELL MY MOM ----
DON'T WANNA --!
I'LL NEVER --
FOR-GET ANY OF YOU!
I'LL COME BACK REAL SOON, I PROMISE!
(MEOW!)
PLEASE DON'T FORGET ME!
GOOD-BYE!
FAREWELL...
DIGIKO...
GOOD-BYE!

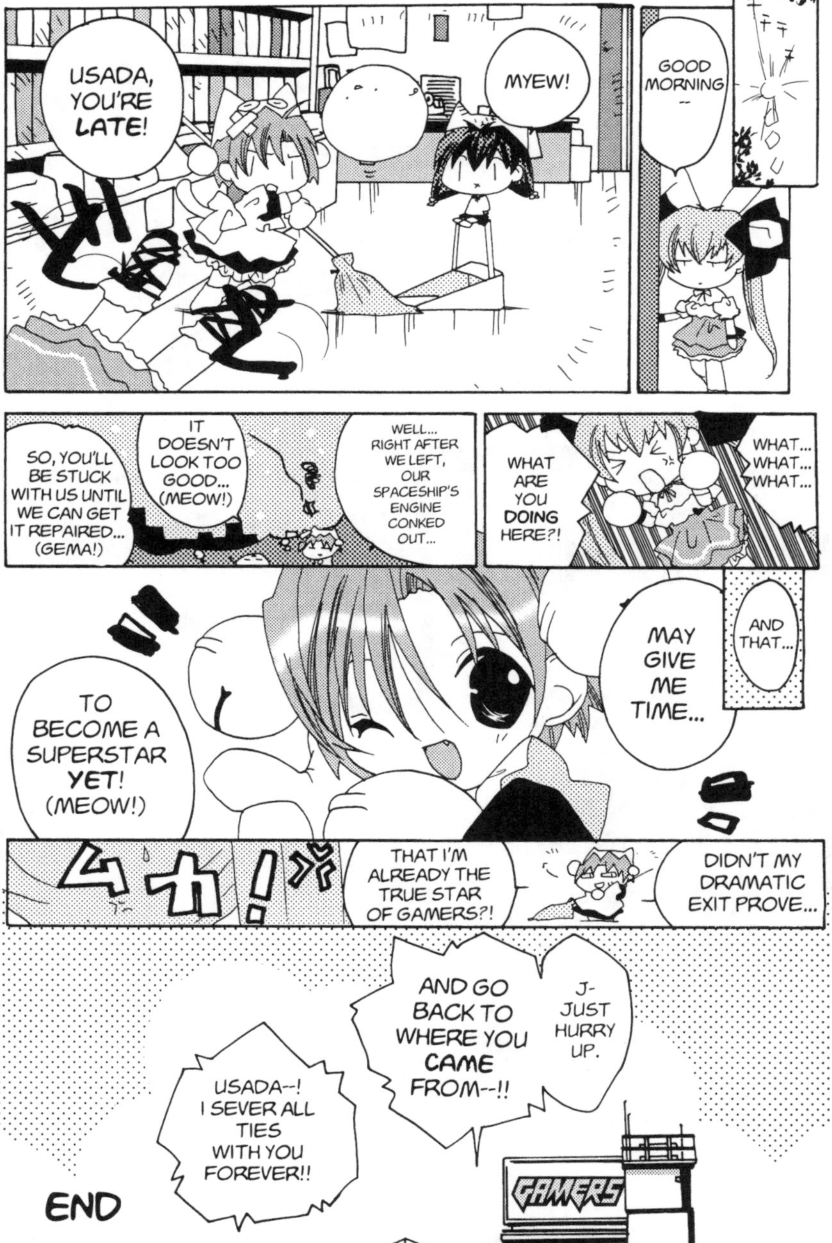
チチチ
GOOD MORNING --
MYEW!
USADA, YOU'RE **LATE**!
WHAT... WHAT... WHAT...
WHAT ARE YOU **DOING** HERE?!
WELL... RIGHT AFTER WE LEFT, OUR SPACESHIP'S ENGINE CONKED OUT...
IT DOESN'T LOOK TOO GOOD... (MEOW!)
SO, YOU'LL BE STUCK WITH US UNTIL WE CAN GET IT REPAIRED... (GEMA!)
AND THAT...
MAY GIVE ME TIME...
TO BECOME A SUPERSTAR **YET**! (MEOW!)
DIDN'T MY DRAMATIC EXIT PROVE...
THAT I'M ALREADY THE TRUE STAR OF GAMERS?!
ムカ!
J- JUST HURRY UP.
AND GO BACK TO WHERE YOU **CAME** FROM--!!
USADA--! I SEVER ALL TIES WITH YOU FOREVER!!
GAMERS
END

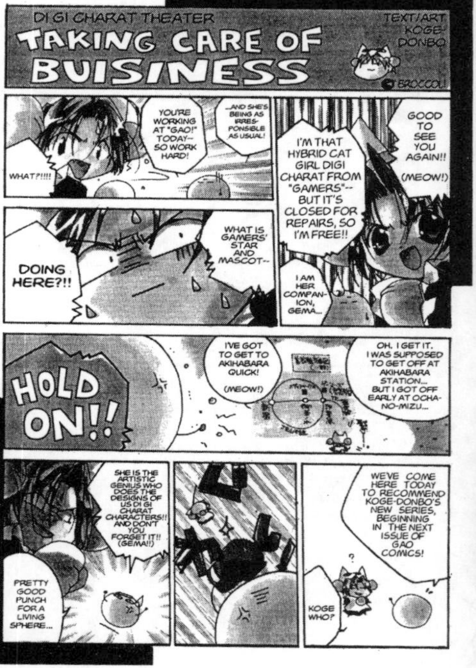
DI GI CHARAT THEATER
TAKING CARE OF BUISINESS
TEXT/ART KOGE-DONBO
© BROCCOLI
GOOD TO SEE YOU AGAIN!! (MEOW!)
I'M THAT HYBRID CAT GIRL DIGI CHARAT FROM "GAMERS"-- BUT IT'S CLOSED FOR REPAIRS, SO I'M FREE!!
I AM HER COMPANION, GEMA...
...AND SHE'S BEING AS IRRESPONSIBLE AS USUAL!
YOU'RE WORKING AT "GAO!" TODAY-- SO WORK HARD!
WHAT?!!!!
WHAT IS GAMERS' STAR AND MASCOT--
DOING HERE?!!
OH, I GET IT. I WAS SUPPOSED TO GET OFF AT AKIHABARA STATION... BUT I GOT OFF EARLY AT OCHA-NO-MIZU...
I'VE GOT TO GET TO AKIHABARA QUICK! (MEOW!)
HOLD ON!!
WE'VE COME HERE TODAY TO RECOMMEND KOGE-DONBO'S NEW SERIES, BEGINNING IN THE NEXT ISSUE OF GAO COMICS!
KOGE WHO?
SHE IS THE ARTISTIC GENIUS WHO DOES THE DESIGNS OF US DI GI CHARAT CHARACTERS!! AND DON'T YOU FORGET IT!! (GEMA!)
PRETTY GOOD PUNCH FOR A LIVING SPHERE...

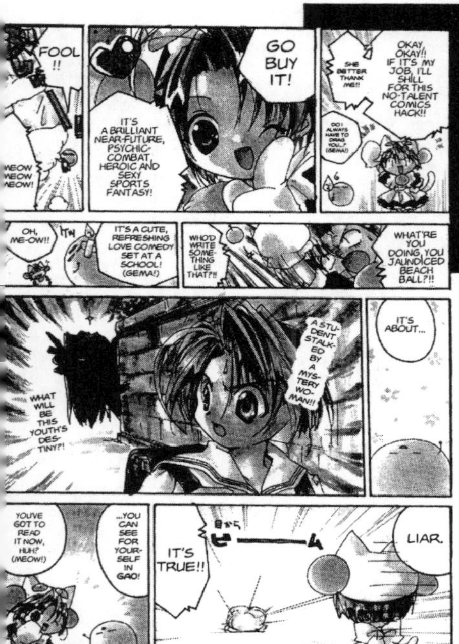
OKAY, OKAY!! IF IT'S MY JOB, I'LL SHILL FOR THIS NO-TALENT COMICS HACK!!
SHE BETTER THANK ME!!
DO I ALWAYS HAVE TO DRAG YOU..? (GEMA!)
GO BUY IT!
IT'S A BRILLIANT NEAR-FUTURE, PSYCHIC-COMBAT, HEROIC AND SEXY SPORTS FANTASY!
FOOL!!
MEOW MEOW MEOW!
WHAT'RE YOU DOING, YOU JAUNDICED BEACH BALL?!!
WHO'D WRITE SOMETHING LIKE THAT?!!
IT'S A CUTE, REFRESHING LOVE COMEDY SET AT A SCHOOL! (GEMA!)
OH, ME-OW!!
IT'S ABOUT...
A STUDENT STALKED BY A MYSTERY WOMAN!!
WHAT WILL BE THIS YOUTH'S DESTINY?!
LIAR.
IT'S TRUE!!
...YOU CAN SEE FOR YOURSELF IN GAO!
YOU'VE GOT TO READ IT NOW, HUH? (MEOW!)

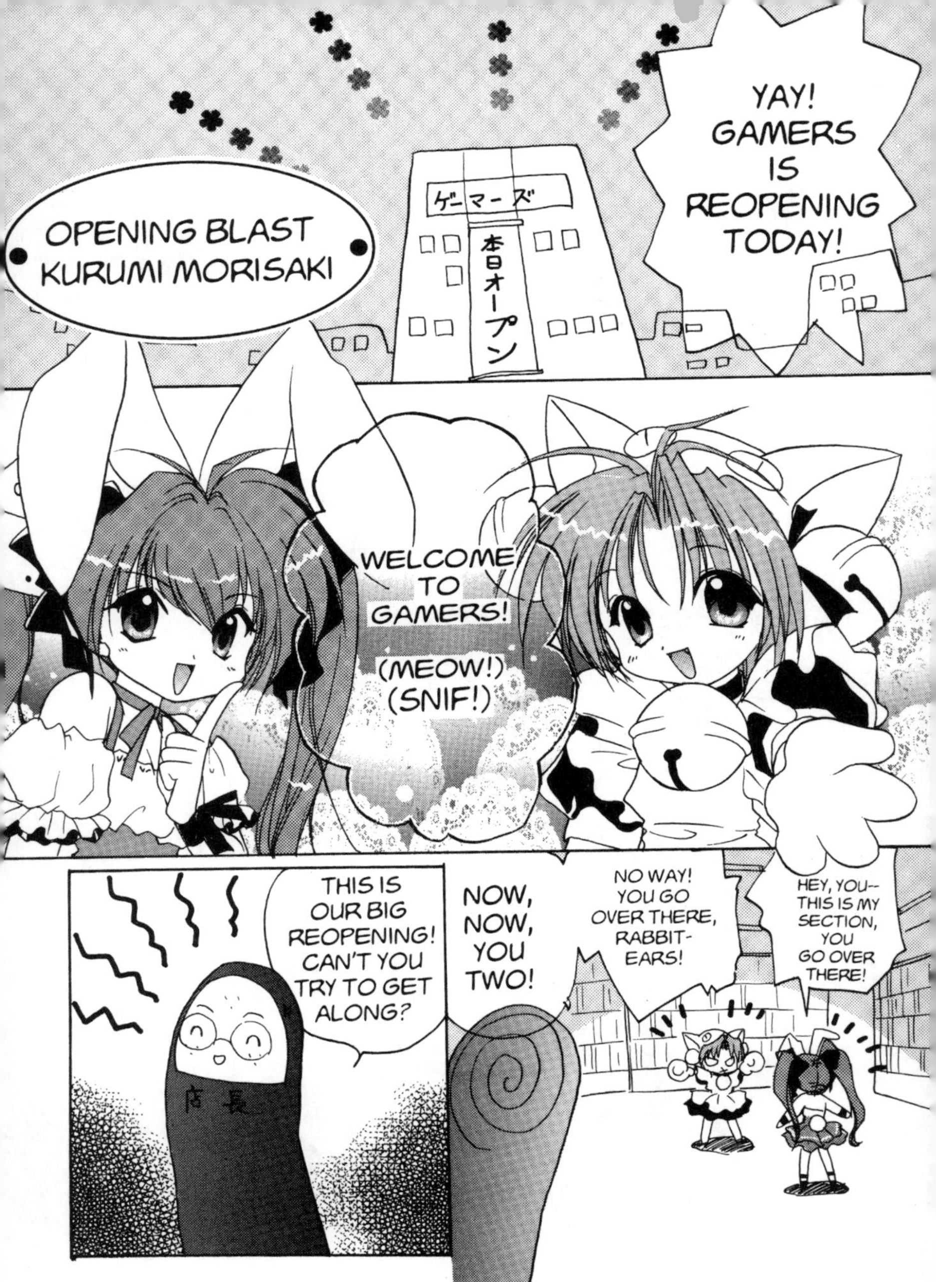
YAY! GAMERS IS REOPENING TODAY!
ゲーマーズ
本日オープン
OPENING BLAST
KURUMI MORISAKI
WELCOME TO GAMERS!
(MEOW!)
(SNIF!)
HEY, YOU-- THIS IS MY SECTION, YOU GO OVER THERE!
NO WAY! YOU GO OVER THERE, RABBIT-EARS!
NOW, NOW, YOU TWO!
THIS IS OUR BIG REOPENING! CAN'T YOU TRY TO GET ALONG?
店長

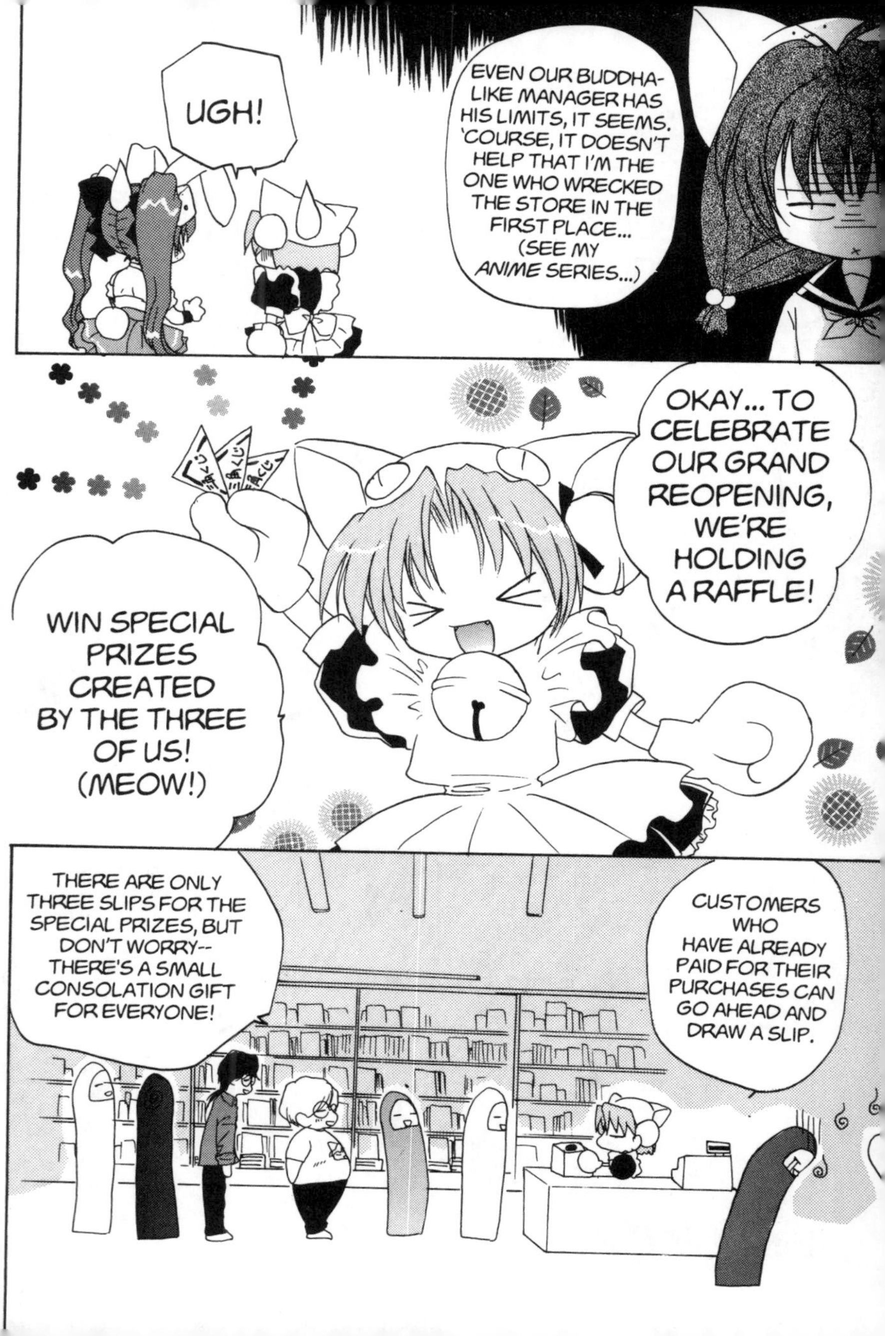
EVEN OUR BUDDHA-LIKE MANAGER HAS HIS LIMITS, IT SEEMS. 'COURSE, IT DOESN'T HELP THAT I'M THE ONE WHO WRECKED THE STORE IN THE FIRST PLACE... (SEE MY *ANIME SERIES*...)
UGH!
OKAY... TO CELEBRATE OUR GRAND REOPENING, WE'RE HOLDING A RAFFLE!
WIN SPECIAL PRIZES CREATED BY THE THREE OF US! (MEOW!)
CUSTOMERS WHO HAVE ALREADY PAID FOR THEIR PURCHASES CAN GO AHEAD AND DRAW A SLIP.
THERE ARE ONLY THREE SLIPS FOR THE SPECIAL PRIZES, BUT DON'T WORRY-- THERE'S A SMALL CONSOLATION GIFT FOR EVERYONE!

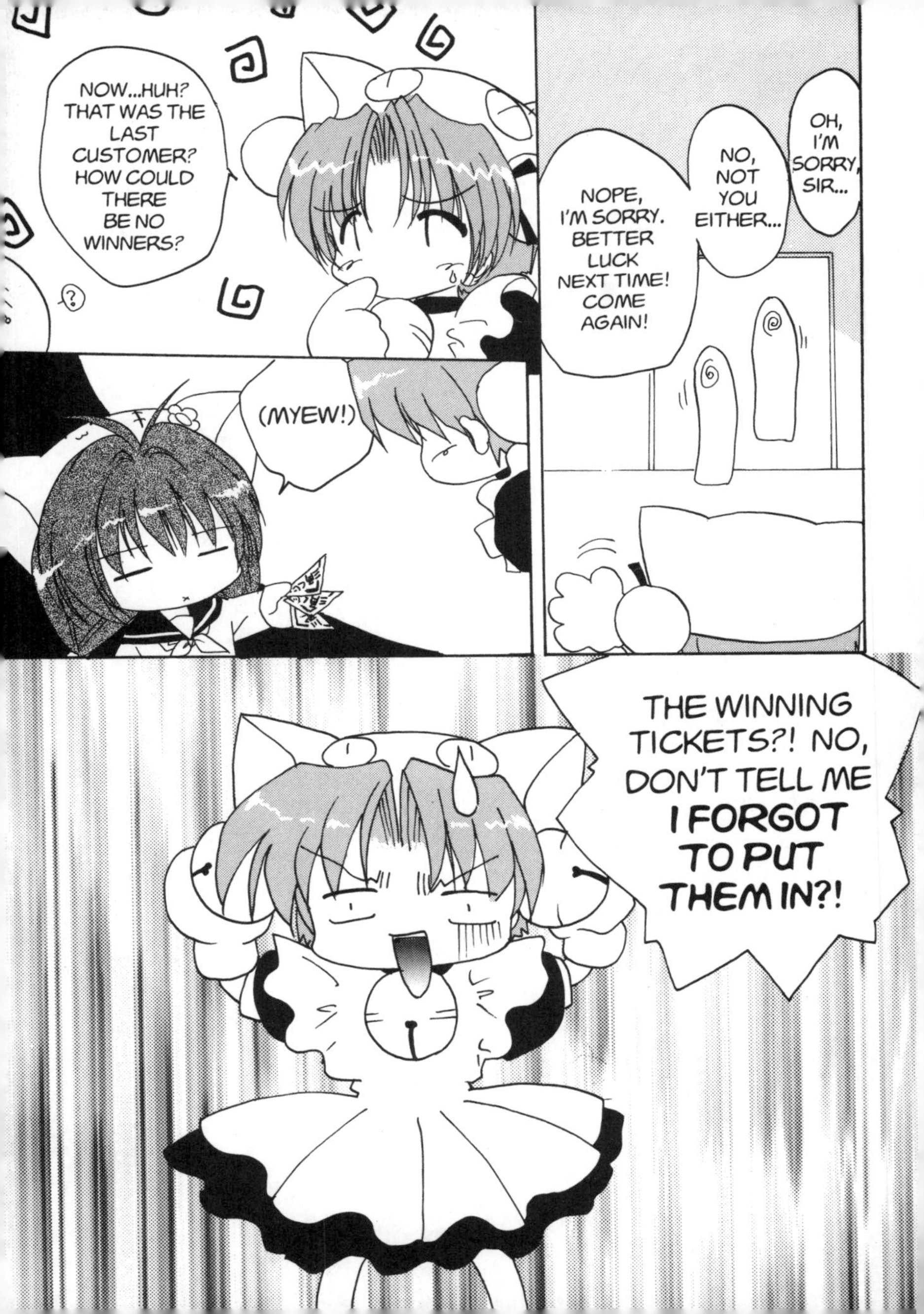

OH, I'M SORRY, SIR...
NO, NOT YOU EITHER...
NOPE, I'M SORRY. BETTER LUCK NEXT TIME! COME AGAIN!
NOW...HUH? THAT WAS THE LAST CUSTOMER? HOW COULD THERE BE NO WINNERS?
?
(MYEW!)
THE WINNING TICKETS?! NO, DON'T TELL ME **I FORGOT TO PUT THEM IN?!**

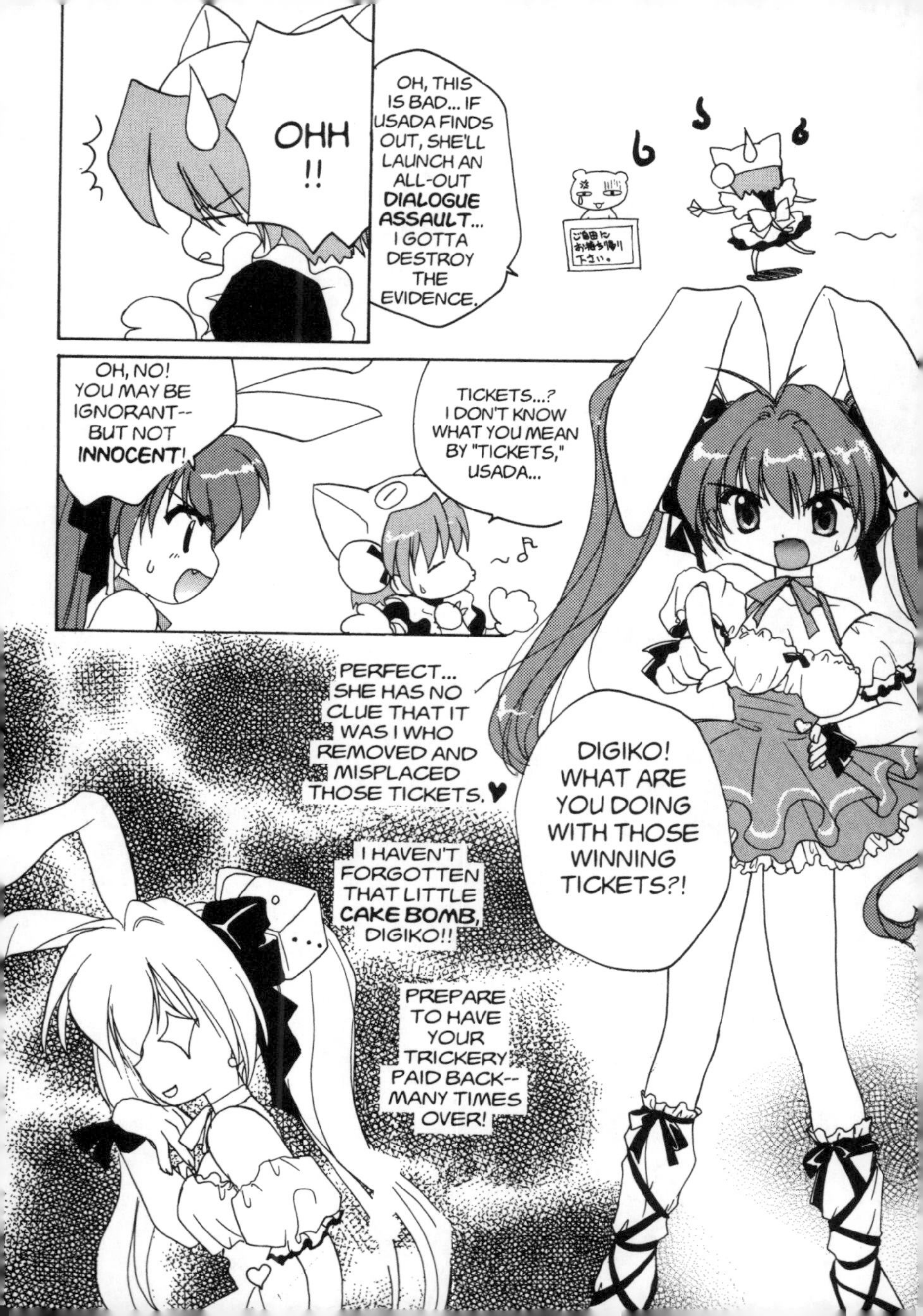
ご自由にお持ち帰り下さい。
OH, THIS IS BAD... IF USADA FINDS OUT, SHE'LL LAUNCH AN ALL-OUT **DIALOGUE ASSAULT**... I GOTTA DESTROY THE EVIDENCE.
OHH !!
DIGIKO! WHAT ARE YOU DOING WITH THOSE WINNING TICKETS?!
TICKETS...? I DON'T KNOW WHAT YOU MEAN BY "TICKETS," USADA...
OH, NO! YOU MAY BE IGNORANT-- BUT NOT **INNOCENT**!
PERFECT... SHE HAS NO CLUE THAT IT WAS I WHO REMOVED AND MISPLACED THOSE TICKETS. ♥
I HAVEN'T FORGOTTEN THAT LITTLE **CAKE BOMB**, DIGIKO!!
PREPARE TO HAVE YOUR TRICKERY PAID BACK-- MANY TIMES OVER!

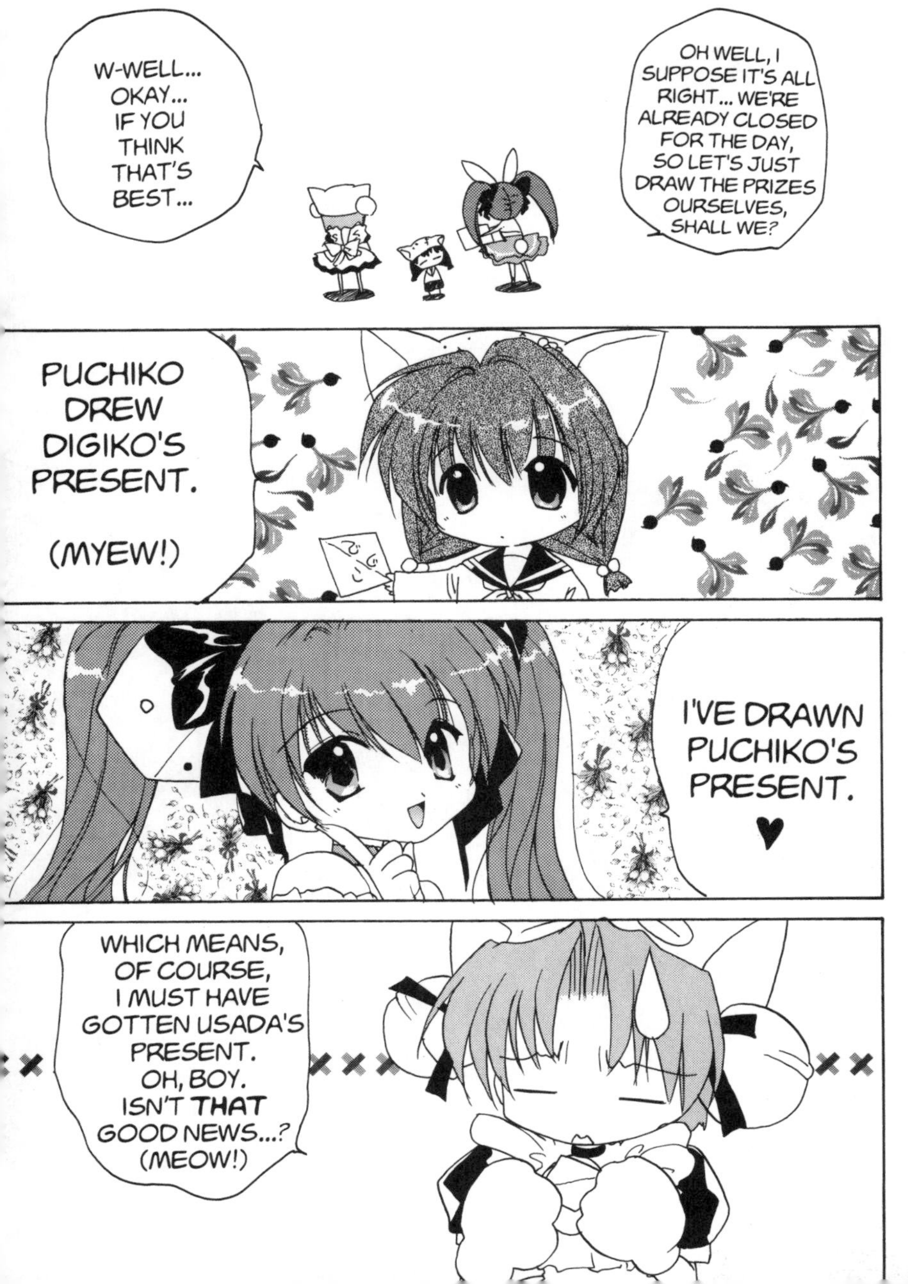
OH WELL, I SUPPOSE IT'S ALL RIGHT... WE'RE ALREADY CLOSED FOR THE DAY, SO LET'S JUST DRAW THE PRIZES OURSELVES, SHALL WE?
W-WELL... OKAY... IF YOU THINK THAT'S BEST...
PUCHIKO DREW DIGIKO'S PRESENT. (MYEW!)
I'VE DRAWN PUCHIKO'S PRESENT. ♥
WHICH MEANS, OF COURSE, I MUST HAVE GOTTEN USADA'S PRESENT. OH, BOY. ISN'T THAT GOOD NEWS...? (MEOW!)

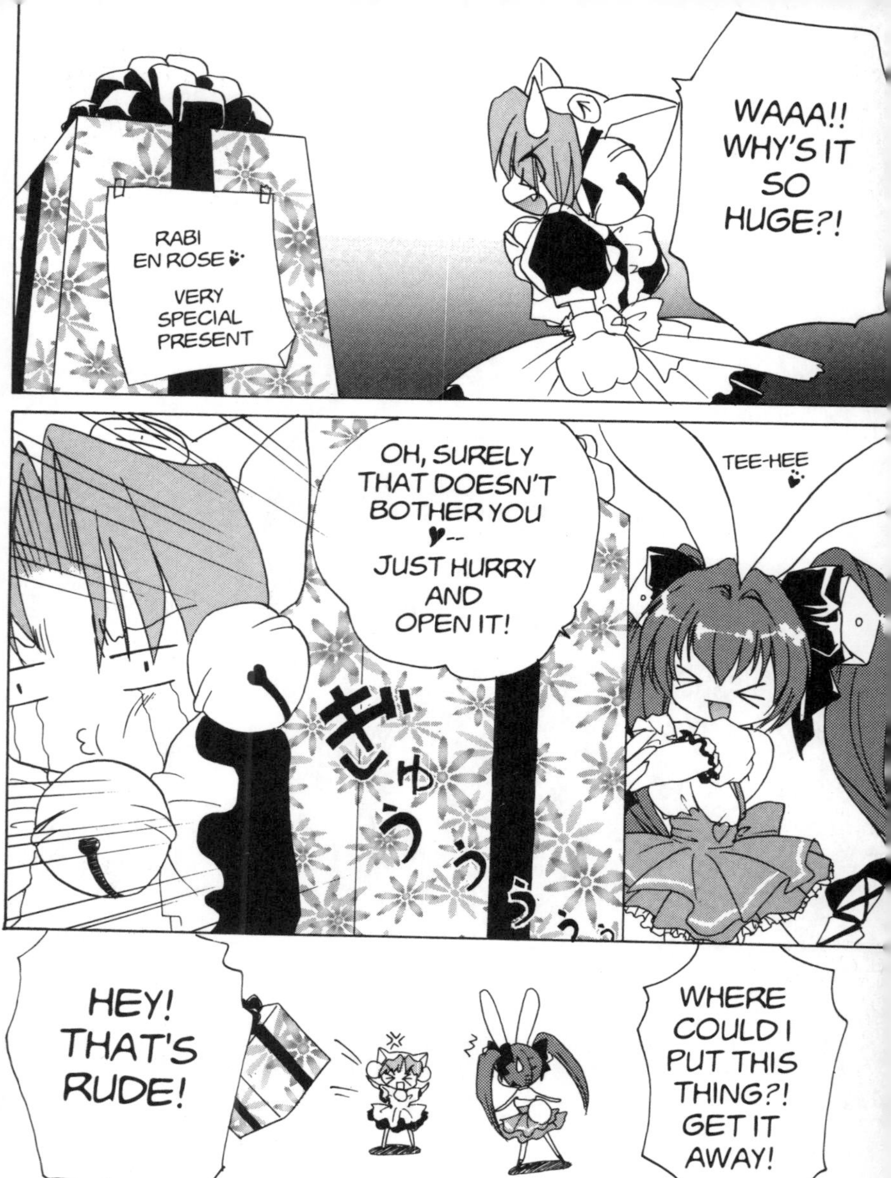
WAAA!! WHY'S IT SO HUGE?!
RABI EN ROSE
VERY SPECIAL PRESENT
TEE-HEE
OH, SURELY THAT DOESN'T BOTHER YOU-- JUST HURRY AND OPEN IT!
ぎゅうううう
WHERE COULD I PUT THIS THING?! GET IT AWAY!
HEY! THAT'S RUDE!

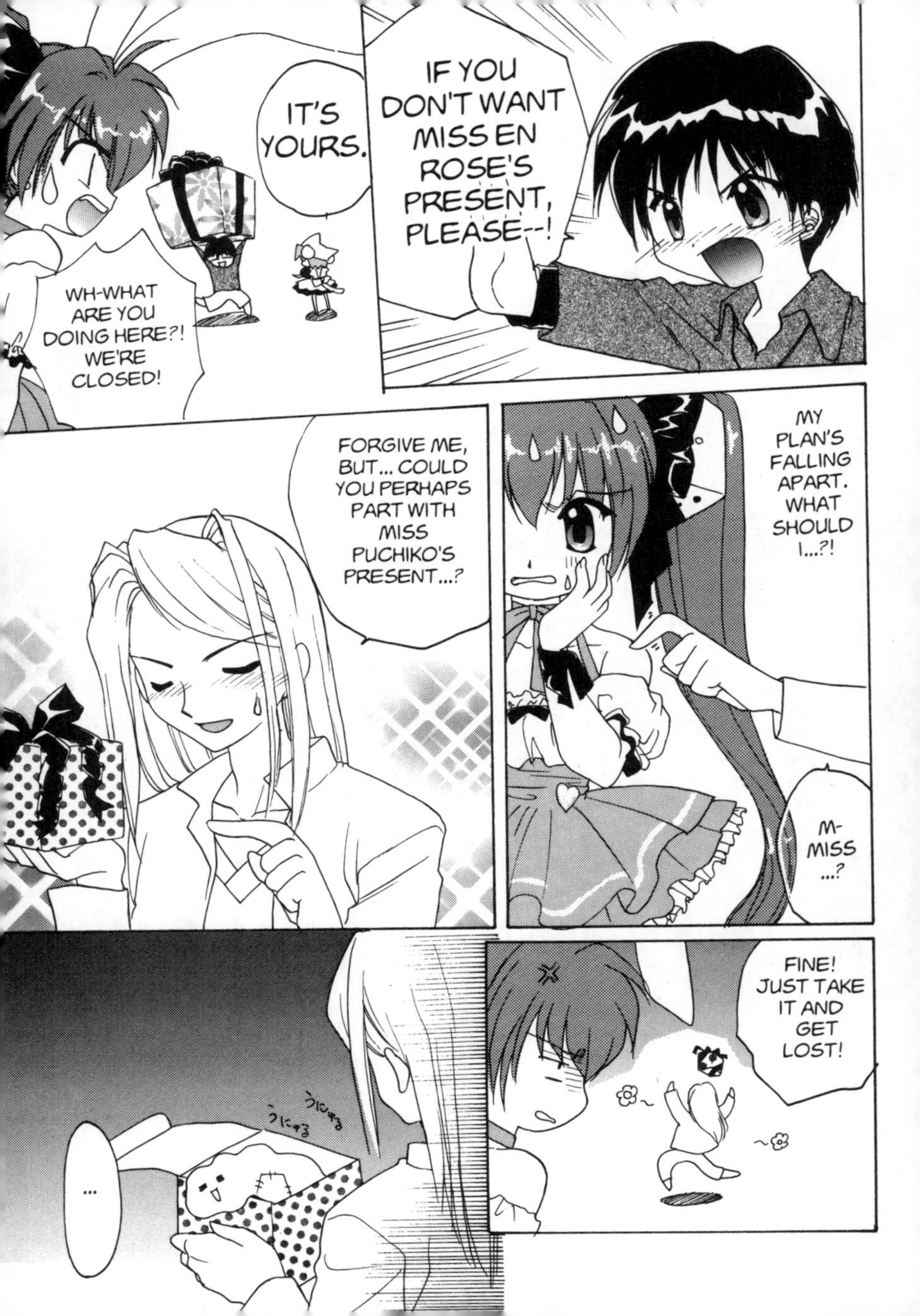
IF YOU DON'T WANT MISS EN ROSE'S PRESENT, PLEASE--!
IT'S YOURS.
WH-WHAT ARE YOU DOING HERE?! WE'RE CLOSED!
MY PLAN'S FALLING APART. WHAT SHOULD I...?!
M-MISS ...?
FORGIVE ME, BUT... COULD YOU PERHAPS PART WITH MISS PUCHIKO'S PRESENT...?
FINE! JUST TAKE IT AND GET LOST!
うにゅる
うにゅる
...

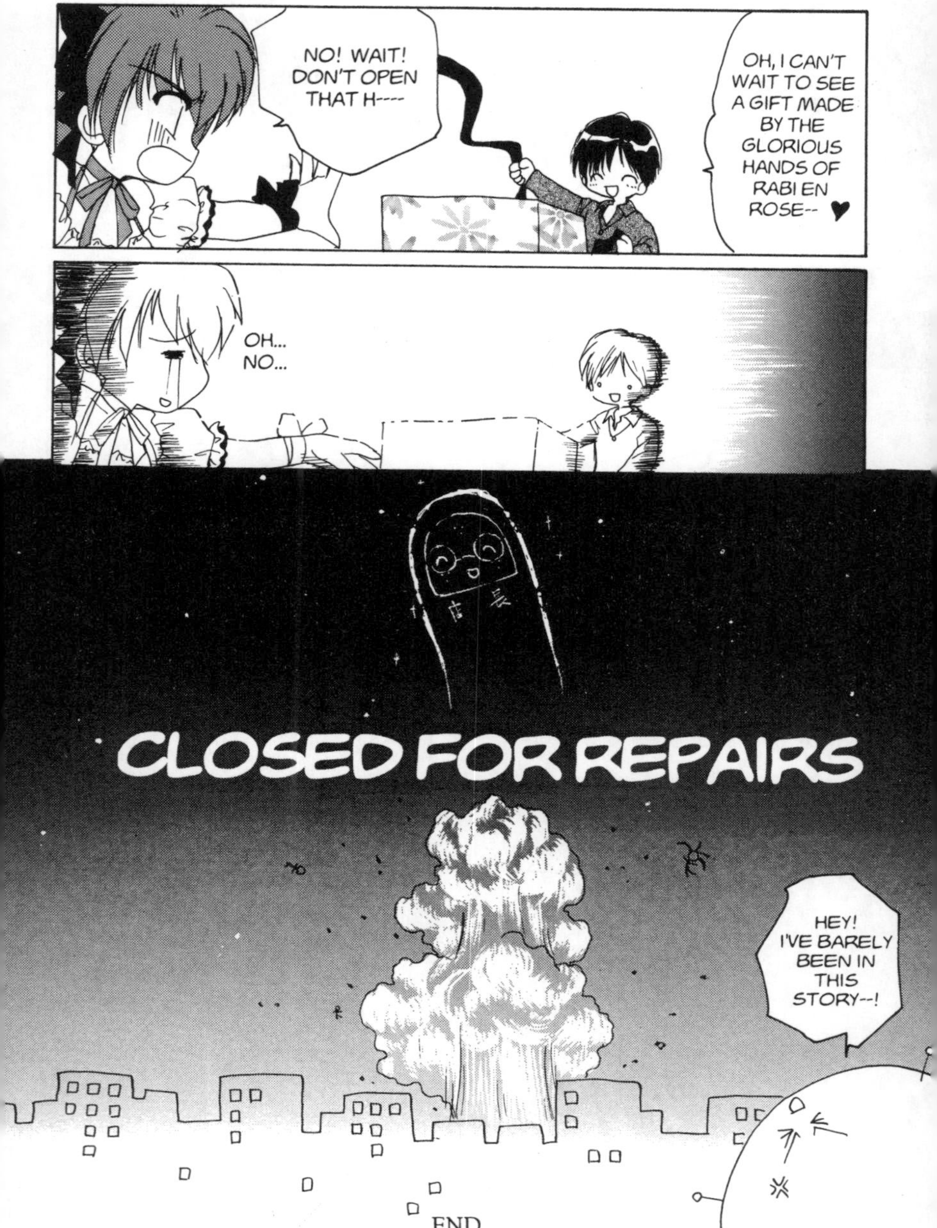
OH, I CAN'T WAIT TO SEE A GIFT MADE BY THE GLORIOUS HANDS OF RABI EN ROSE-- ♥
NO! WAIT! DON'T OPEN THAT H----
OH... NO...
CLOSED FOR REPAIRS
HEY! I'VE BARELY BEEN IN THIS STORY--!

END

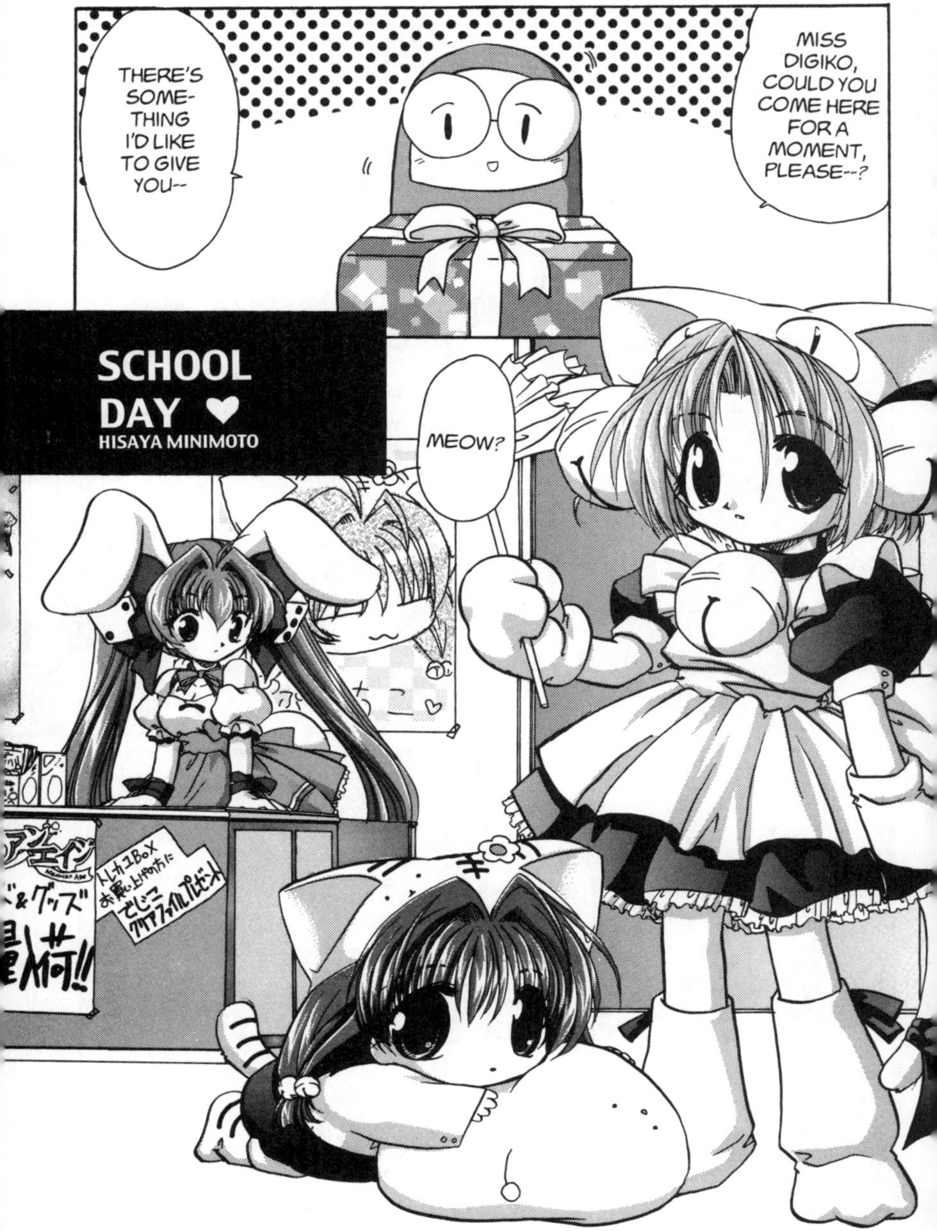
MISS DIGIKO, COULD YOU COME HERE FOR A MOMENT, PLEASE--?
THERE'S SOME-THING I'D LIKE TO GIVE YOU--
SCHOOL DAY ♥
HISAYA MINIMOTO
MEOW?
トレカ1BOX お買い上げの方に でじこ クリアファイル プレゼント

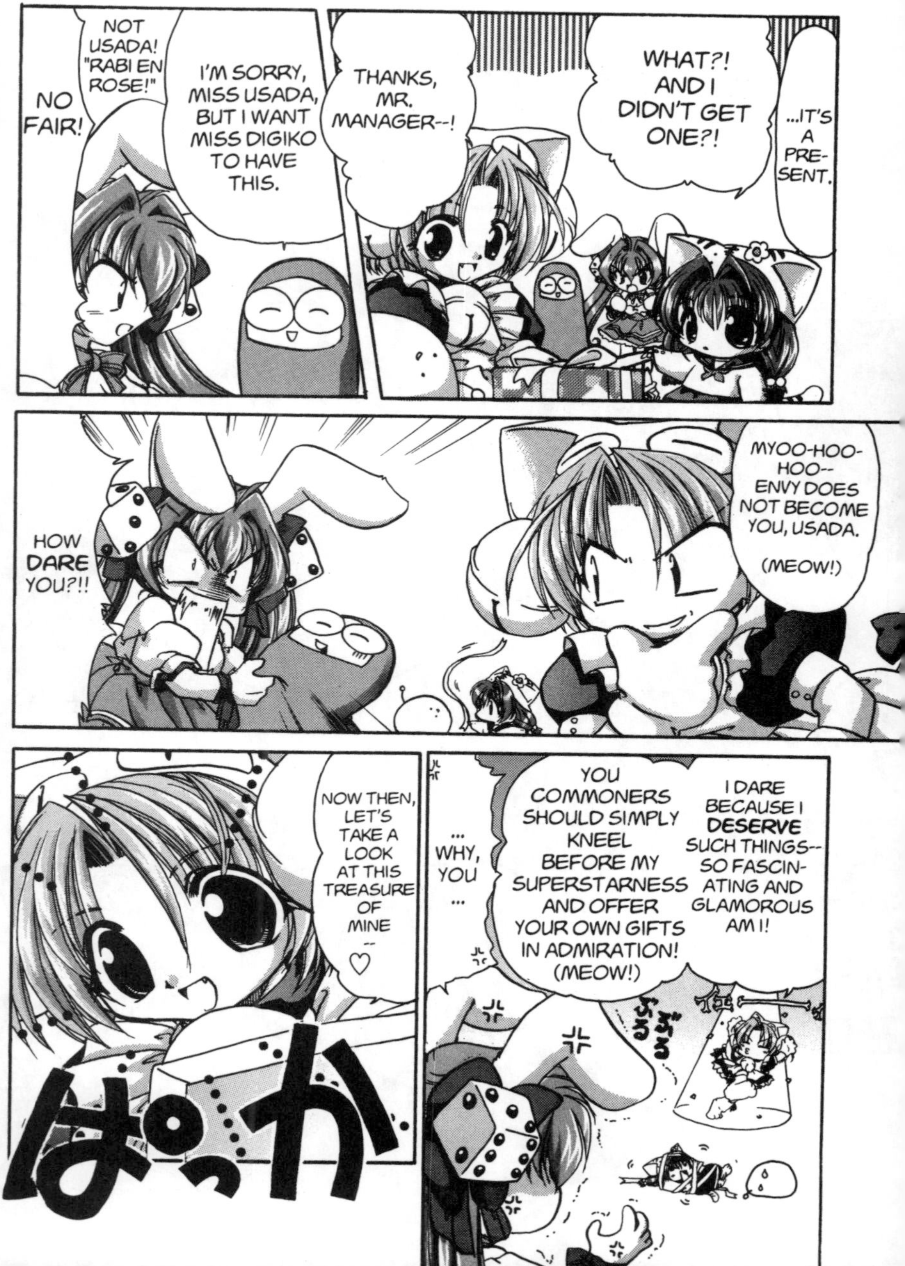
...IT'S A PRESENT.
WHAT?! AND I DIDN'T GET ONE?!
THANKS, MR. MANAGER--!
I'M SORRY, MISS USADA, BUT I WANT MISS DIGIKO TO HAVE THIS.
NOT USADA! "RABI EN ROSE!"
NO FAIR!
MYOO-HOO-HOO-- ENVY DOES NOT BECOME YOU, USADA.
(MEOW!)
HOW DARE YOU?!!
I DARE BECAUSE I DESERVE SUCH THINGS-- SO FASCINATING AND GLAMOROUS AM I!
YOU COMMONERS SHOULD SIMPLY KNEEL BEFORE MY SUPERSTARNESS AND OFFER YOUR OWN GIFTS IN ADMIRATION! (MEOW!)
... WHY, YOU ...
NOW THEN, LET'S TAKE A LOOK AT THIS TREASURE OF MINE --♡
ぱっか

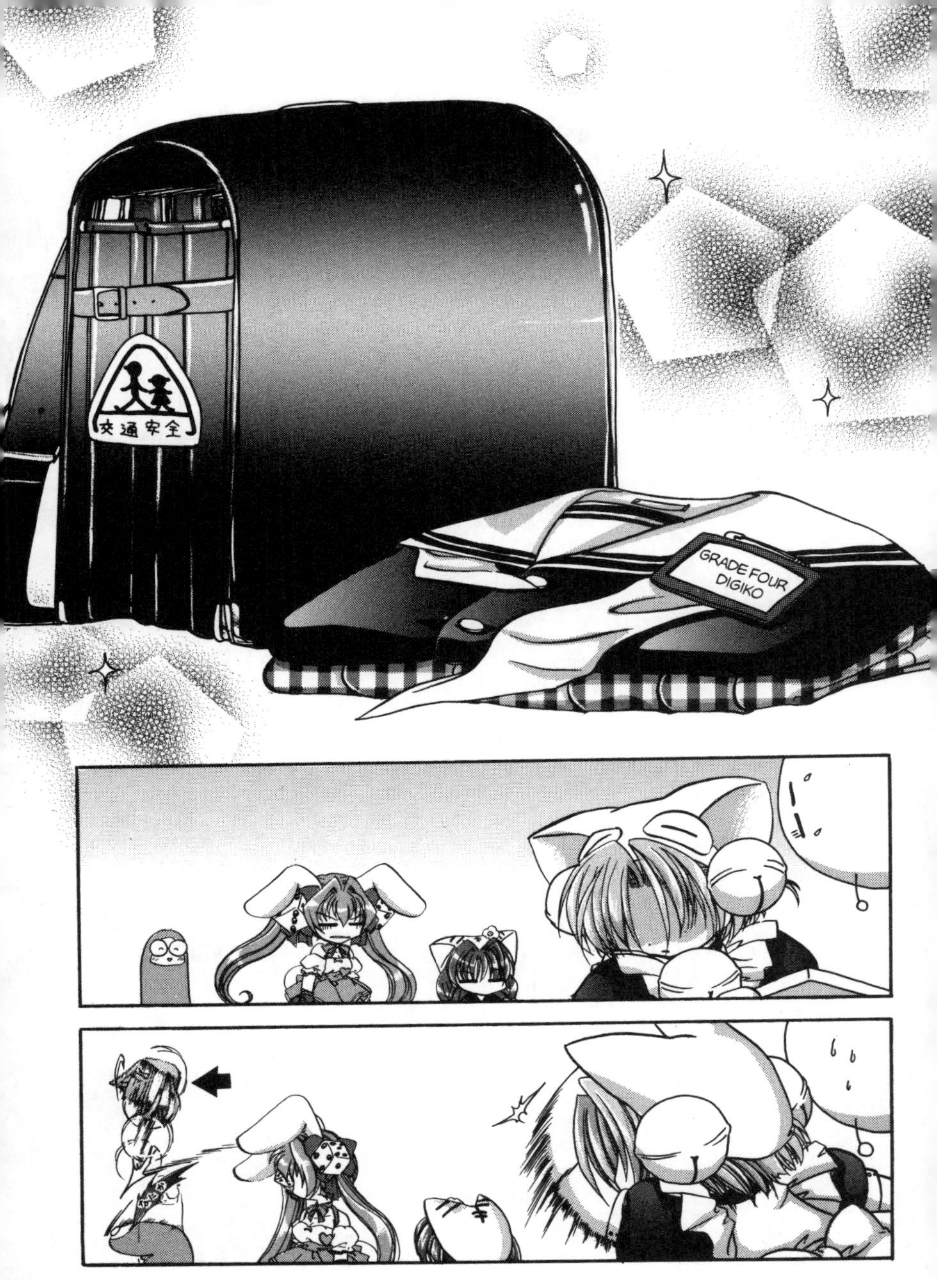
交通安全
GRADE FOUR DIGIKO

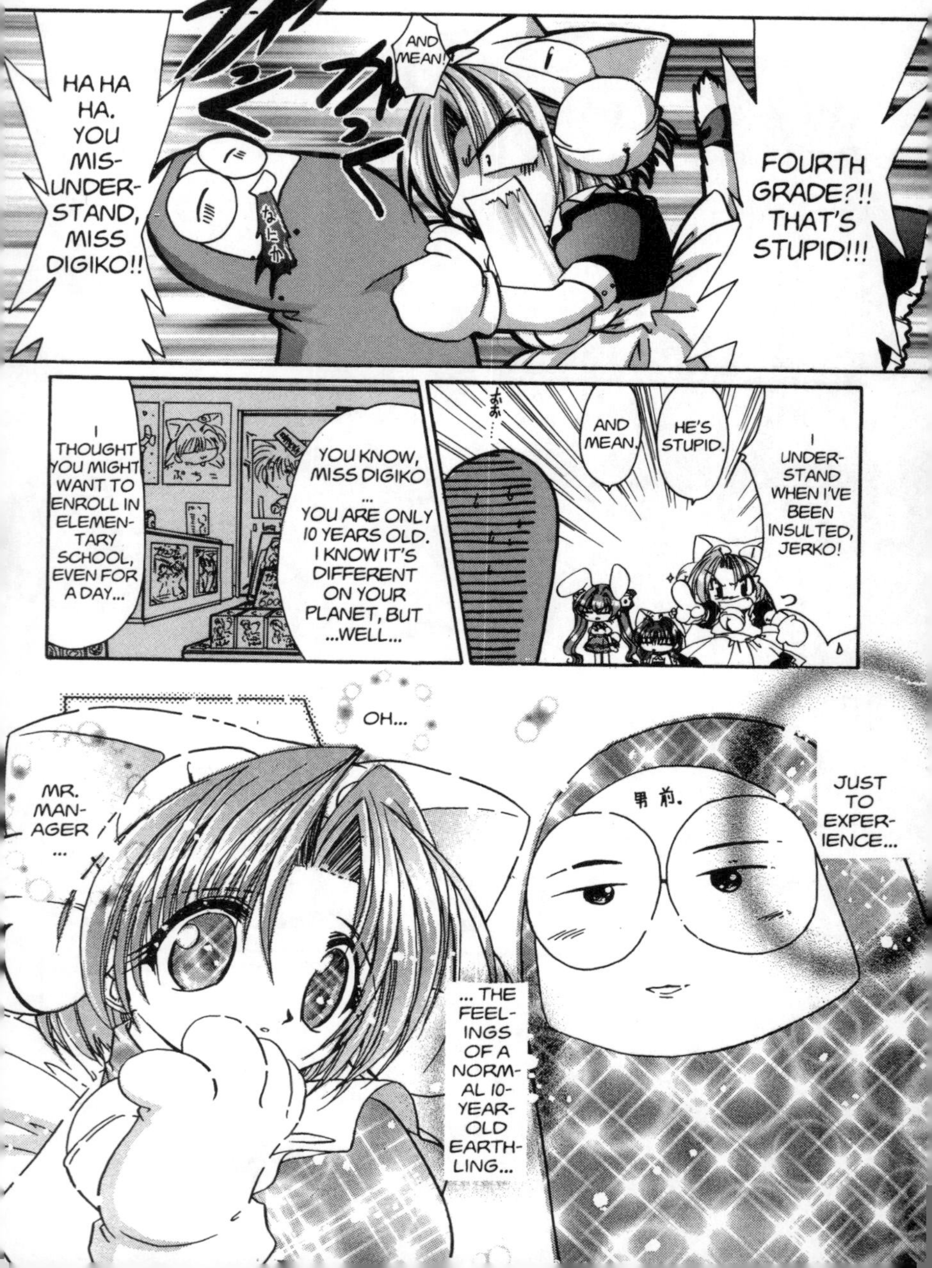
FOURTH GRADE?!! THAT'S STUPID!!!
AND MEAN!!
HA HA HA. YOU MISUNDERSTAND, MISS DIGIKO!!
I UNDERSTAND WHEN I'VE BEEN INSULTED, JERKO!
HE'S STUPID.
AND MEAN.
YOU KNOW, MISS DIGIKO ... YOU ARE ONLY 10 YEARS OLD. I KNOW IT'S DIFFERENT ON YOUR PLANET, BUT ...WELL...
I THOUGHT YOU MIGHT WANT TO ENROLL IN ELEMENTARY SCHOOL, EVEN FOR A DAY...
JUST TO EXPERIENCE...
男前。
OH...
MR. MANAGER ...
... THE FEELINGS OF A NORMAL 10-YEAR-OLD EARTHLING...

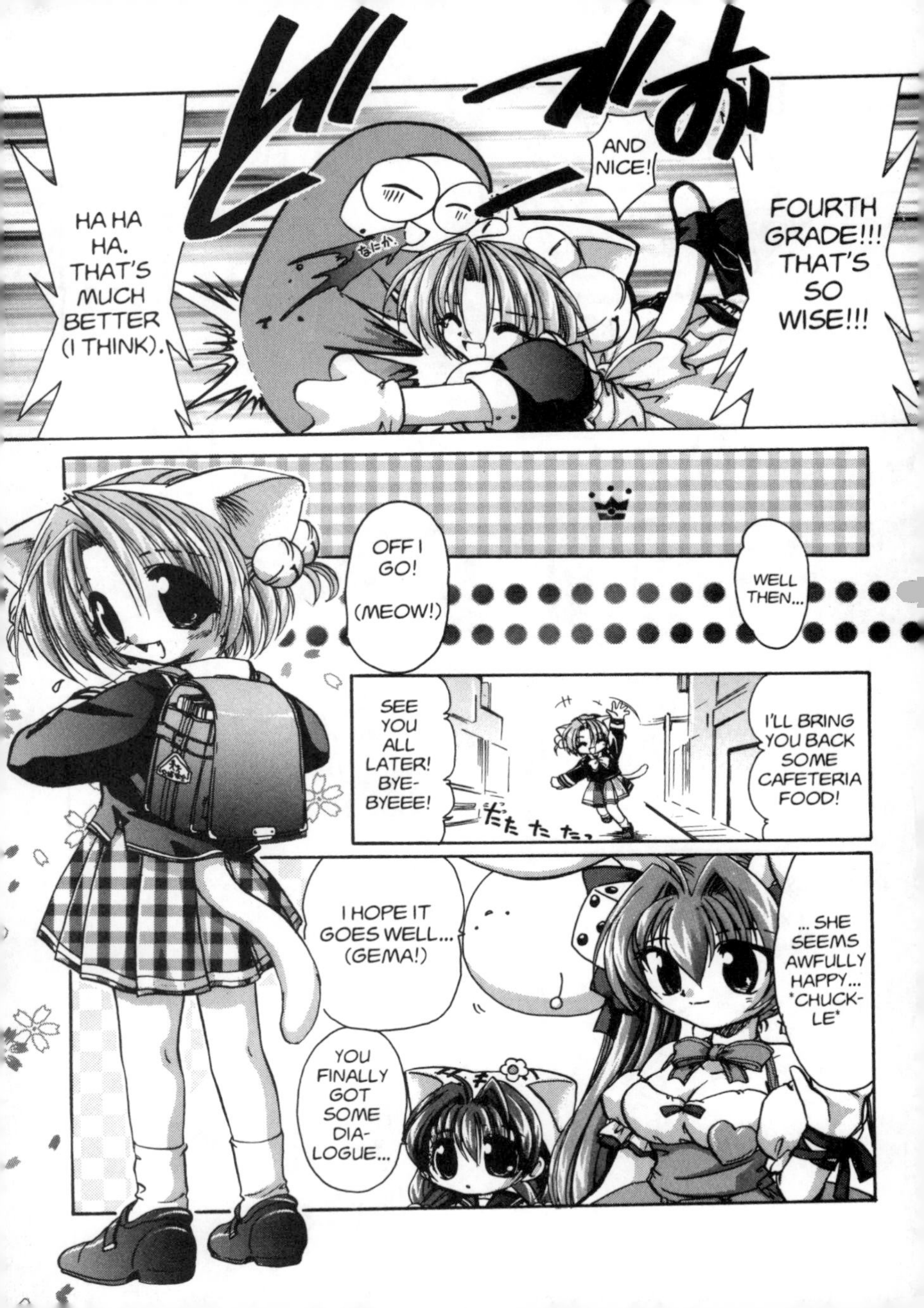
FOURTH GRADE!!! THAT'S SO WISE!!!
AND NICE!
HA HA HA. THAT'S MUCH BETTER (I THINK).
WELL THEN...
OFF I GO! (MEOW!)
I'LL BRING YOU BACK SOME CAFETERIA FOOD!
SEE YOU ALL LATER! BYE-BYEEE!
だたたたっ
... SHE SEEMS AWFULLY HAPPY... *CHUCKLE*
I HOPE IT GOES WELL... (GEMA!)
YOU FINALLY GOT SOME DIA-LOGUE...

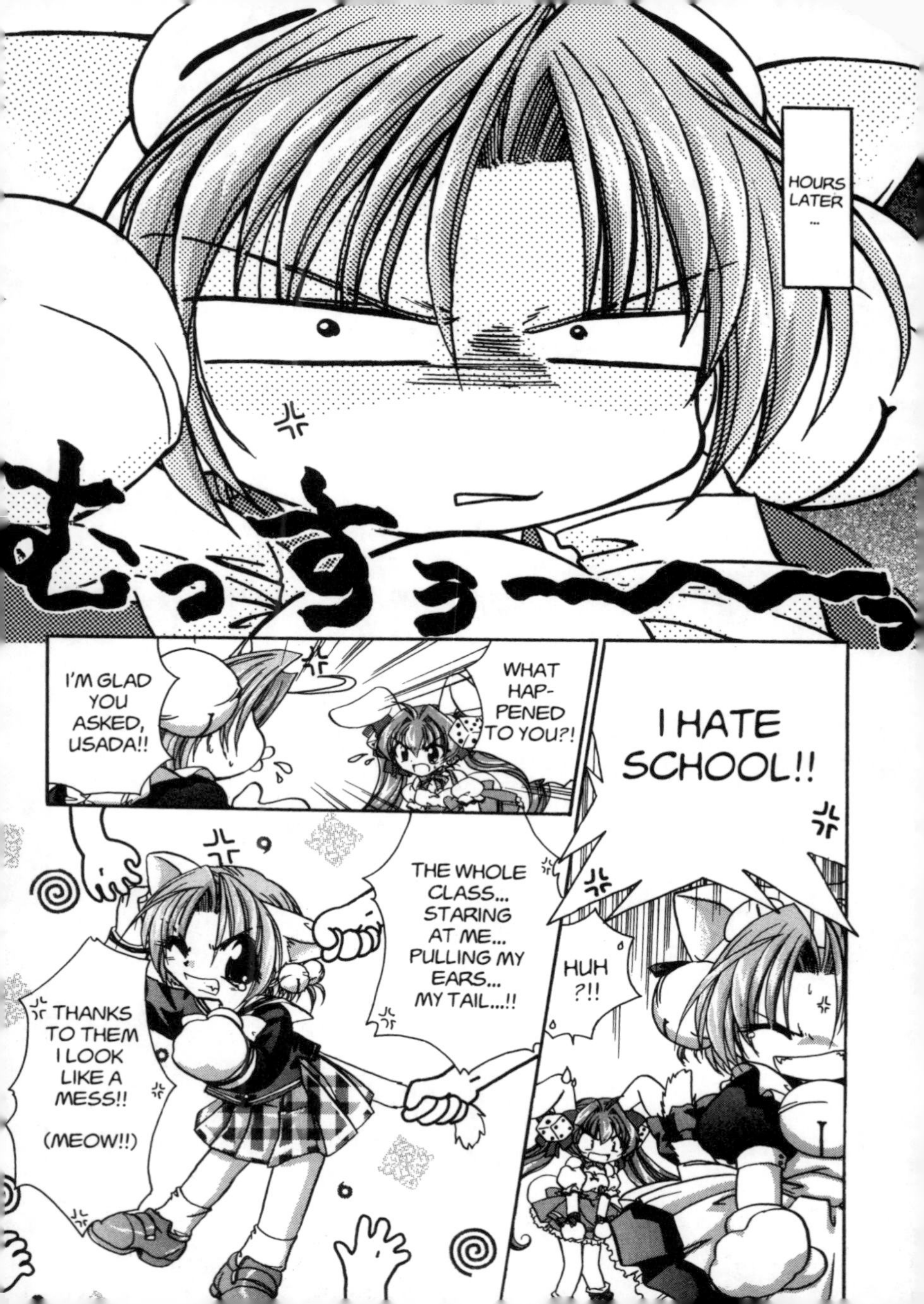
HOURS LATER ...
むっすぅ～～～っ
I HATE SCHOOL!!
HUH ?!!
WHAT HAP-PENED TO YOU?!
I'M GLAD YOU ASKED, USADA!!
THE WHOLE CLASS... STARING AT ME... PULLING MY EARS... MY TAIL...!!
THANKS TO THEM I LOOK LIKE A MESS!!
(MEOW!!)

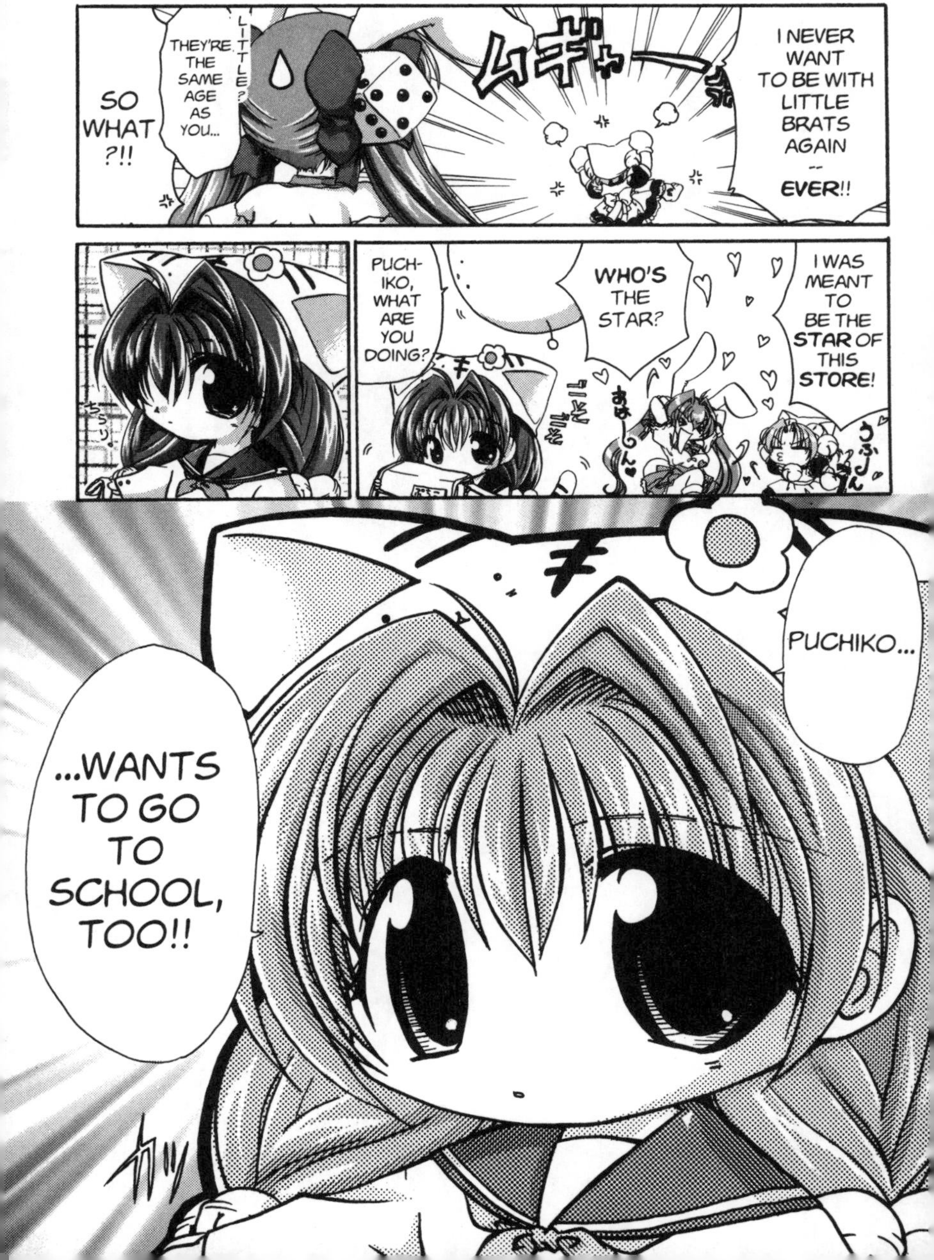
I NEVER WANT TO BE WITH LITTLE BRATS AGAIN -- **EVER**!!
ムギャーー
LITTLE?
THEY'RE THE SAME AGE AS YOU...
SO WHAT?!!
I WAS MEANT TO BE THE **STAR** OF THIS **STORE**!
WHO'S THE STAR?
PUCHIKO, WHAT ARE YOU DOING?
ちらり
PUCHIKO...
...WANTS TO GO TO SCHOOL, TOO!!

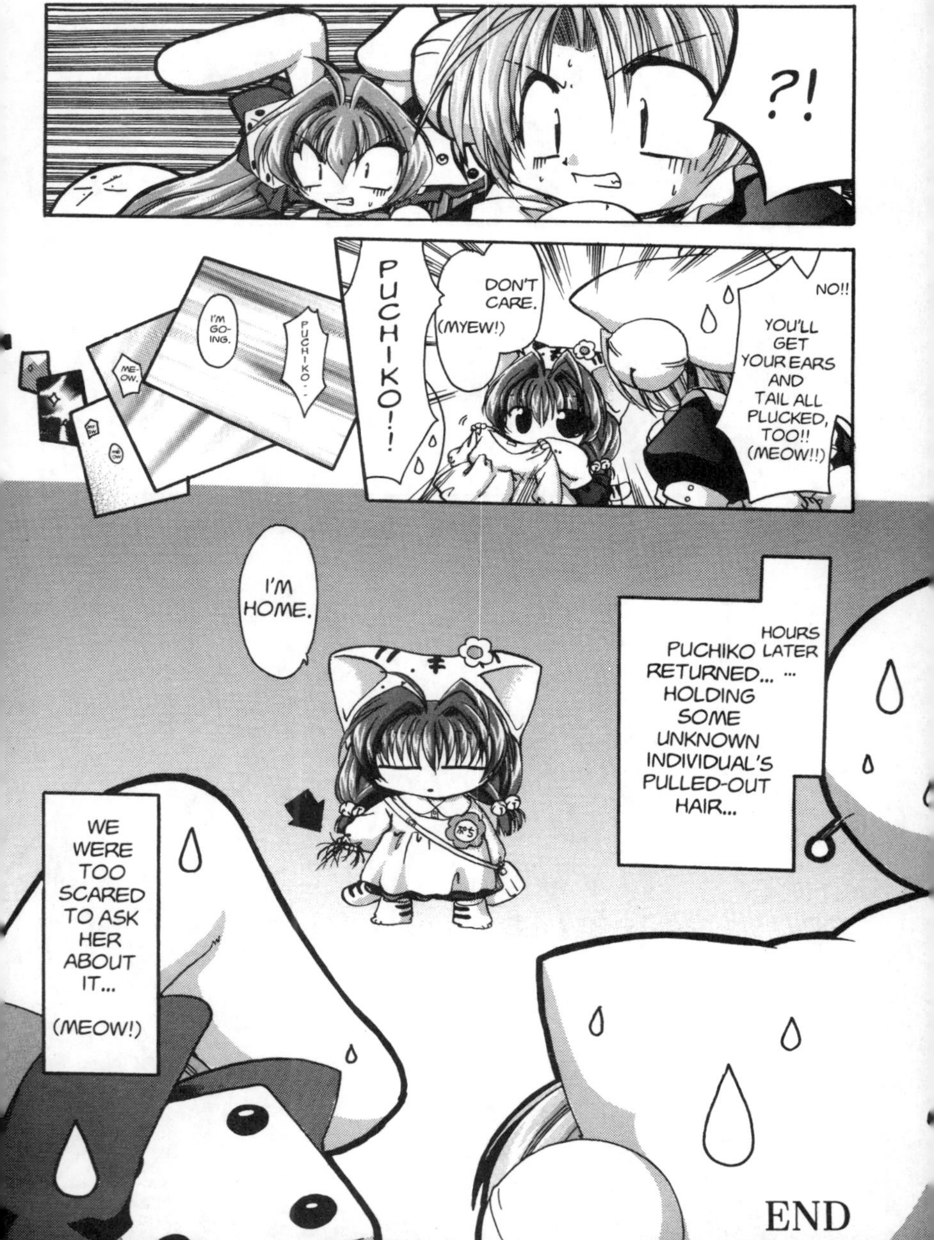
?!
NO!!
YOU'LL GET YOUR EARS AND TAIL ALL PLUCKED, TOO!! (MEOW!!)
DON'T CARE. (MYEW!)
PUCHIKO!!
PUCHIKO...
I'M GO-ING.
ME-OW.
HOURS LATER PUCHIKO RETURNED... ... HOLDING SOME UNKNOWN INDIVIDUAL'S PULLED-OUT HAIR...
I'M HOME.
WE WERE TOO SCARED TO ASK HER ABOUT IT... (MEOW!)
END

A comment about Di Gi Charat

I **LOVE** PUCHIKO ♥

THE DI GI CHARAT ANIME WAS QUITE FUN.
THE CHARACTERS'
PERSONALITIES WERE
PRESENTED REALLY
WELL IN A SHORT
PERIOD OF TIME. I
MUST ADMIT I LIKE
PUCHIKO MORE THAN
DIGIKO. SHE HAS
SUCH A NICE
PERSONALITY...
OF COURSE, USADA
IS AWFULLY PRECIOUS,
TOO. I WAS PLEASED
AT HOW LIKABLE
EVERY CHARACTER
WAS. I HOPE THEY
DO MORE ANIME
SOON!

MORISAK.K

MURASAKI KONNO

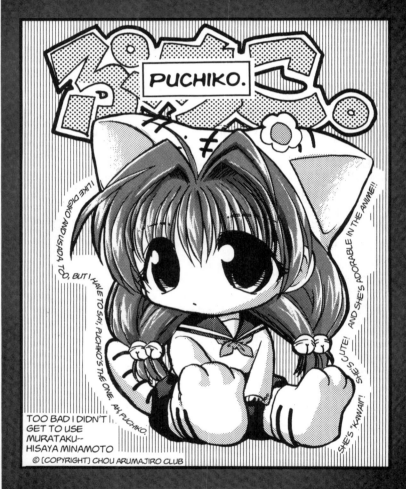

A comment abou

Di Gi Charat

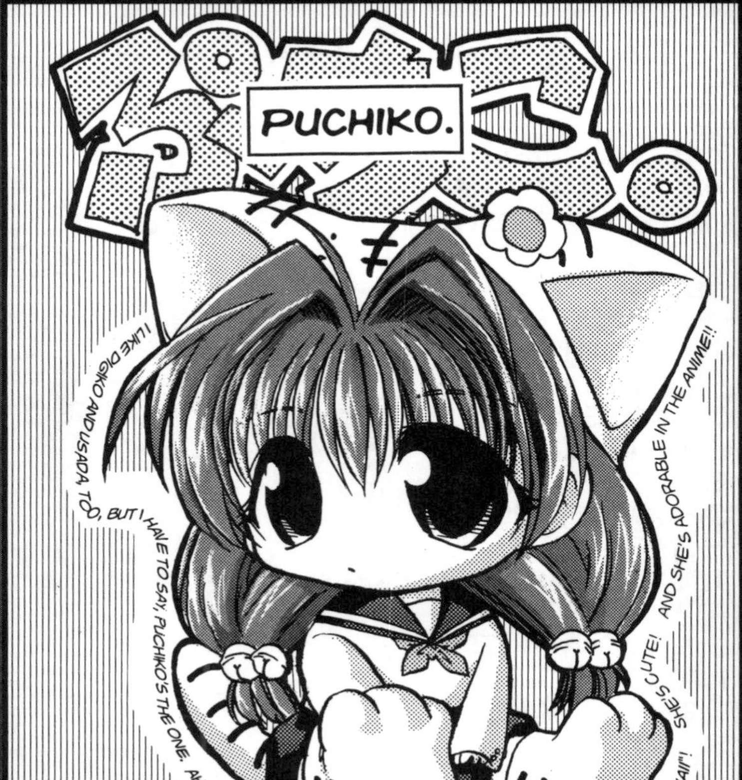

PUCHIKO.
AND SHE'S ADORABLE IN THE ANIME!!
SHE'S CUTE!
SHE'S "KAWAII"!
I LIKE DIGIKO AND USADA, TOO, BUT I HAVE TO SAY, PUCHIKO'S THE ONE. AH, PUCHIKO.
TOO BAD I DIDN'T GET TO USE MURATAKU-- HISAYA MINAMOTO
© [COPYRIGHT] CHOU ARUMAJIRO CLUB

HISAYA
MINAMOTO

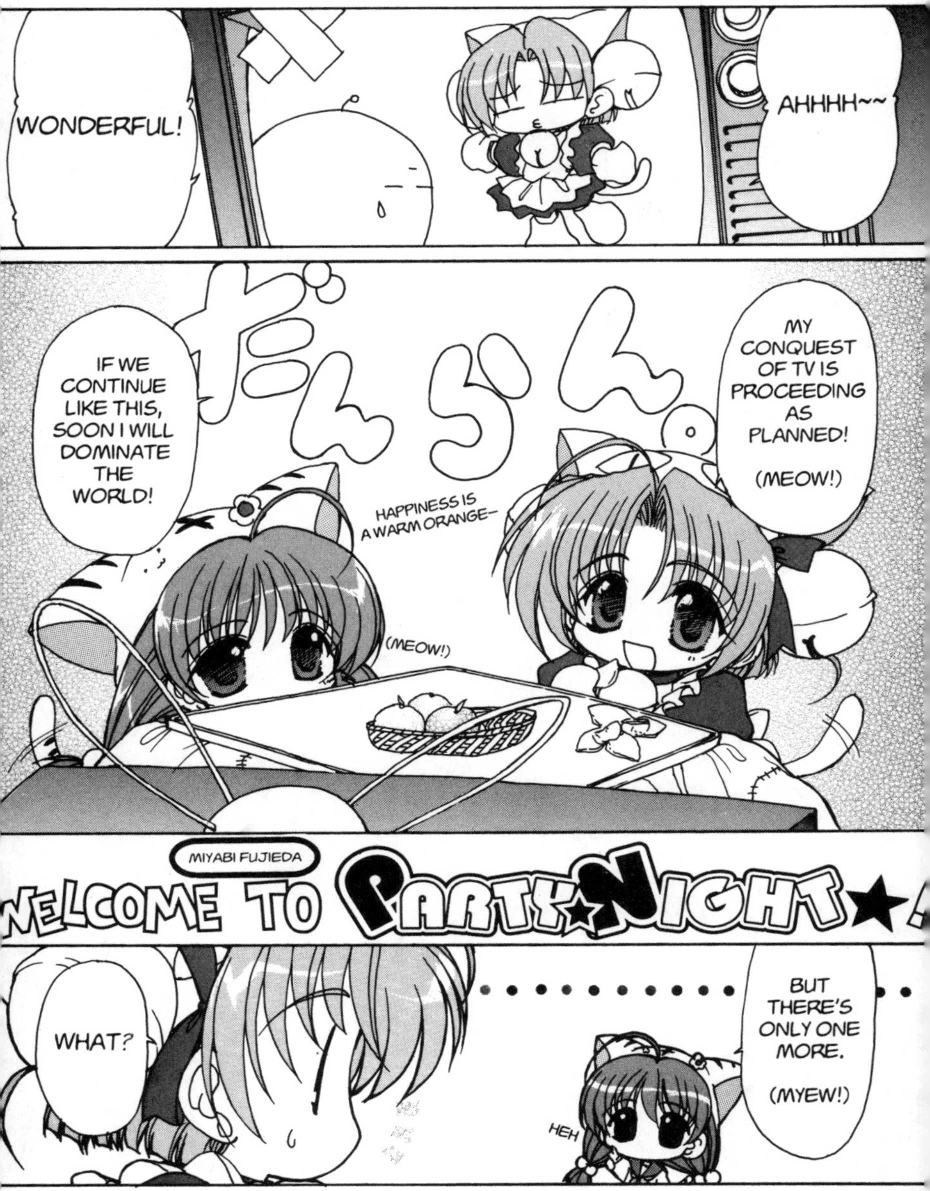
AHHHH~~
WONDERFUL!
MY CONQUEST OF TV IS PROCEEDING AS PLANNED!
(MEOW!)
だんらん。
HAPPINESS IS A WARM ORANGE-
IF WE CONTINUE LIKE THIS, SOON I WILL DOMINATE THE WORLD!
(MEOW!)
MIYABI FUJIEDA
WELCOME TO PARTY★NIGHT★!
BUT THERE'S ONLY ONE MORE.
(MYEW!)
HEH
WHAT?

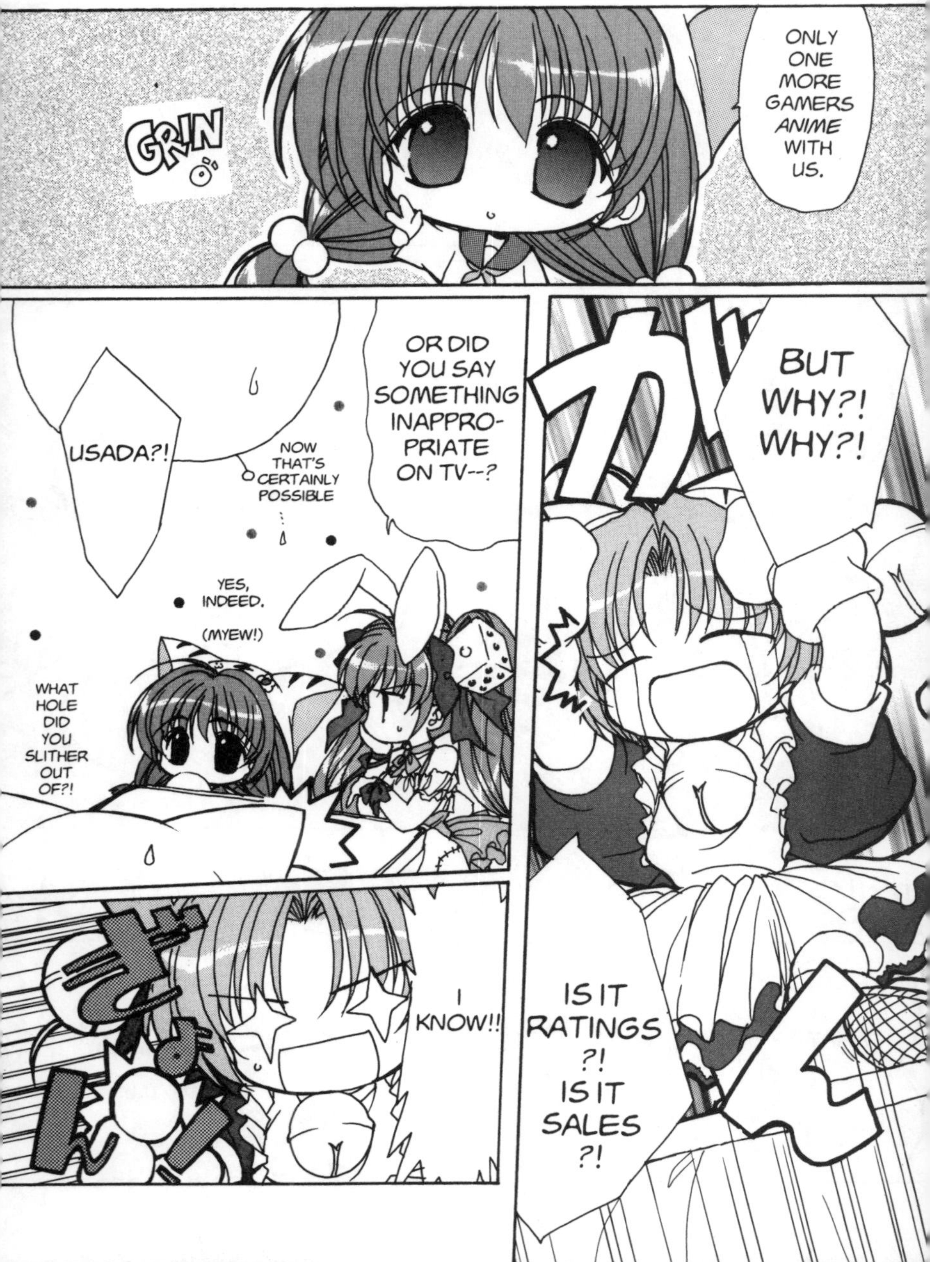
GRIN
ONLY ONE MORE GAMERS ANIME WITH US.
BUT WHY?! WHY?!
IS IT RATINGS?! IS IT SALES?!
OR DID YOU SAY SOMETHING INAPPRO-PRIATE ON TV--?
NOW THAT'S CERTAINLY POSSIBLE
USADA?!
YES, INDEED.
(MYEW!)
WHAT HOLE DID YOU SLITHER OUT OF?!
I KNOW!!

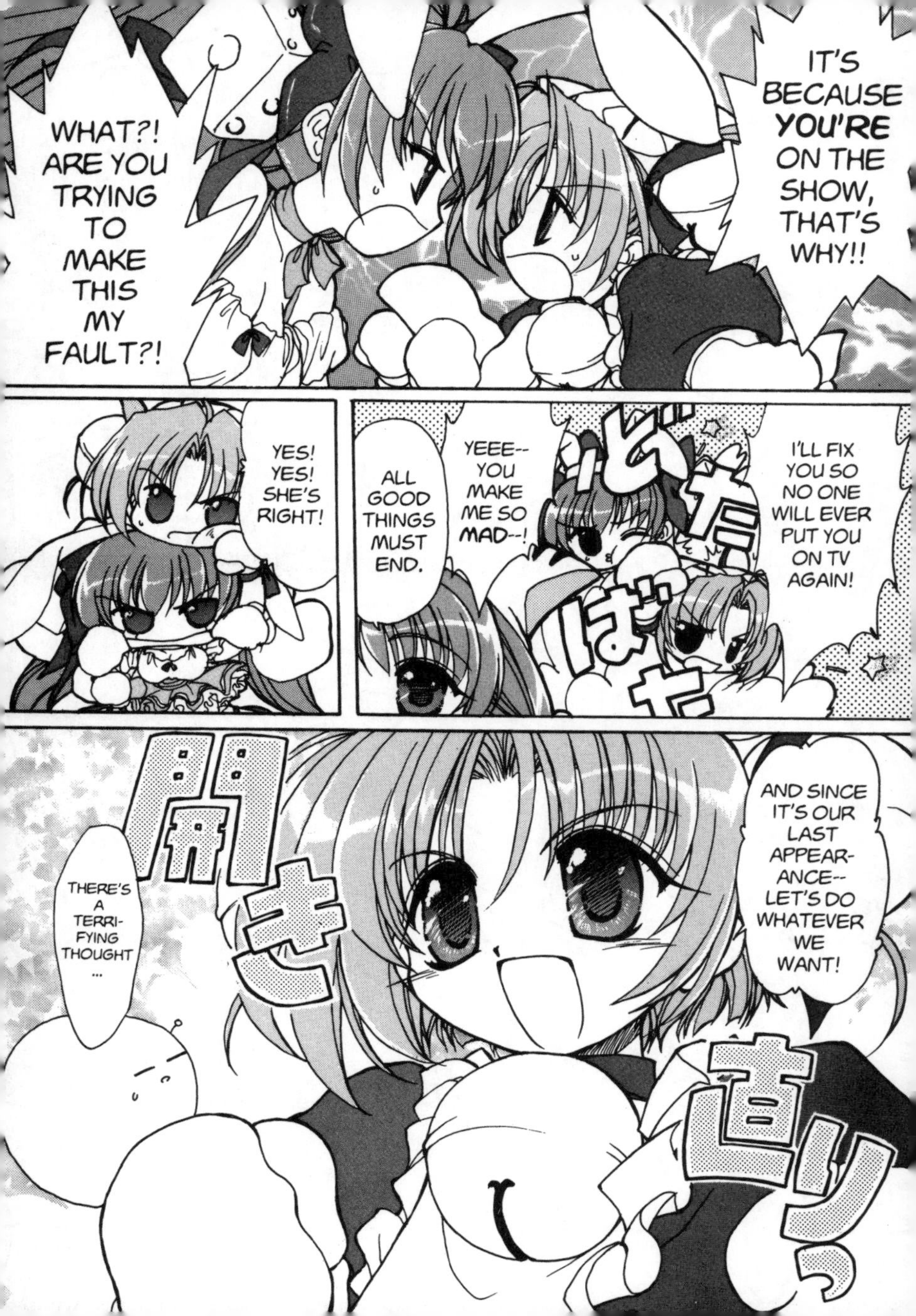
IT'S BECAUSE **YOU'RE** ON THE SHOW, THAT'S WHY!!
WHAT?! ARE YOU TRYING TO MAKE THIS MY FAULT?!
I'LL FIX YOU SO NO ONE WILL EVER PUT YOU ON TV AGAIN!
YEEE-- YOU MAKE ME SO **MAD**--!
どたばた
ALL GOOD THINGS MUST END.
YES! YES! SHE'S RIGHT!
AND SINCE IT'S OUR LAST APPEAR-ANCE-- LET'S DO WHATEVER WE WANT!
開き直りっ
THERE'S A TERRI-FYING THOUGHT ...

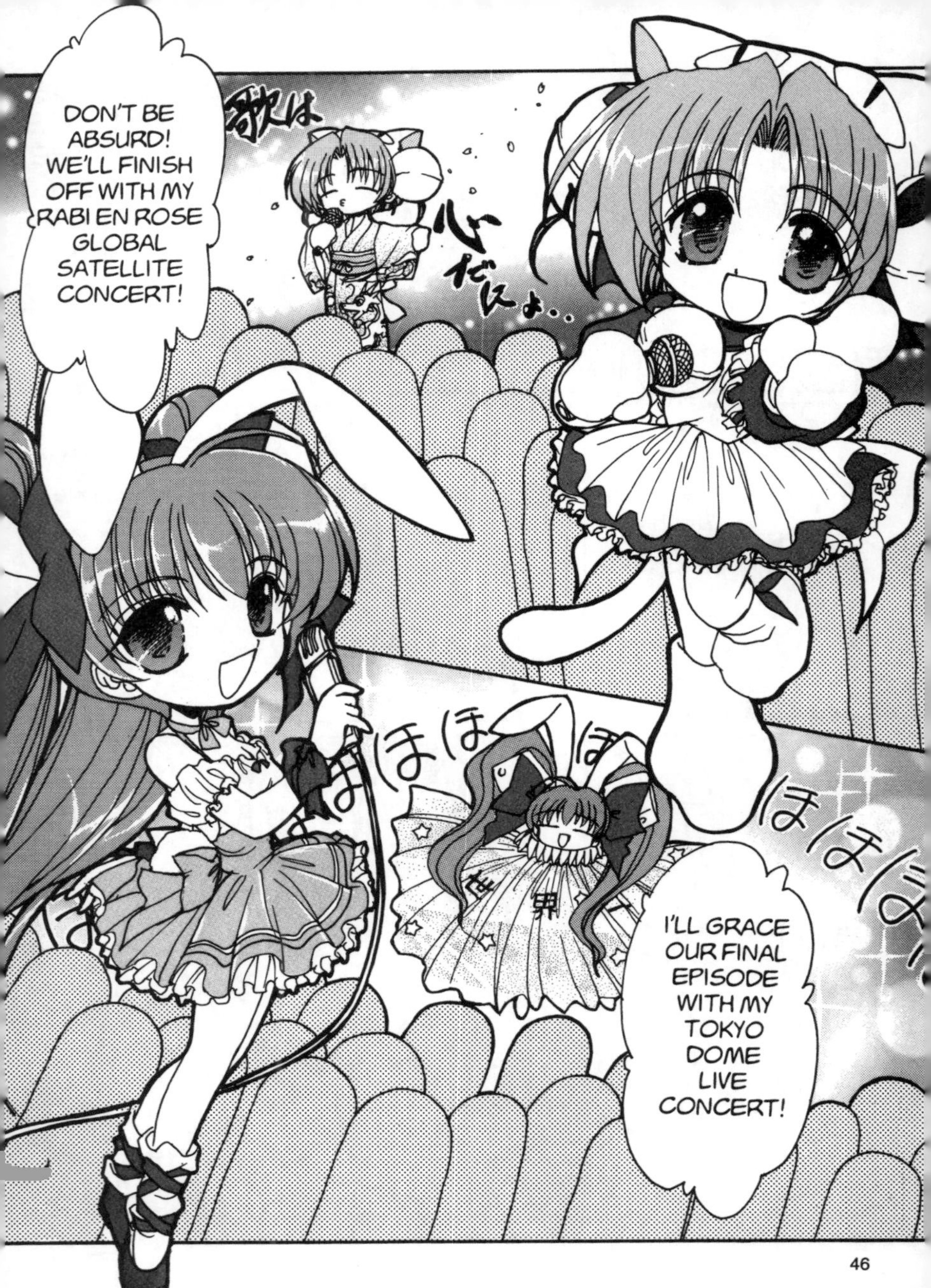
歌は心だにょ..
DON'T BE ABSURD! WE'LL FINISH OFF WITH MY RABI EN ROSE GLOBAL SATELLITE CONCERT!
I'LL GRACE OUR FINAL EPISODE WITH MY TOKYO DOME LIVE CONCERT!

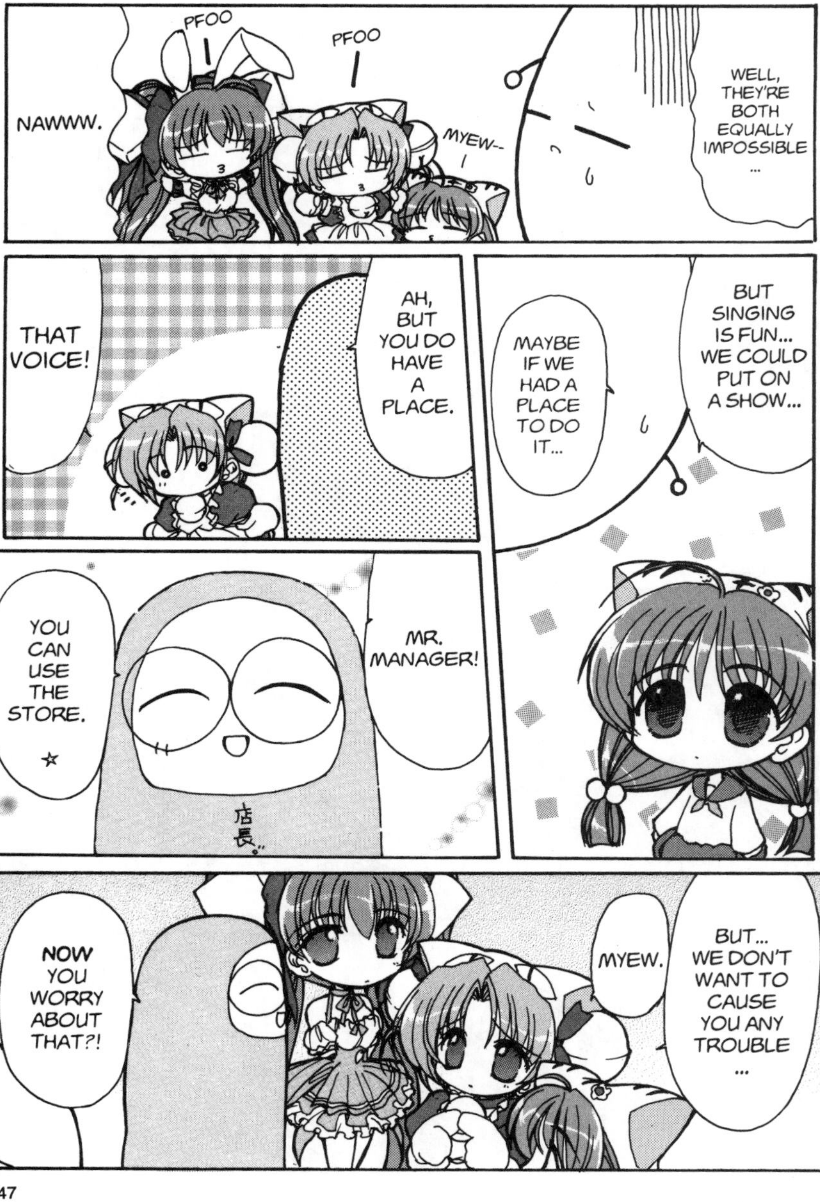
WELL, THEY'RE BOTH EQUALLY IMPOSSIBLE ...
MYEW--
PFOO
PFOO
NAWWW.
BUT SINGING IS FUN... WE COULD PUT ON A SHOW...
MAYBE IF WE HAD A PLACE TO DO IT...
AH, BUT YOU DO HAVE A PLACE.
THAT VOICE!
MR. MANAGER!
YOU CAN USE THE STORE. ☆
店長
BUT... WE DON'T WANT TO CAUSE YOU ANY TROUBLE ...
MYEW.
NOW YOU WORRY ABOUT THAT?!

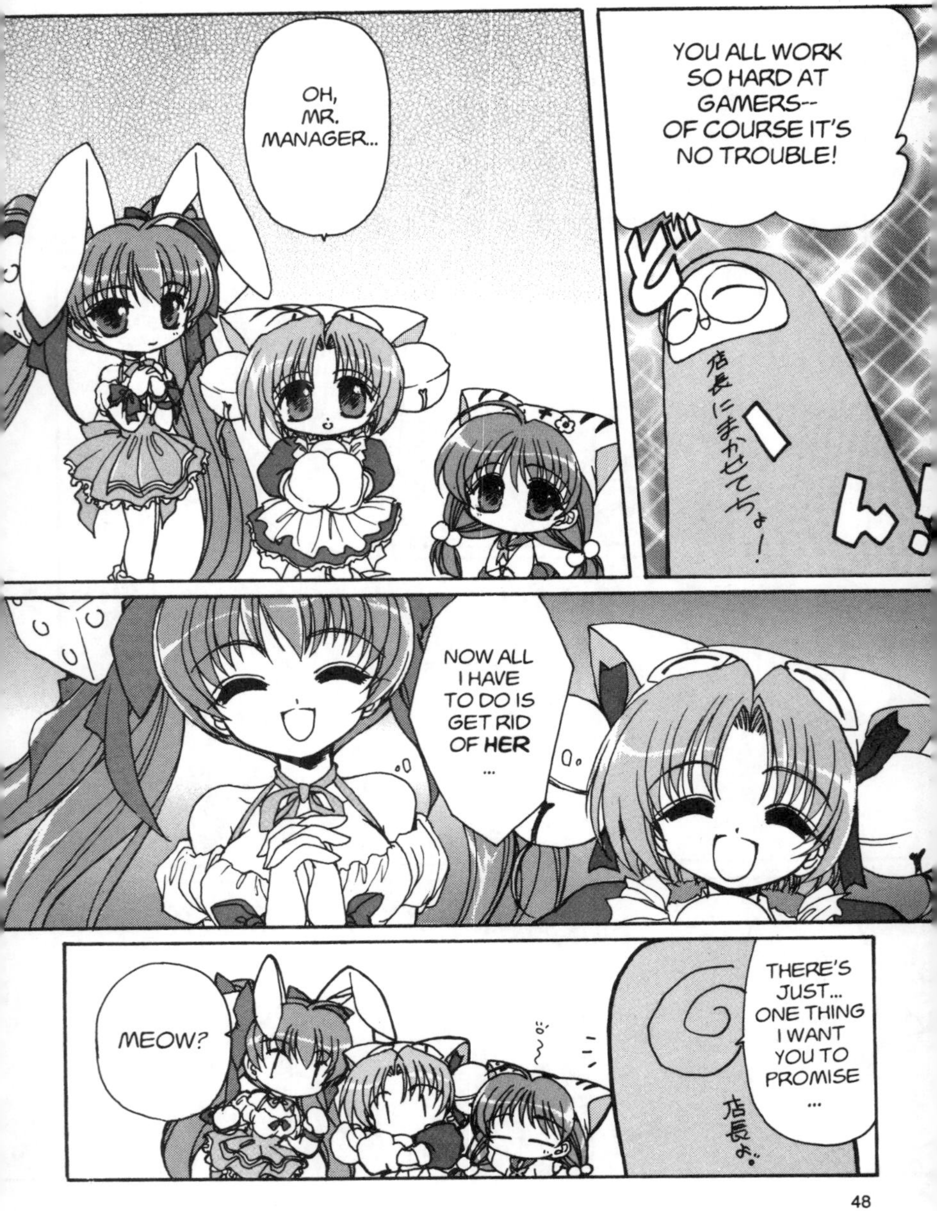
YOU ALL WORK SO HARD AT GAMERS-- OF COURSE IT'S NO TROUBLE!
店長にまかせてちょ!
OH, MR. MANAGER...
NOW ALL I HAVE TO DO IS GET RID OF HER ...
THERE'S JUST... ONE THING I WANT YOU TO PROMISE ...
店長よ。
MEOW?

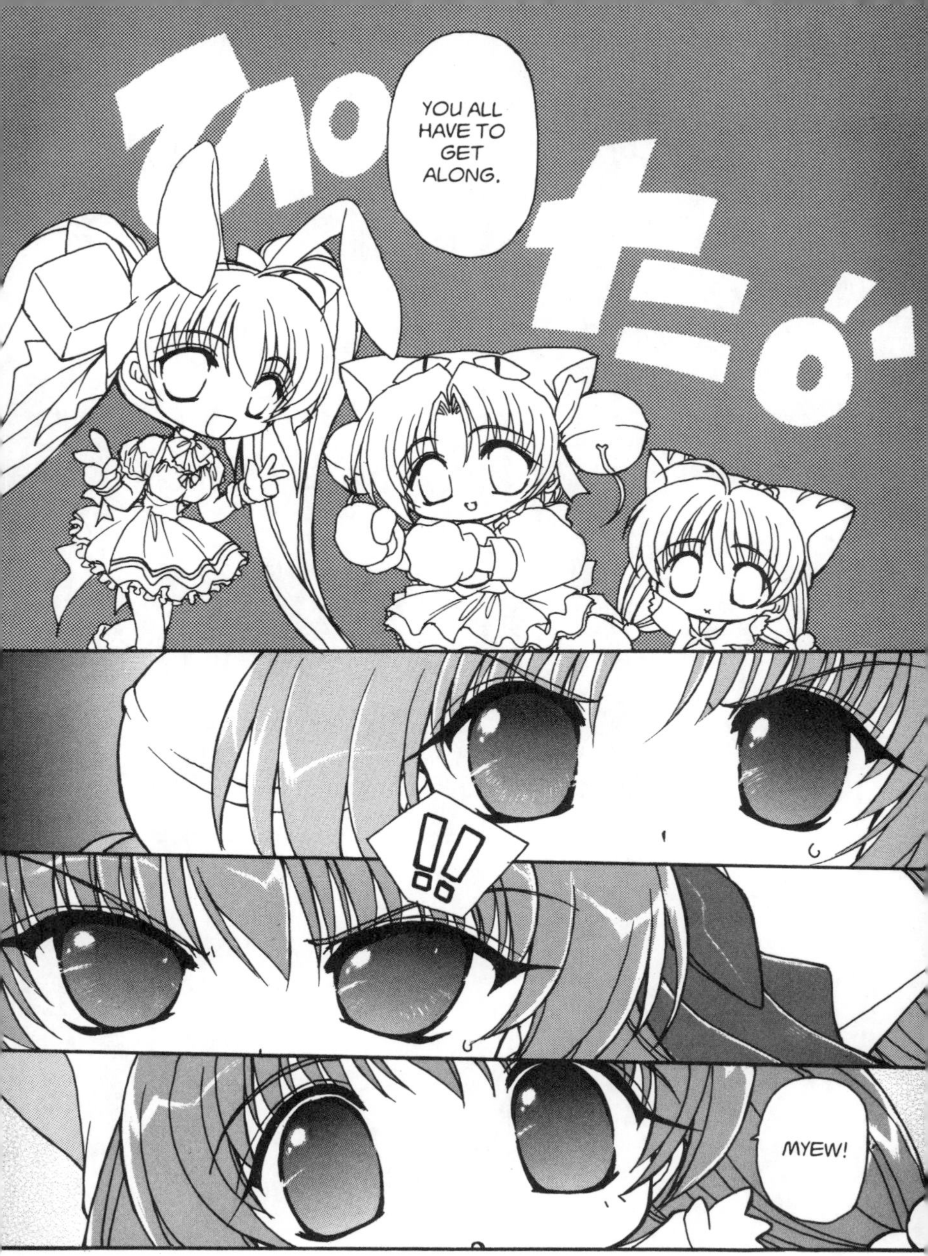
YOU ALL HAVE TO GET ALONG.
!!
MYEW!

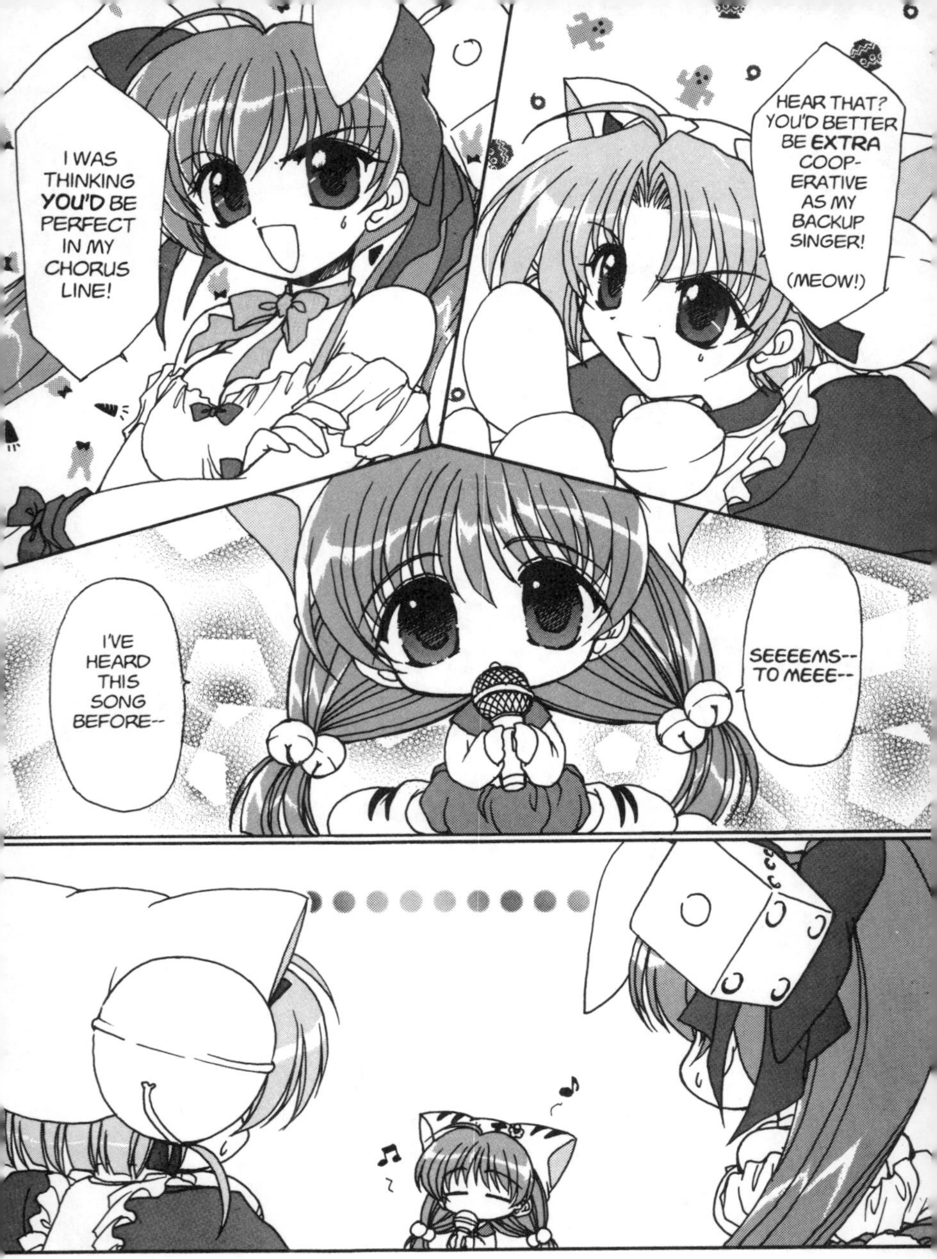
HEAR THAT? YOU'D BETTER BE **EXTRA** COOP-ERATIVE AS MY BACKUP SINGER!
(MEOW!)
I WAS THINKING **YOU'D** BE PERFECT IN MY CHORUS LINE!
SEEEEMS-- TO MEEE--
I'VE HEARD THIS SONG BEFORE--

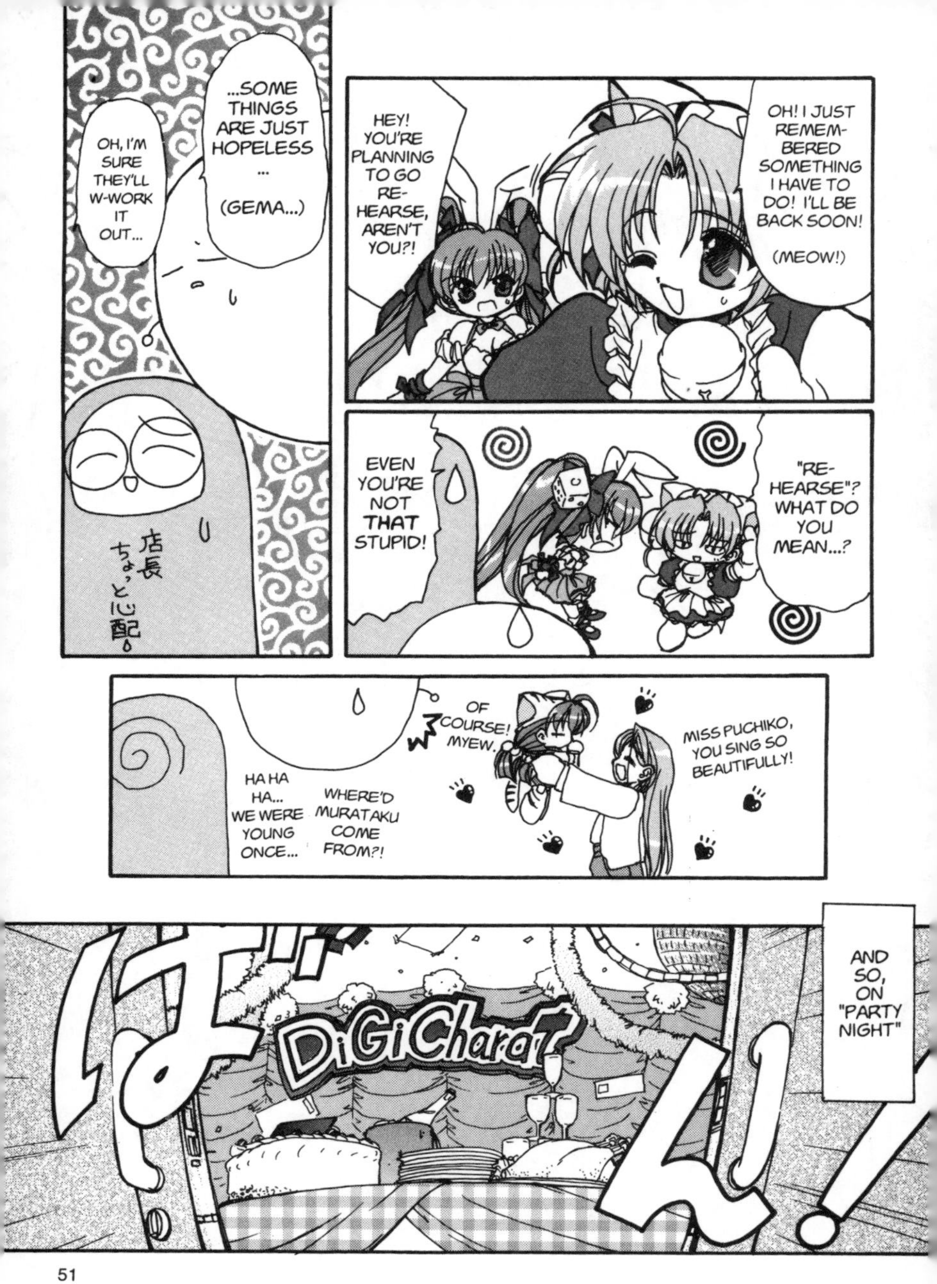
OH! I JUST REMEMBERED SOMETHING I HAVE TO DO! I'LL BE BACK SOON!
(MEOW!)
HEY! YOU'RE PLANNING TO GO REHEARSE, AREN'T YOU?!
"REHEARSE"? WHAT DO YOU MEAN...?
EVEN YOU'RE NOT THAT STUPID!
...SOME THINGS ARE JUST HOPELESS ...
(GEMA...)
OH, I'M SURE THEY'LL W-WORK IT OUT...
店長ちょっと心配。
MISS PUCHIKO, YOU SING SO BEAUTIFULLY!
OF COURSE! MYEW.
WHERE'D MURATAKU COME FROM?!
HA HA HA... WE WERE YOUNG ONCE...
AND SO, ON "PARTY NIGHT"
DiGiCharaT

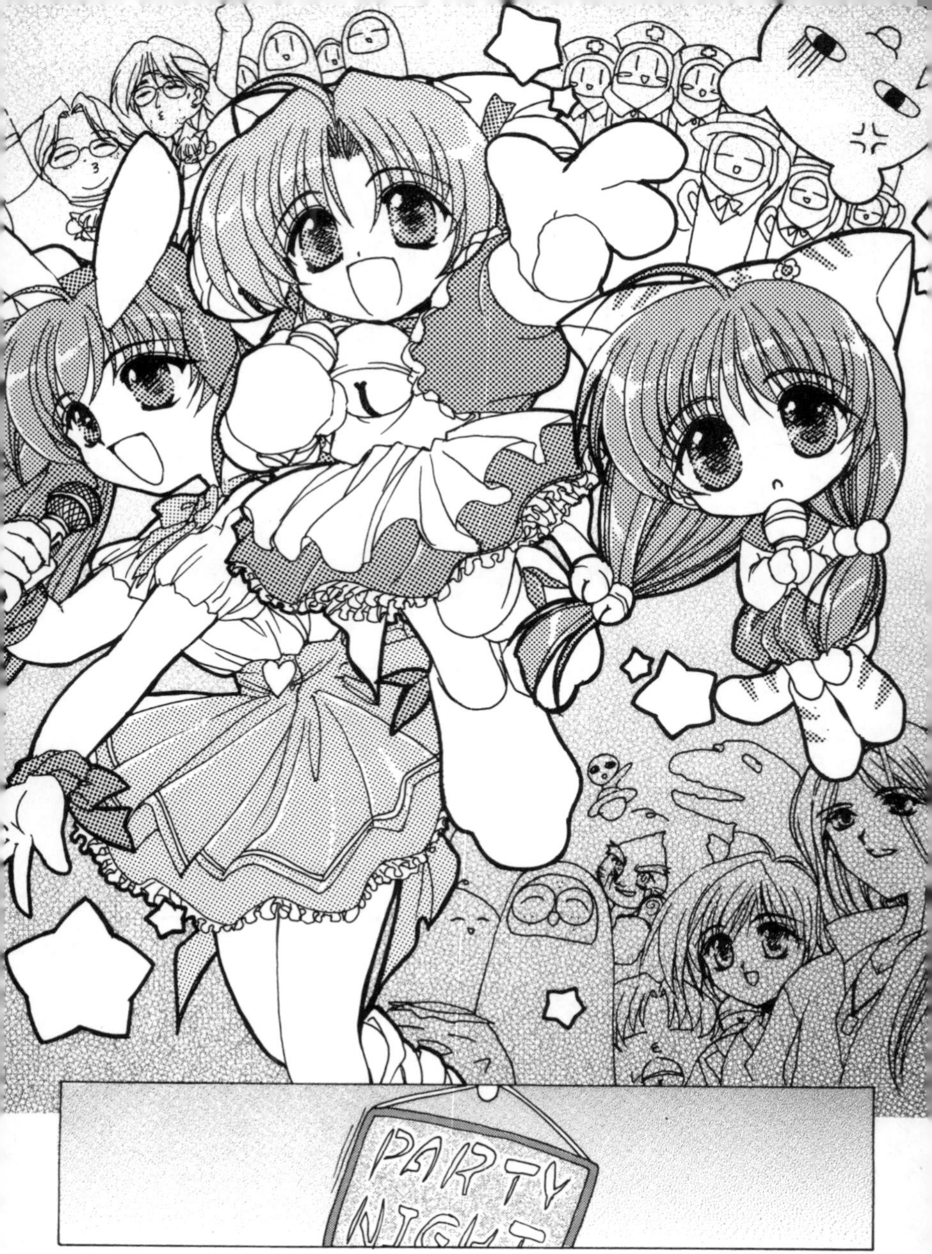
PARTY NIGHT

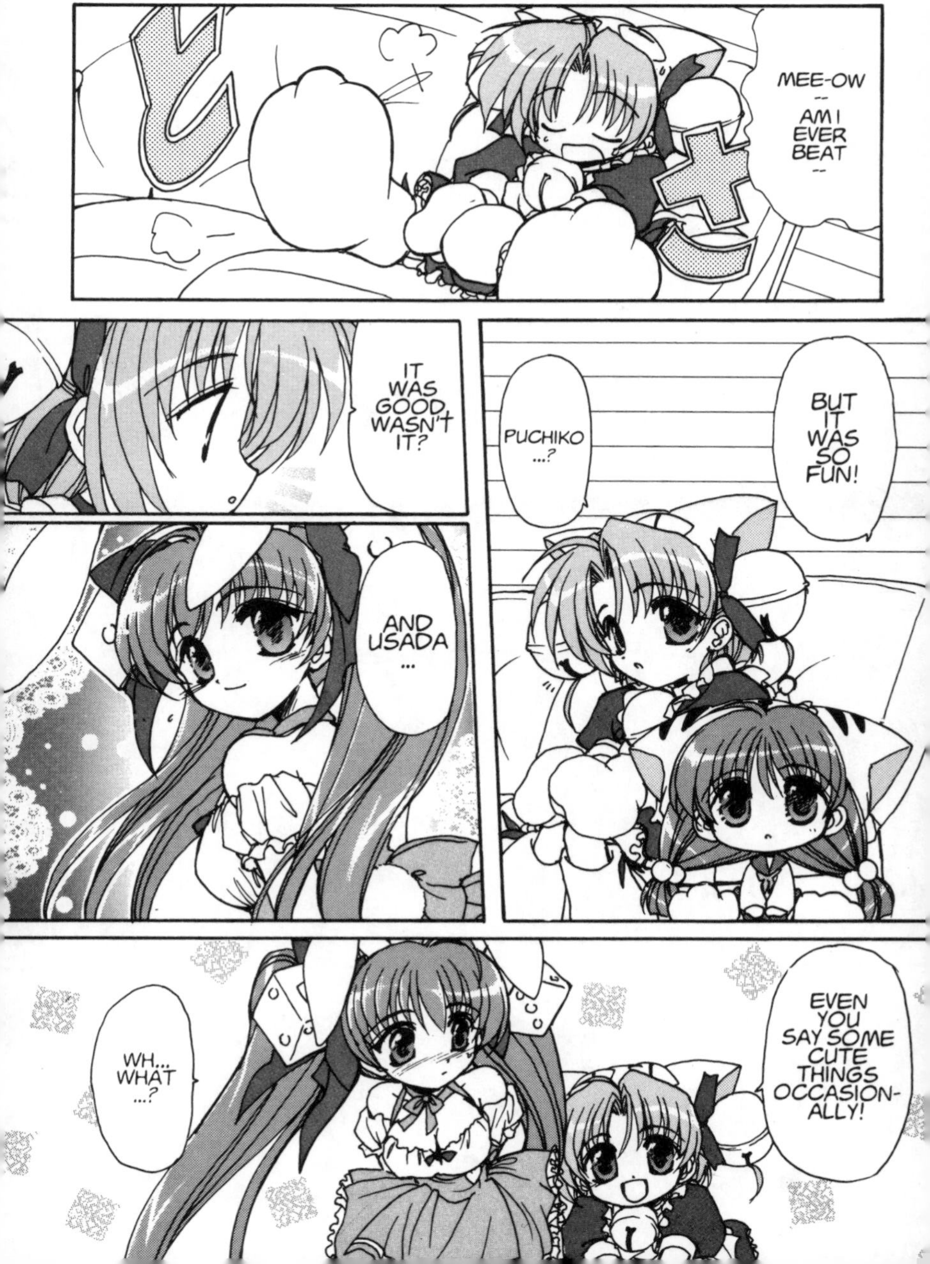
MEE-OW -- AM I EVER BEAT --
BUT IT WAS SO FUN!
PUCHIKO ...?
IT WAS GOOD WASN'T IT?
AND USADA ...
EVEN YOU SAY SOME CUTE THINGS OCCASION-ALLY!
WH... WHAT ...?

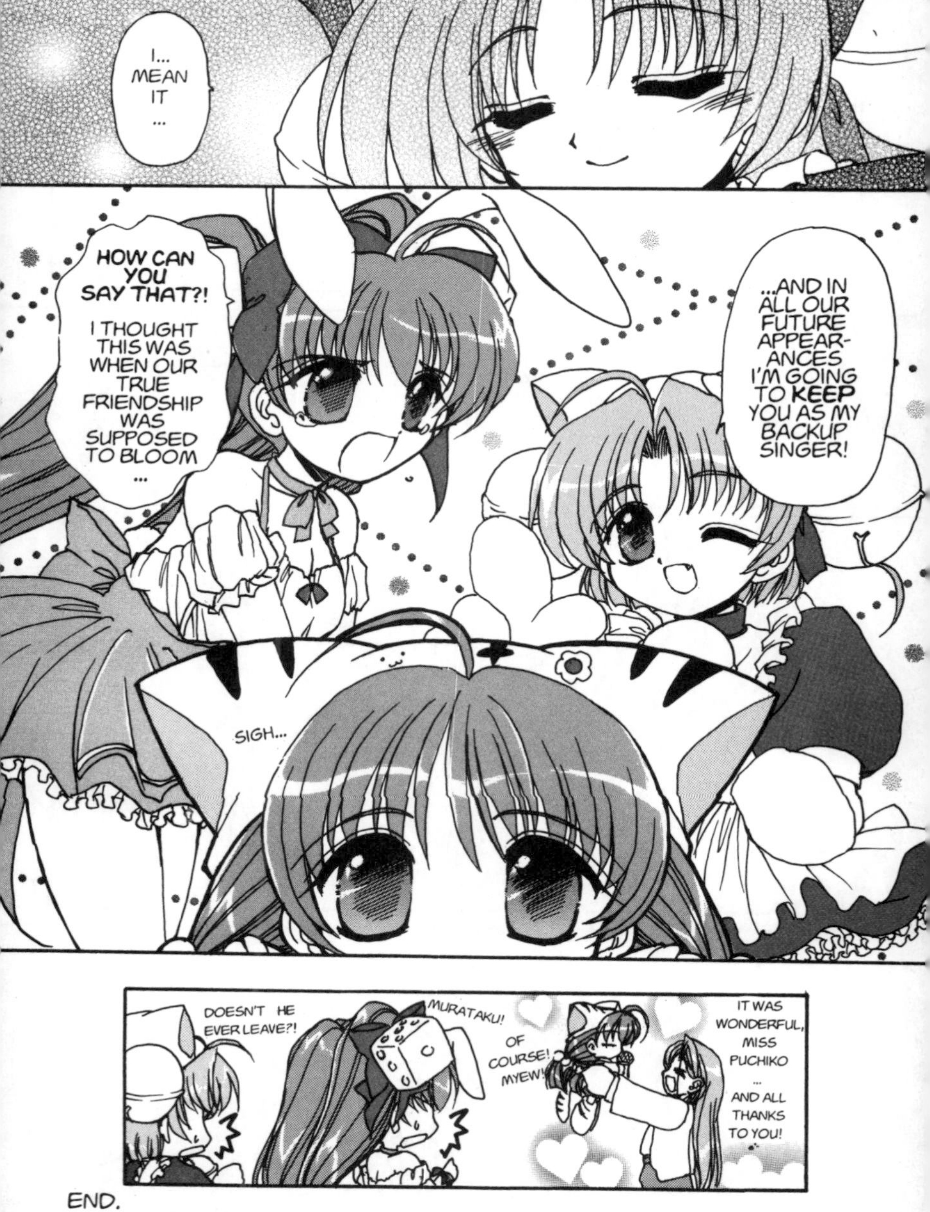
I... MEAN IT ...
...AND IN ALL OUR FUTURE APPEARANCES I'M GOING TO **KEEP** YOU AS MY BACKUP SINGER!
HOW CAN YOU SAY THAT?!
I THOUGHT THIS WAS WHEN OUR TRUE FRIENDSHIP WAS SUPPOSED TO BLOOM ...
SIGH...
IT WAS WONDERFUL, MISS PUCHIKO ... AND ALL THANKS TO YOU!
OF COURSE! MYEW!
MURATAKU!
DOESN'T HE EVER LEAVE?!

END.

A comment about Di Gi Charat

"I LOVE DIGIKO!"

I FELL IN LOVE WITH HER AT FIRST SIGHT WHEN SHE FIRST APPEARED IN "FROM GAMERS" MAGAZINE. SO I LOVED HAVING THE CHANCE TO DO THIS GIG.

IT'S AN ODD MANGA, I ADMIT, BUT WE DIGIKO FANS LOVE IT...

MIYABI FUJIEDA

MIYABI FUJIEDA

KAPPA:

"A GREAT MAGICIAN IS NEVER CAUGHT DOING TRICKS."

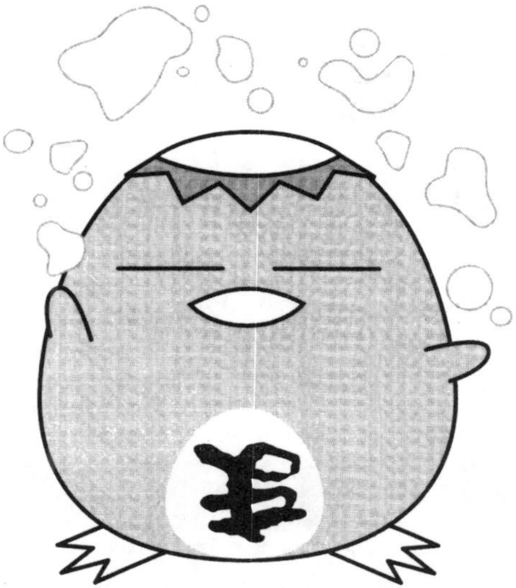

ILLUSTRATION/KURIMU

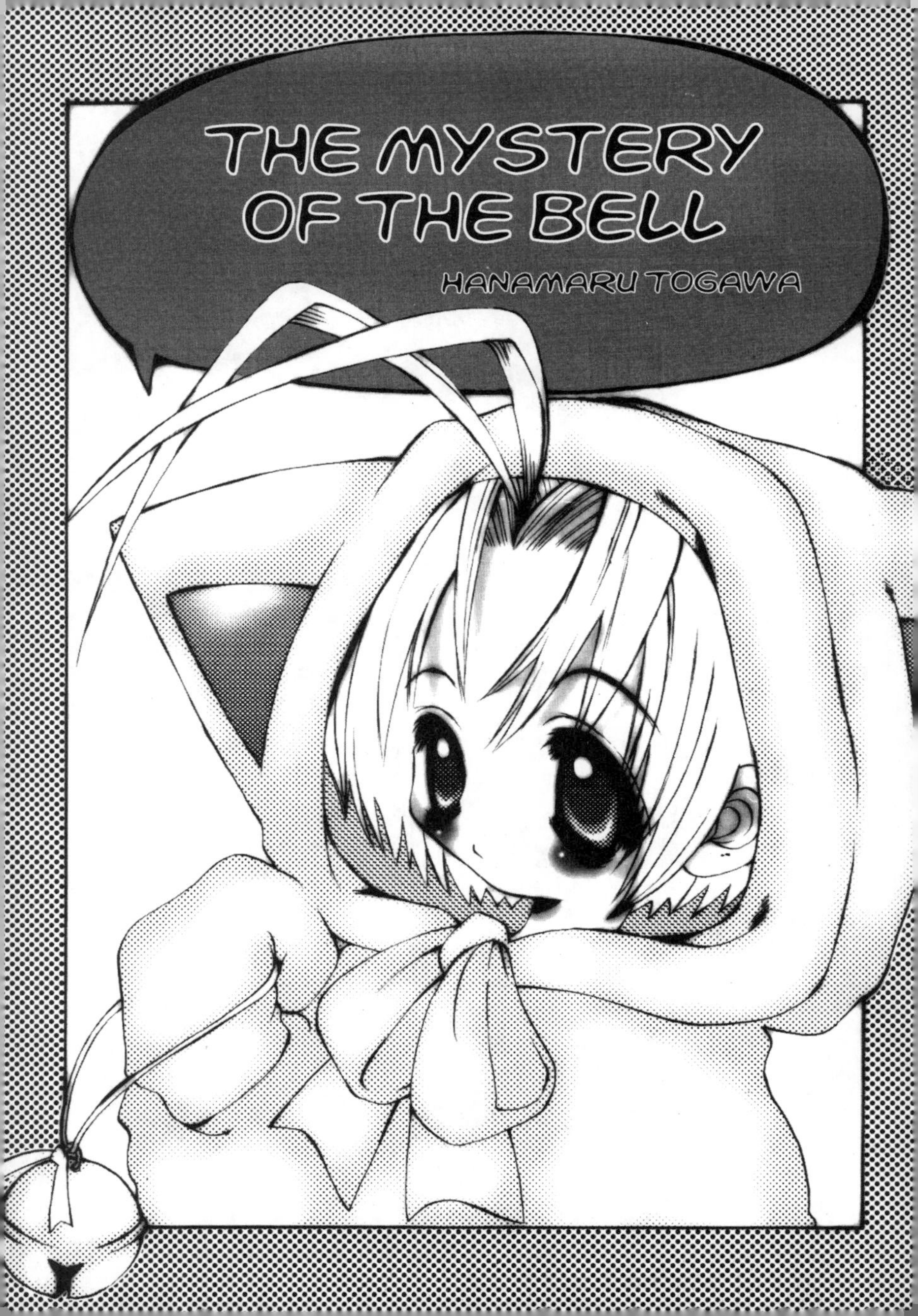
THE MYSTERY OF THE BELL
HANAMARU TOGAWA

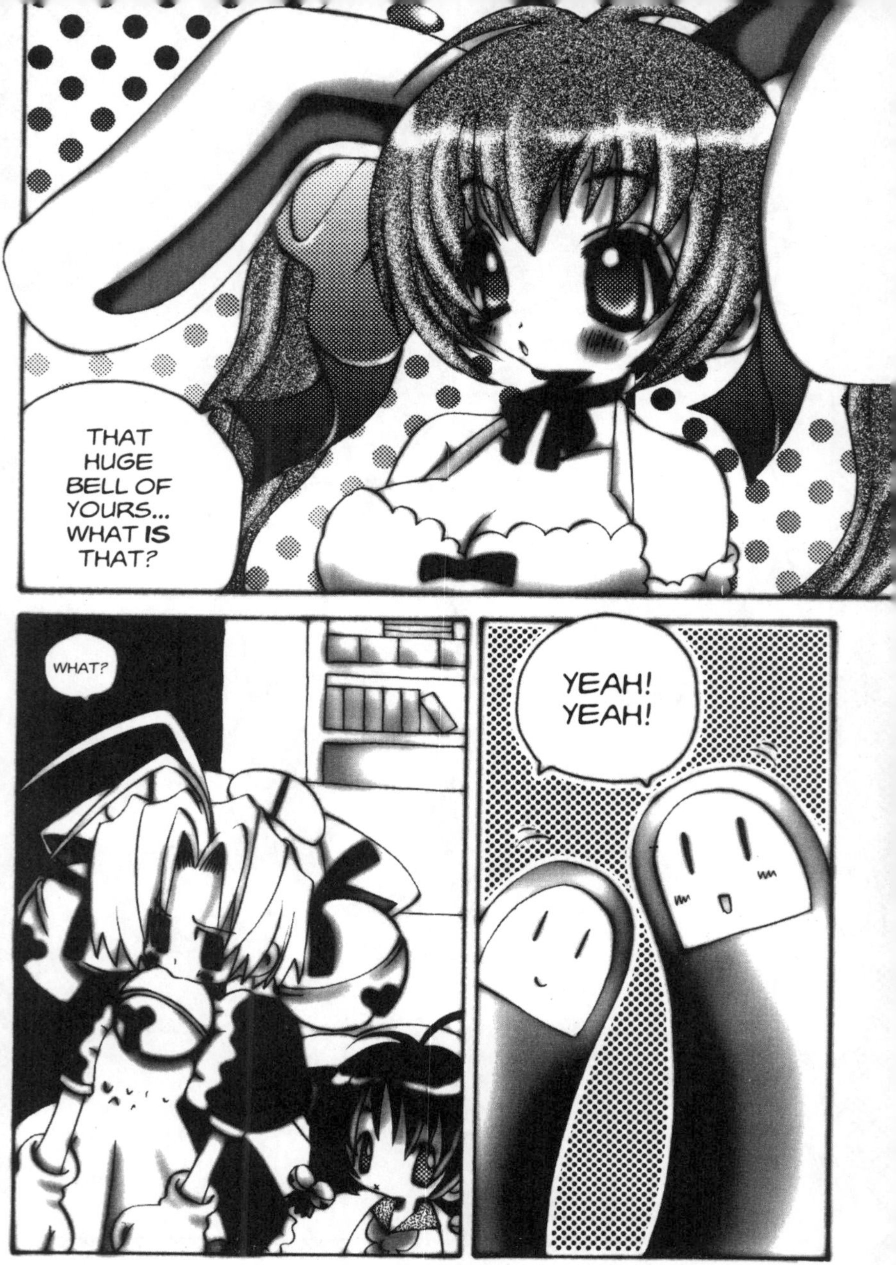
THAT HUGE BELL OF YOURS... WHAT **IS** THAT?
YEAH! YEAH!
WHAT?

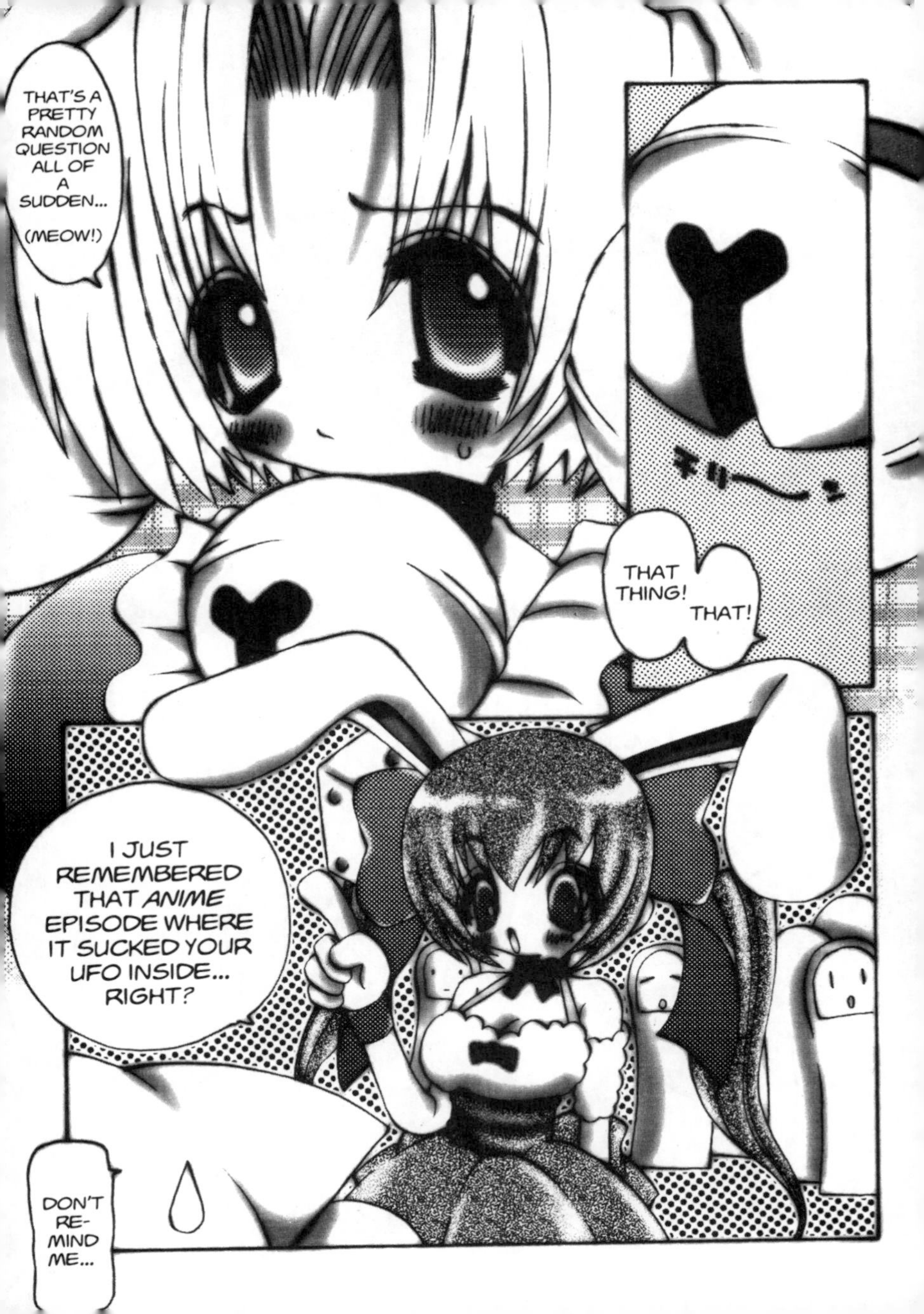
THAT THING! THAT!
THAT'S A PRETTY RANDOM QUESTION ALL OF A SUDDEN... (MEOW!)
I JUST REMEMBERED THAT *ANIME* EPISODE WHERE IT SUCKED YOUR UFO INSIDE... RIGHT?
DON'T RE-MIND ME...

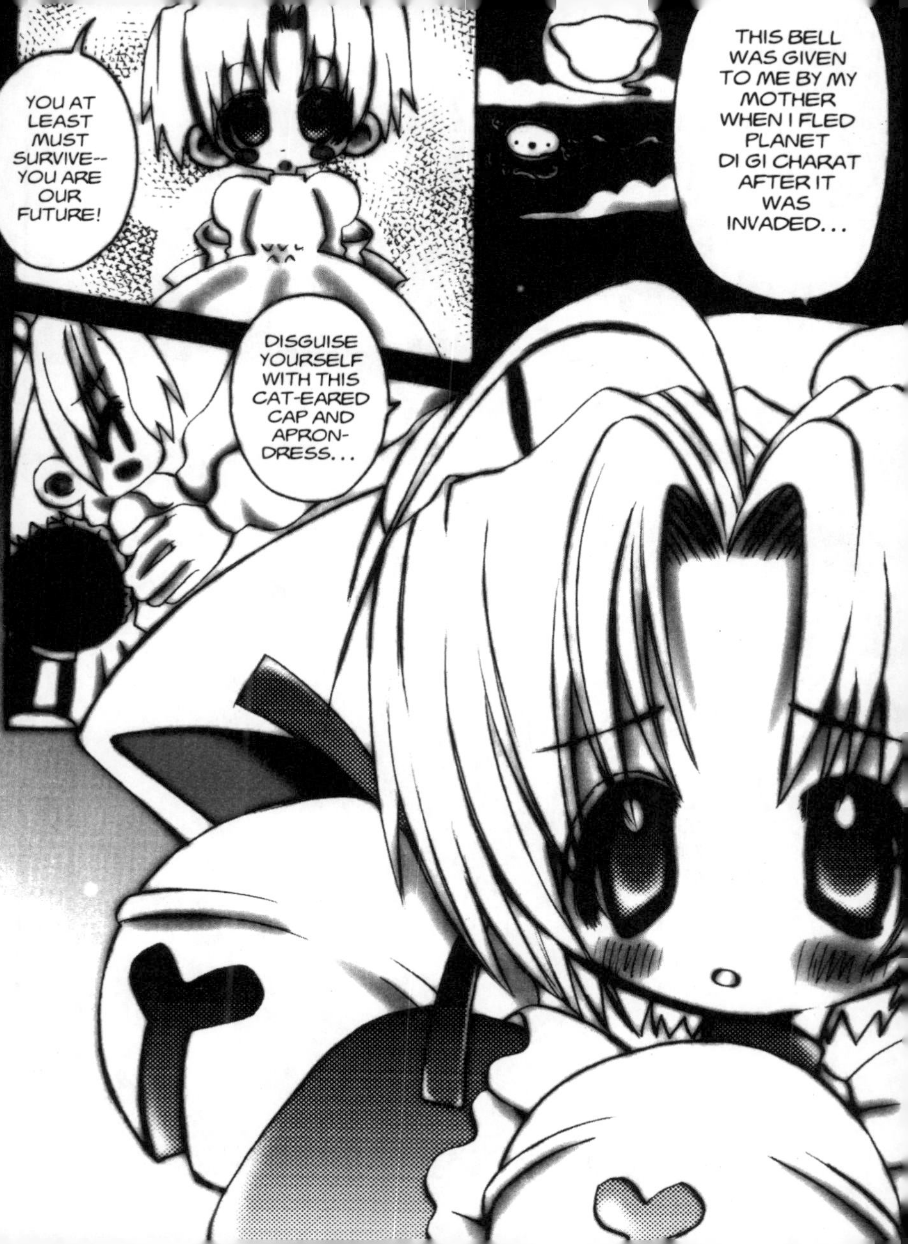
THIS BELL WAS GIVEN TO ME BY MY MOTHER WHEN I FLED PLANET DI GI CHARAT AFTER IT WAS INVADED...
YOU AT LEAST MUST SURVIVE--YOU ARE OUR FUTURE!
DISGUISE YOURSELF WITH THIS CAT-EARED CAP AND APRON-DRESS...

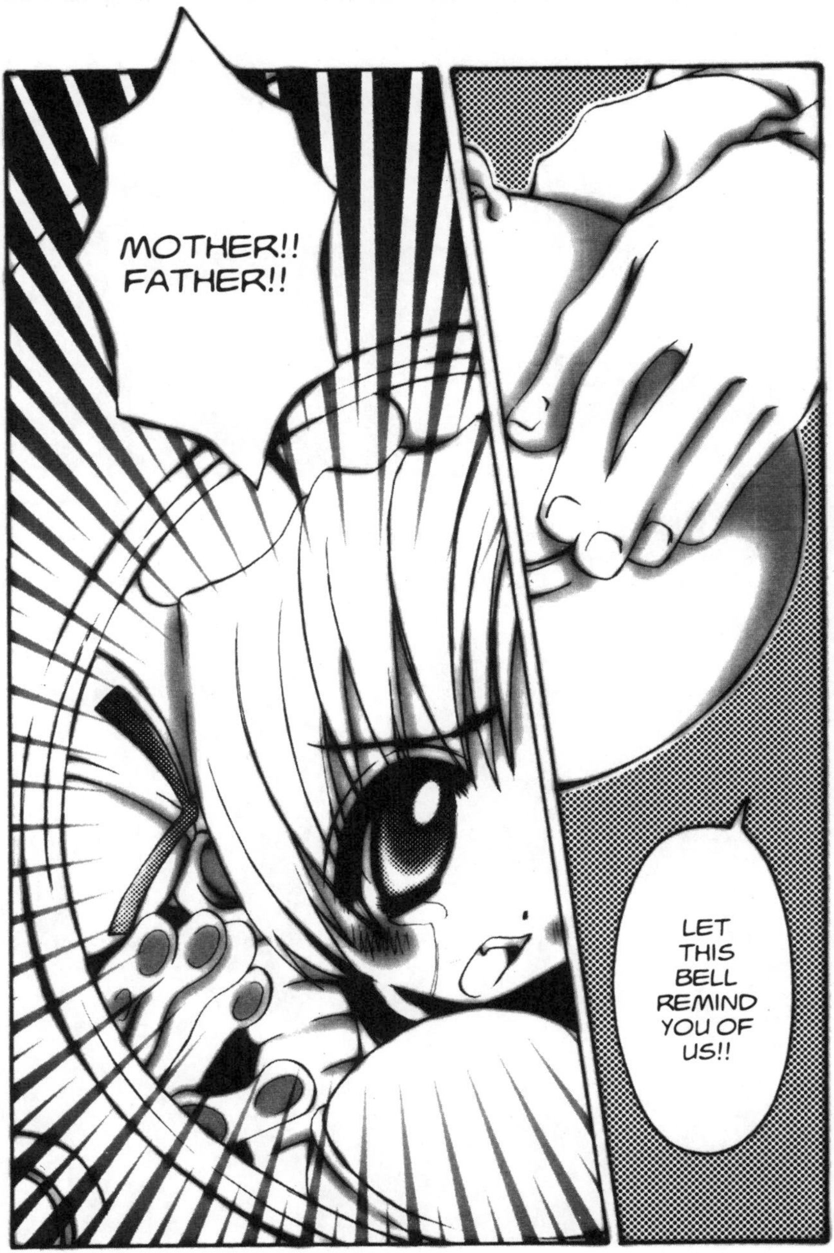
LET THIS BELL REMIND YOU OF US!!
MOTHER!! FATHER!!

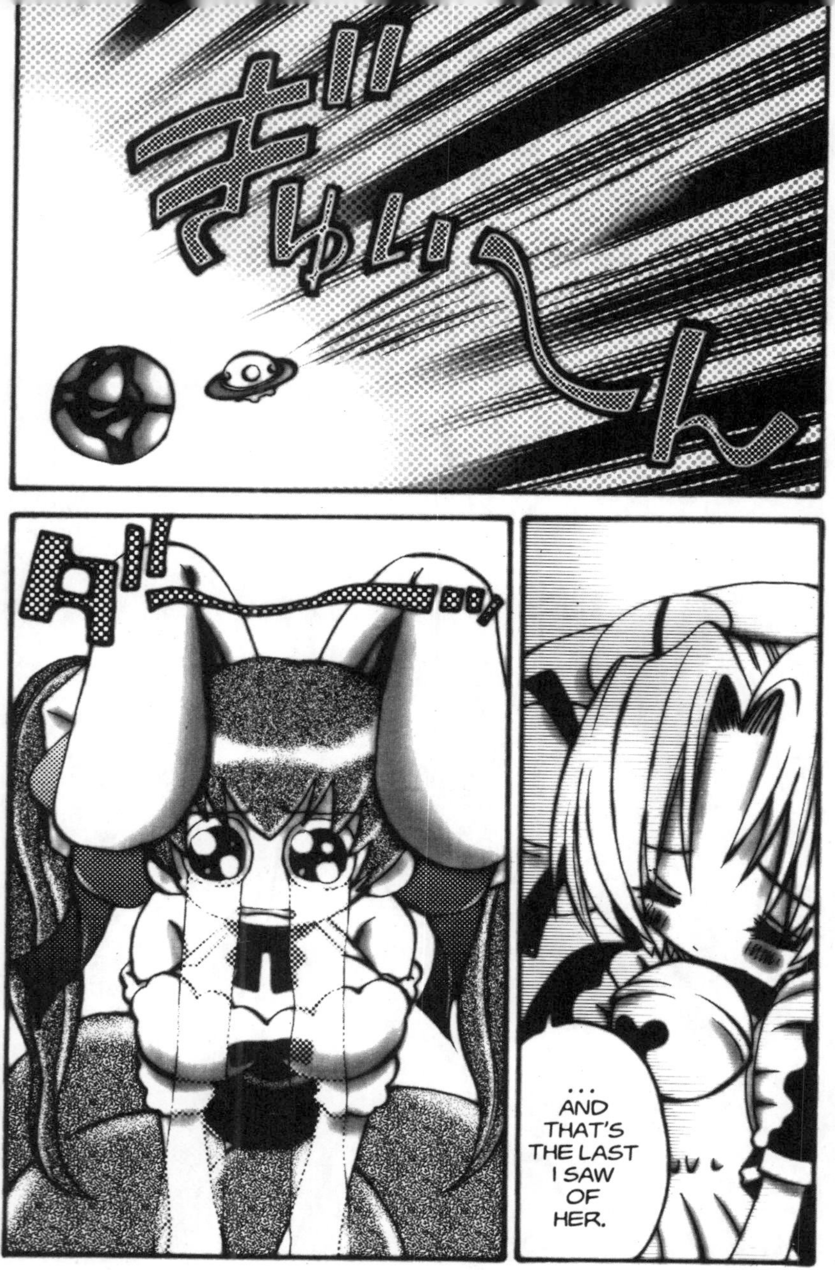
...
AND THAT'S THE LAST I SAW OF HER.

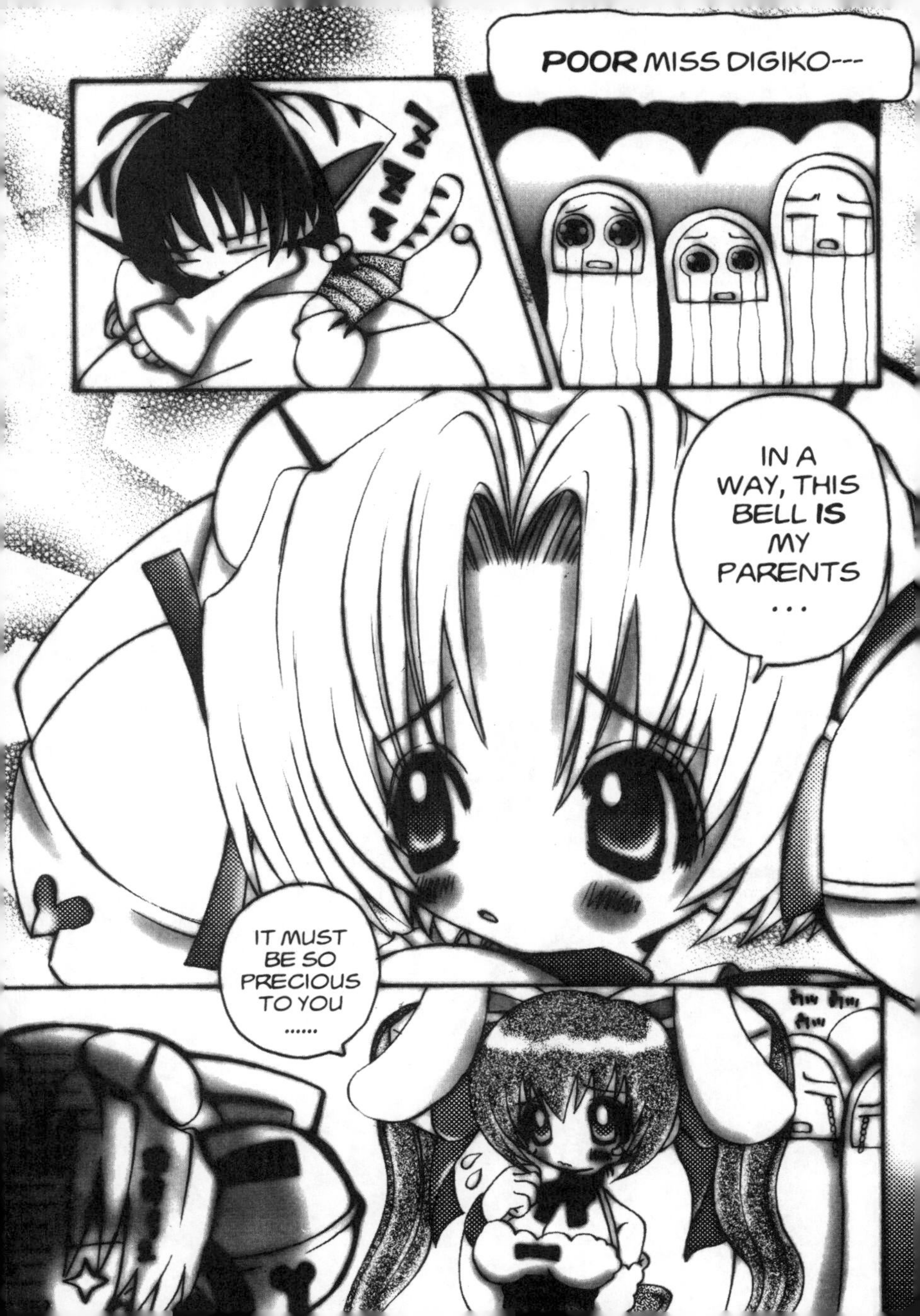
POOR MISS DIGIKO---
IN A WAY, THIS BELL IS MY PARENTS ...
IT MUST BE SO PRECIOUS TO YOU ......

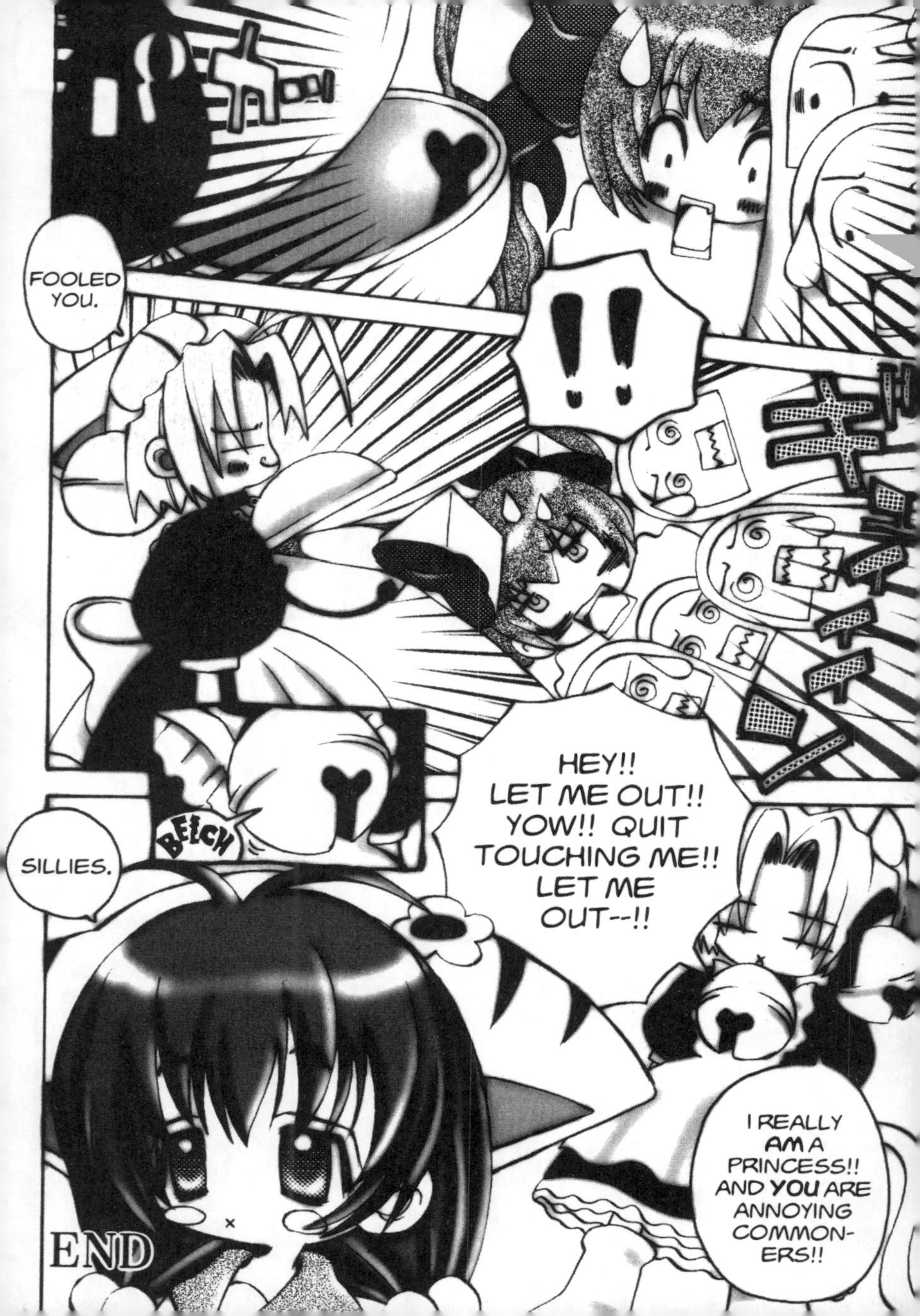
FOOLED YOU.
!!
HEY!! LET ME OUT!! YOW!! QUIT TOUCHING ME!! LET ME OUT--!!
BELCH
SILLIES.
I REALLY **AM** A PRINCESS!! AND **YOU** ARE ANNOYING COMMONERS!!
END

A comment about Di Gi Charat

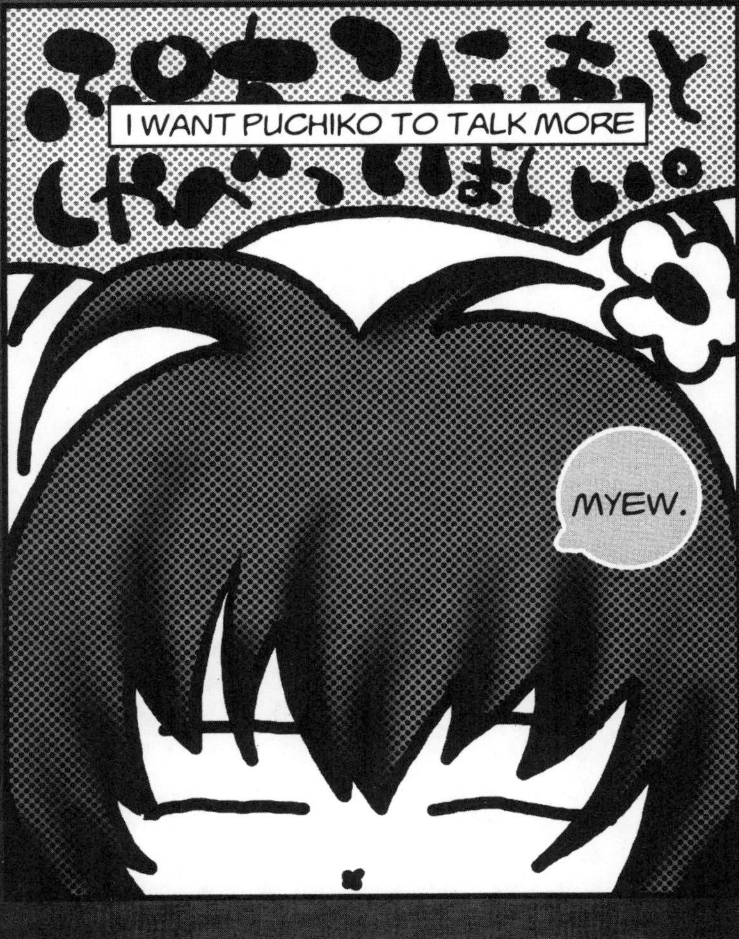
ぷちこにもっとしゃべってほしい。
I WANT PUCHIKO TO TALK MORE
MYEW.

HANAMARU TOGAWA

KAPPA:
"EVEN
WATER-
IMPS
CAN BE
WASHED
AWAY."

ILLUSTRATION/KURIMU

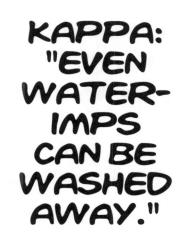

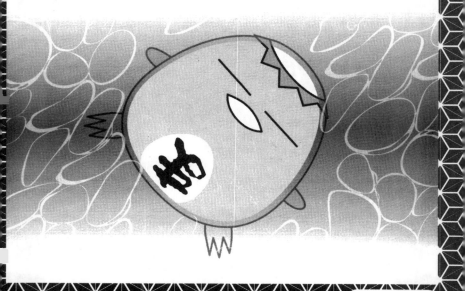

MAY YOUR FUTURE BE BRIGHT!

TAKAHIRO AKIDUKI

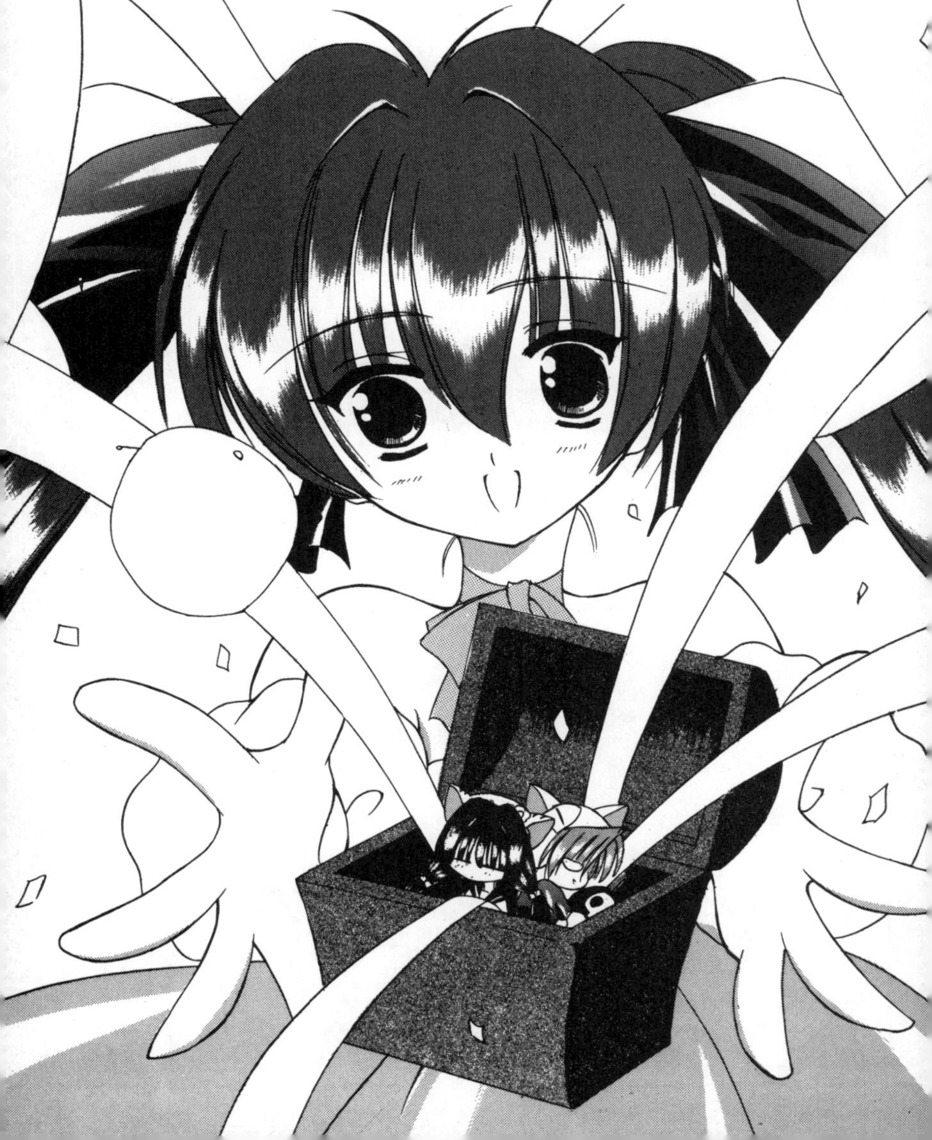

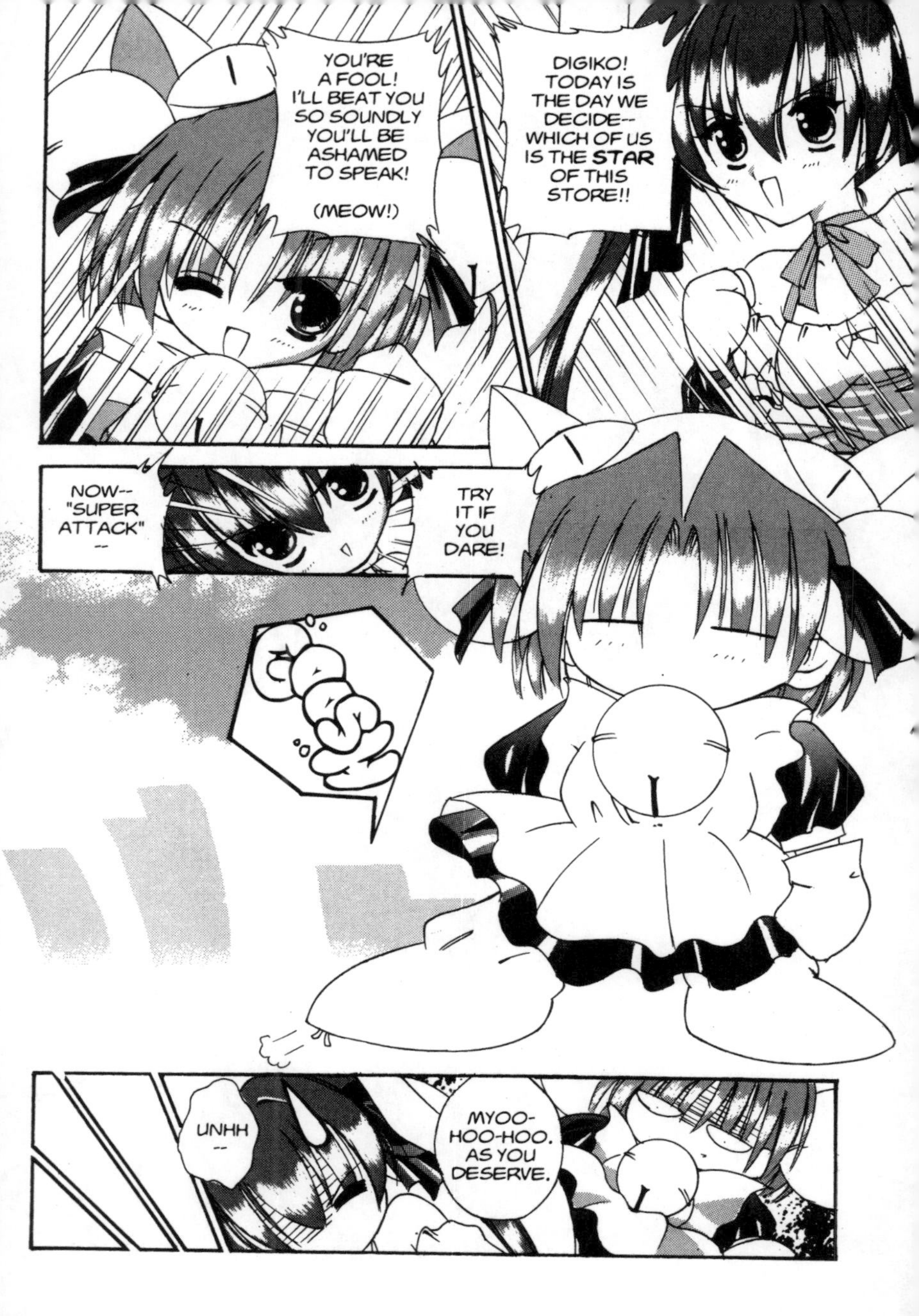
DIGIKO! TODAY IS THE DAY WE DECIDE-- WHICH OF US IS THE **STAR** OF THIS STORE!!
YOU'RE A FOOL! I'LL BEAT YOU SO SOUNDLY YOU'LL BE ASHAMED TO SPEAK!
(MEOW!)
TRY IT IF YOU DARE!
NOW-- "SUPER ATTACK" --
MYOO-HOO-HOO. AS YOU DESERVE.
UNHH --

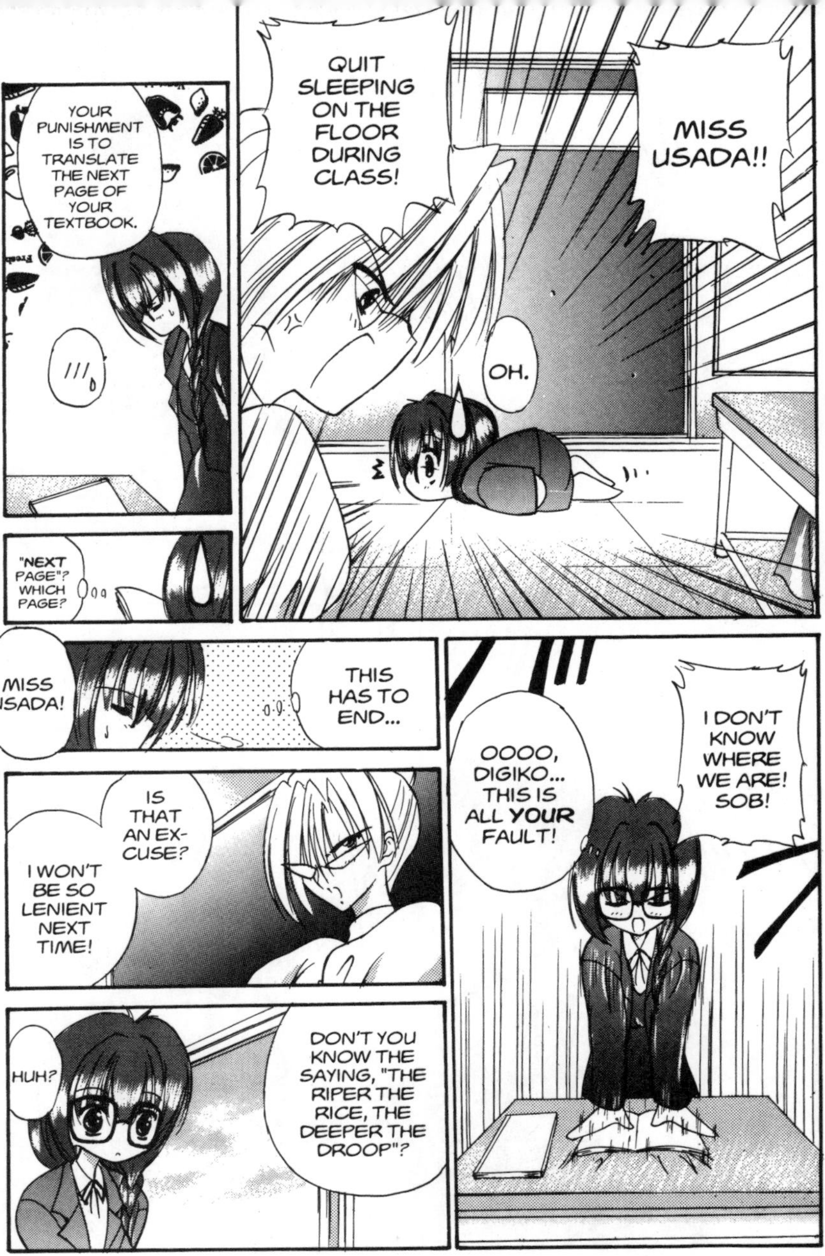
MISS USADA!!
QUIT SLEEPING ON THE FLOOR DURING CLASS!
OH.
YOUR PUNISHMENT IS TO TRANSLATE THE NEXT PAGE OF YOUR TEXTBOOK.
///
"NEXT PAGE"? WHICH PAGE?
I DON'T KNOW WHERE WE ARE! SOB!
OOOO, DIGIKO... THIS IS ALL YOUR FAULT!
THIS HAS TO END...
MISS USADA!
IS THAT AN EXCUSE?
I WON'T BE SO LENIENT NEXT TIME!
DON'T YOU KNOW THE SAYING, "THE RIPER THE RICE, THE DEEPER THE DROOP"?
HUH?

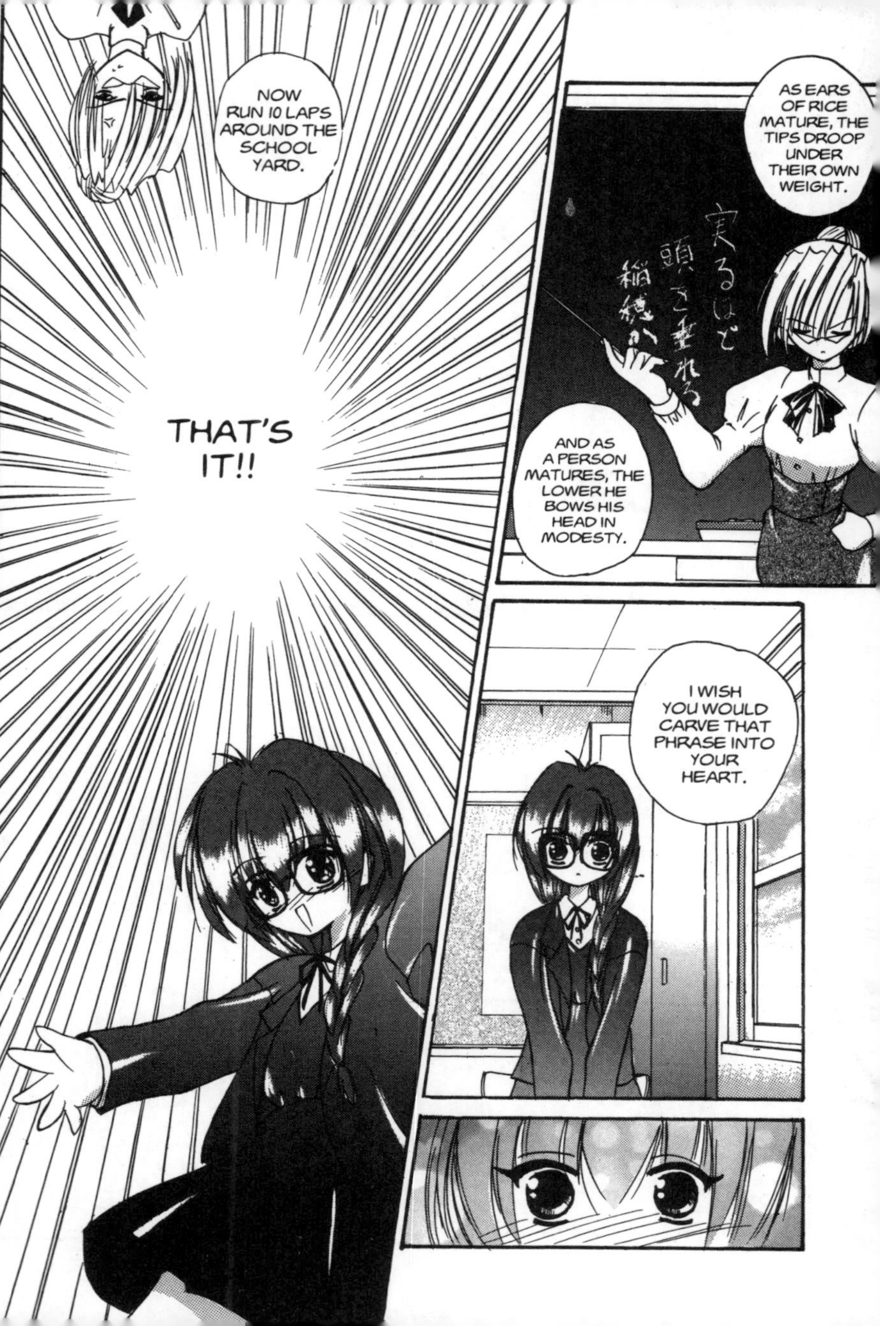
AS EARS OF RICE MATURE, THE TIPS DROOP UNDER THEIR OWN WEIGHT.
実るほど頭を垂れる稲穂かな
AND AS A PERSON MATURES, THE LOWER HE BOWS HIS HEAD IN MODESTY.
I WISH YOU WOULD CARVE THAT PHRASE INTO YOUR HEART.
NOW RUN 10 LAPS AROUND THE SCHOOL YARD.
THAT'S IT!!

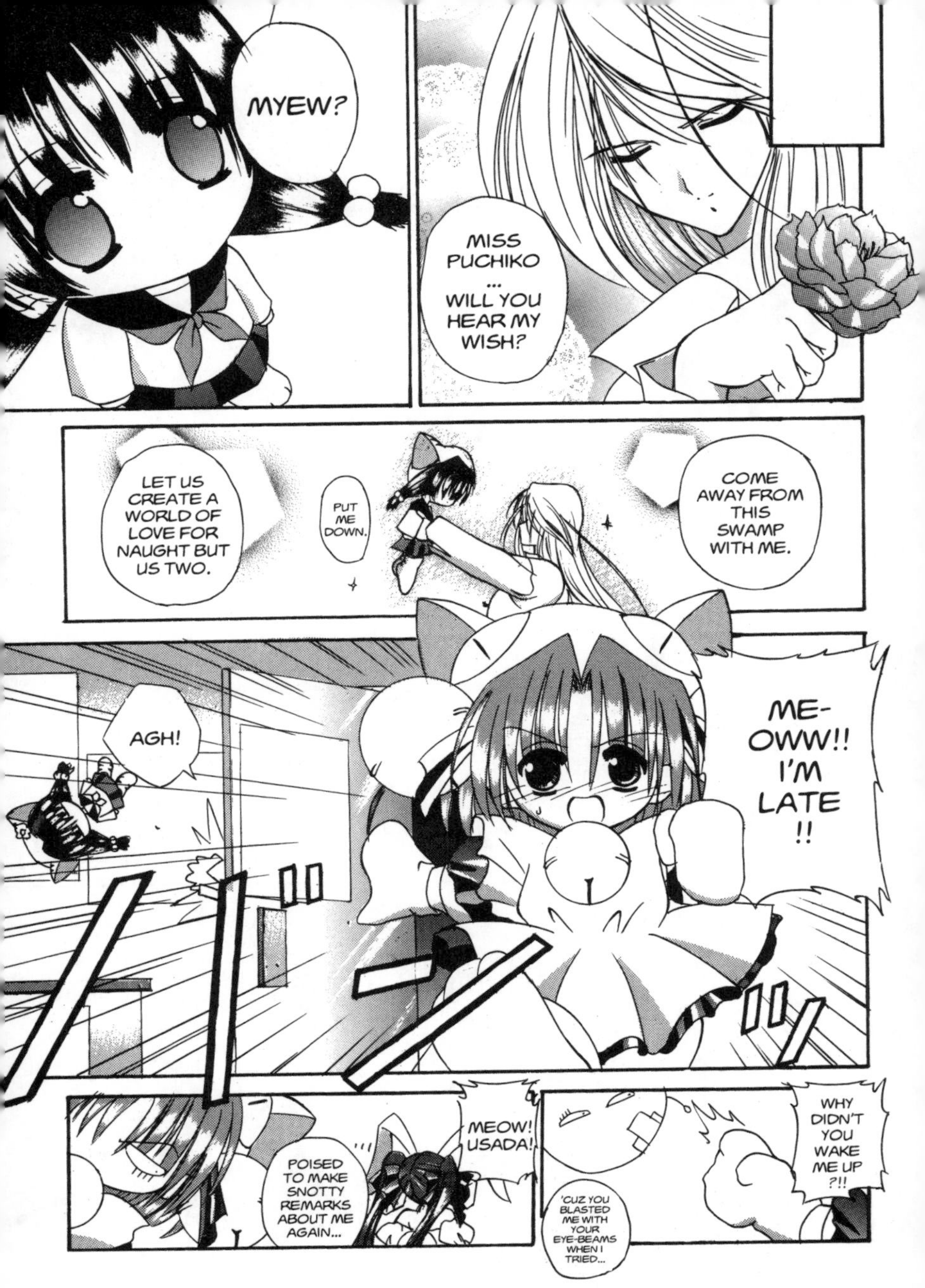
MISS PUCHIKO ... WILL YOU HEAR MY WISH?
MYEW?
COME AWAY FROM THIS SWAMP WITH ME.
PUT ME DOWN.
LET US CREATE A WORLD OF LOVE FOR NAUGHT BUT US TWO.
ME-OWW!! I'M LATE !!
AGH!
WHY DIDN'T YOU WAKE ME UP ?!!
'CUZ YOU BLASTED ME WITH YOUR EYE-BEAMS WHEN I TRIED...
MEOW! USADA!
POISED TO MAKE SNOTTY REMARKS ABOUT ME AGAIN...

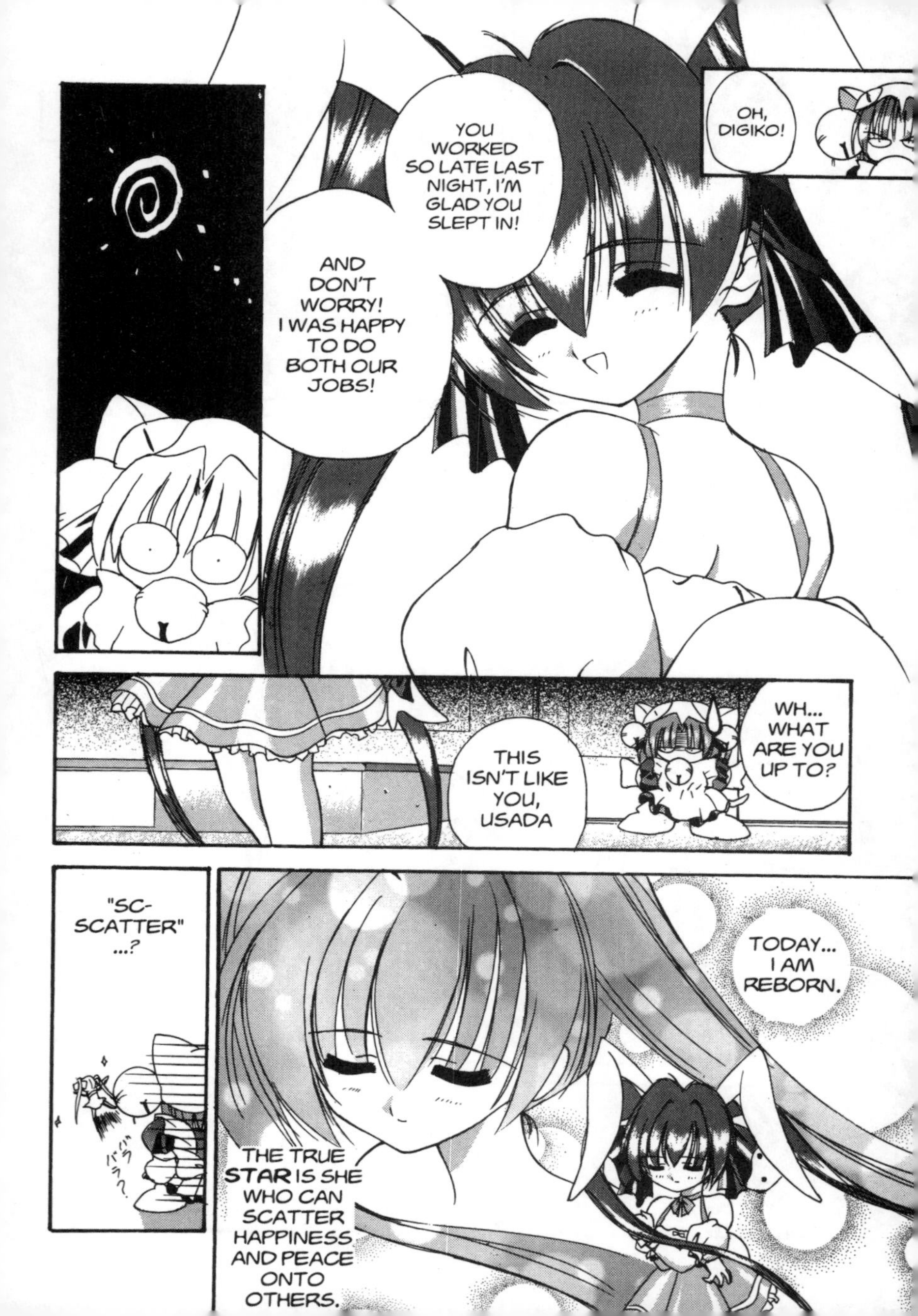
OH, DIGIKO!
YOU WORKED SO LATE LAST NIGHT, I'M GLAD YOU SLEPT IN!
AND DON'T WORRY! I WAS HAPPY TO DO BOTH OUR JOBS!
WH... WHAT ARE YOU UP TO?
THIS ISN'T LIKE YOU, USADA
TODAY... I AM REBORN.
THE TRUE **STAR** IS SHE WHO CAN SCATTER HAPPINESS AND PEACE ONTO OTHERS.
"SC-SCATTER" ...?

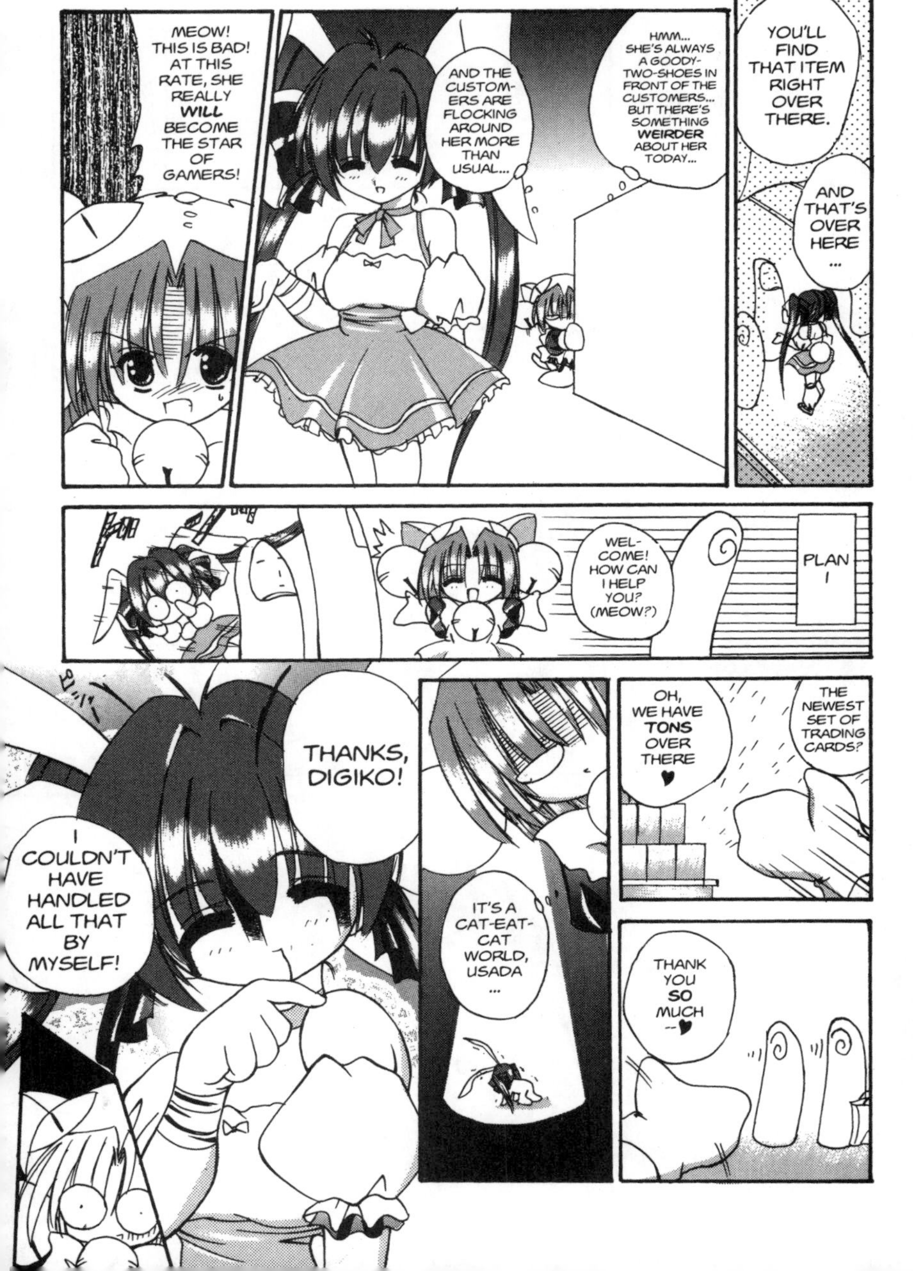
YOU'LL FIND THAT ITEM RIGHT OVER THERE.
AND THAT'S OVER HERE ...
HMM... SHE'S ALWAYS A GOODY-TWO-SHOES IN FRONT OF THE CUSTOMERS... BUT THERE'S SOMETHING **WEIRDER** ABOUT HER TODAY...
AND THE CUSTOM-ERS ARE FLOCKING AROUND HER MORE THAN USUAL...
MEOW! THIS IS BAD! AT THIS RATE, SHE REALLY **WILL** BECOME THE STAR OF GAMERS!
PLAN 1
WEL-COME! HOW CAN I HELP YOU? (MEOW?)
THE NEWEST SET OF TRADING CARDS?
OH, WE HAVE **TONS** OVER THERE ♥
THANK YOU **SO** MUCH --♥
IT'S A CAT-EAT-CAT WORLD, USADA ...
THANKS, DIGIKO!
I COULDN'T HAVE HANDLED ALL THAT BY MYSELF!

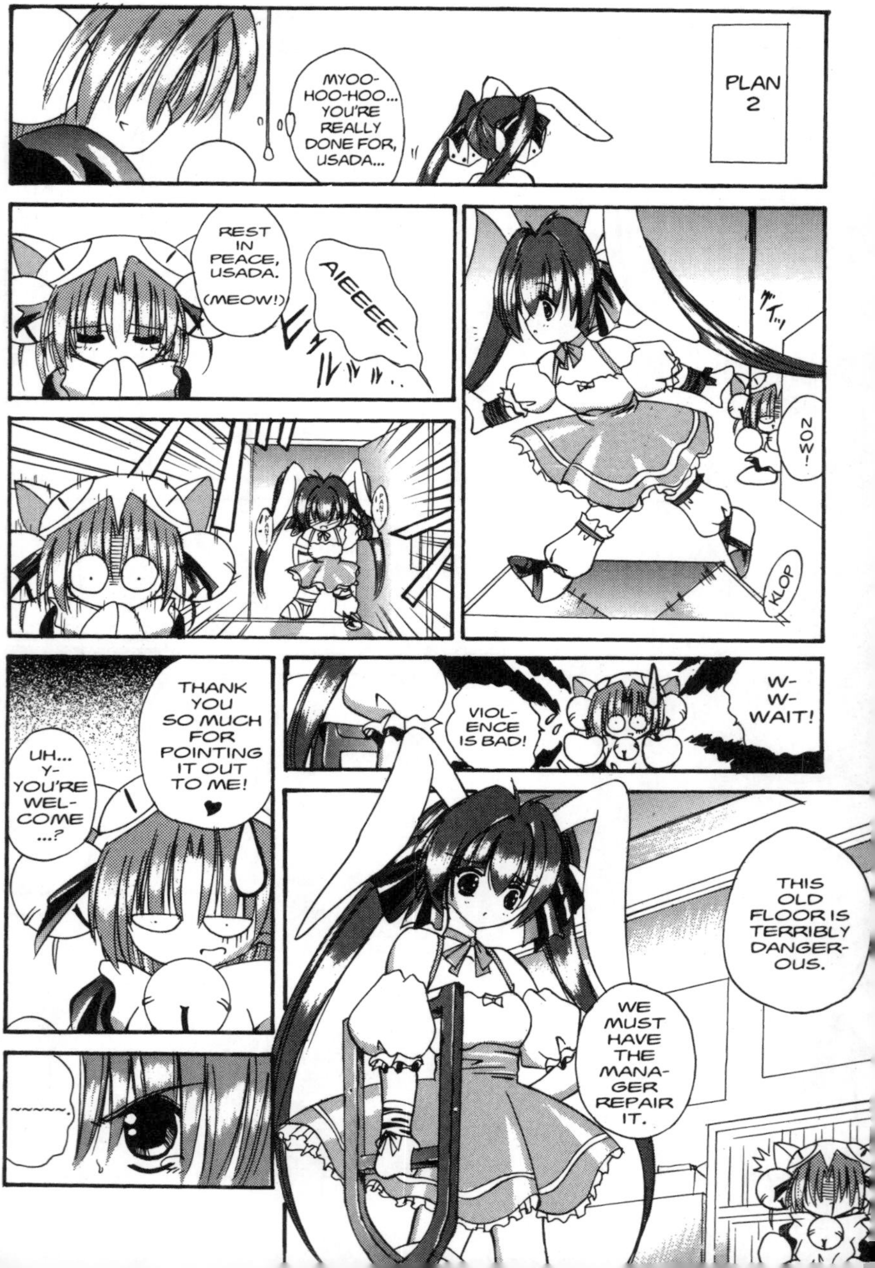
PLAN 2
MYOO-HOO-HOO... YOU'RE REALLY DONE FOR, USADA...
NOW!
KLOP
AIEEEEE--
REST IN PEACE, USADA.
(MEOW!)
PANT
PANT
W-W-WAIT!
VIOLENCE IS BAD!
THIS OLD FLOOR IS TERRIBLY DANGEROUS.
WE MUST HAVE THE MANAGER REPAIR IT.
THANK YOU SO MUCH FOR POINTING IT OUT TO ME! ♥
UH... Y-YOU'RE WELCOME...?
~~~~~.
~~~~~

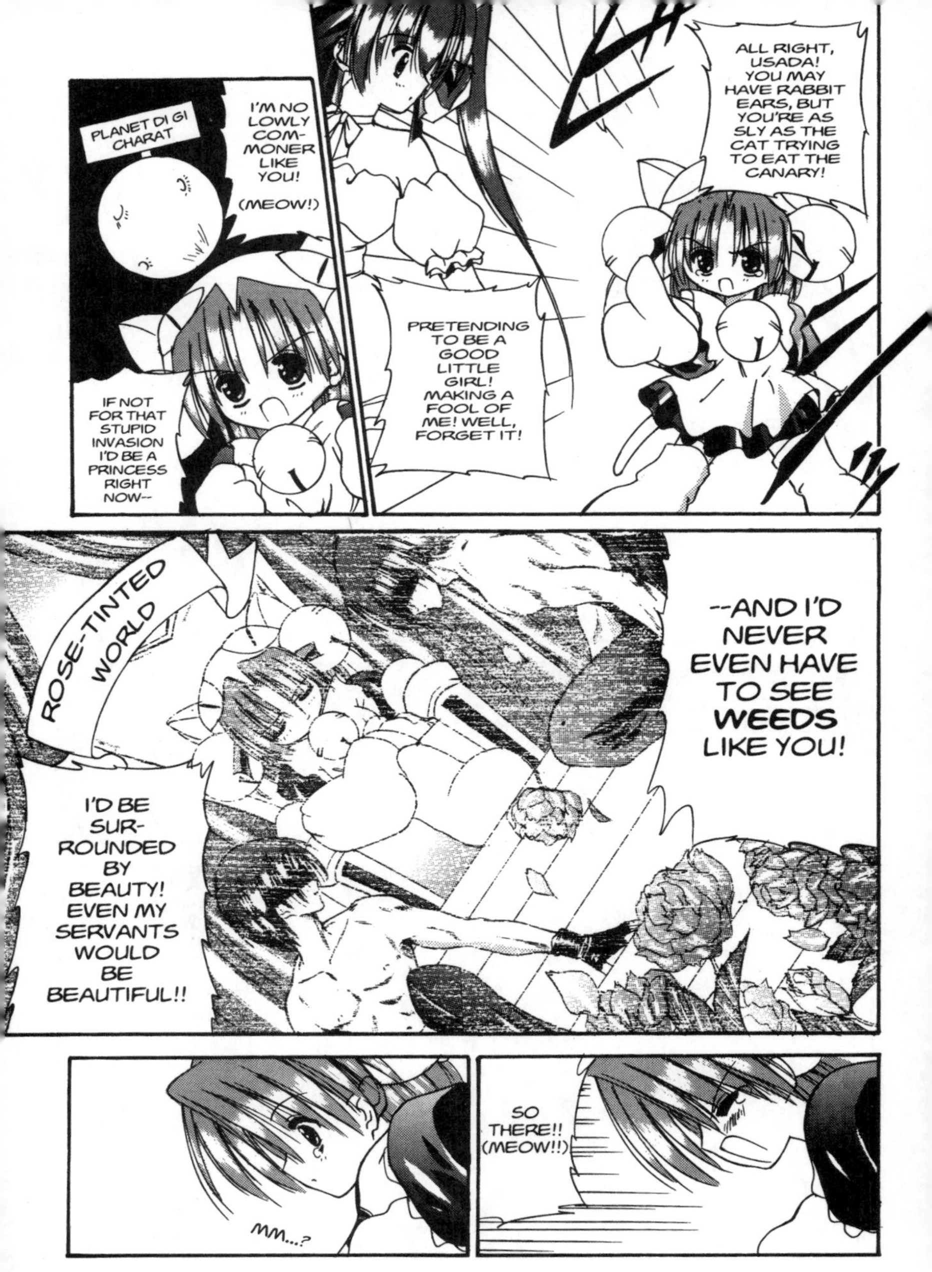

ALL RIGHT, USADA! YOU MAY HAVE RABBIT EARS, BUT YOU'RE AS SLY AS THE CAT TRYING TO EAT THE CANARY!
PRETENDING TO BE A GOOD LITTLE GIRL! MAKING A FOOL OF ME! WELL, FORGET IT!
I'M NO LOWLY COM-MONER LIKE YOU!
(MEOW!)
PLANET DI GI CHARAT
IF NOT FOR THAT STUPID INVASION I'D BE A PRINCESS RIGHT NOW--
--AND I'D NEVER EVEN HAVE TO SEE **WEEDS** LIKE YOU!
ROSE-TINTED WORLD
I'D BE SUR-ROUNDED BY BEAUTY! EVEN MY SERVANTS WOULD BE BEAUTIFUL!!
SO THERE!! (MEOW!!)
MM...?

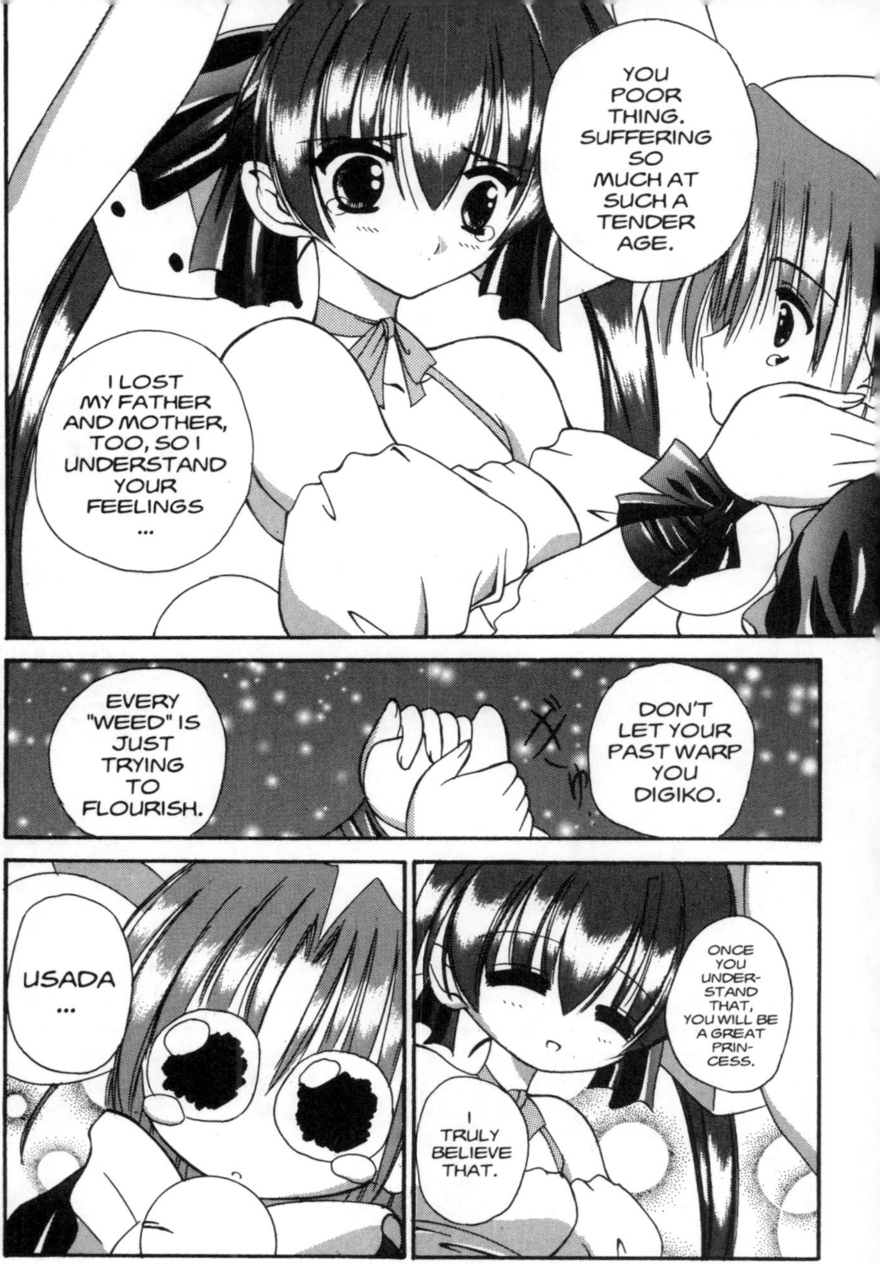
YOU POOR THING. SUFFERING SO MUCH AT SUCH A TENDER AGE.
I LOST MY FATHER AND MOTHER, TOO, SO I UNDERSTAND YOUR FEELINGS ...
DON'T LET YOUR PAST WARP YOU DIGIKO.
EVERY "WEED" IS JUST TRYING TO FLOURISH.
ONCE YOU UNDER-STAND THAT, YOU WILL BE A GREAT PRIN-CESS.
I TRULY BELIEVE THAT.
USADA ...

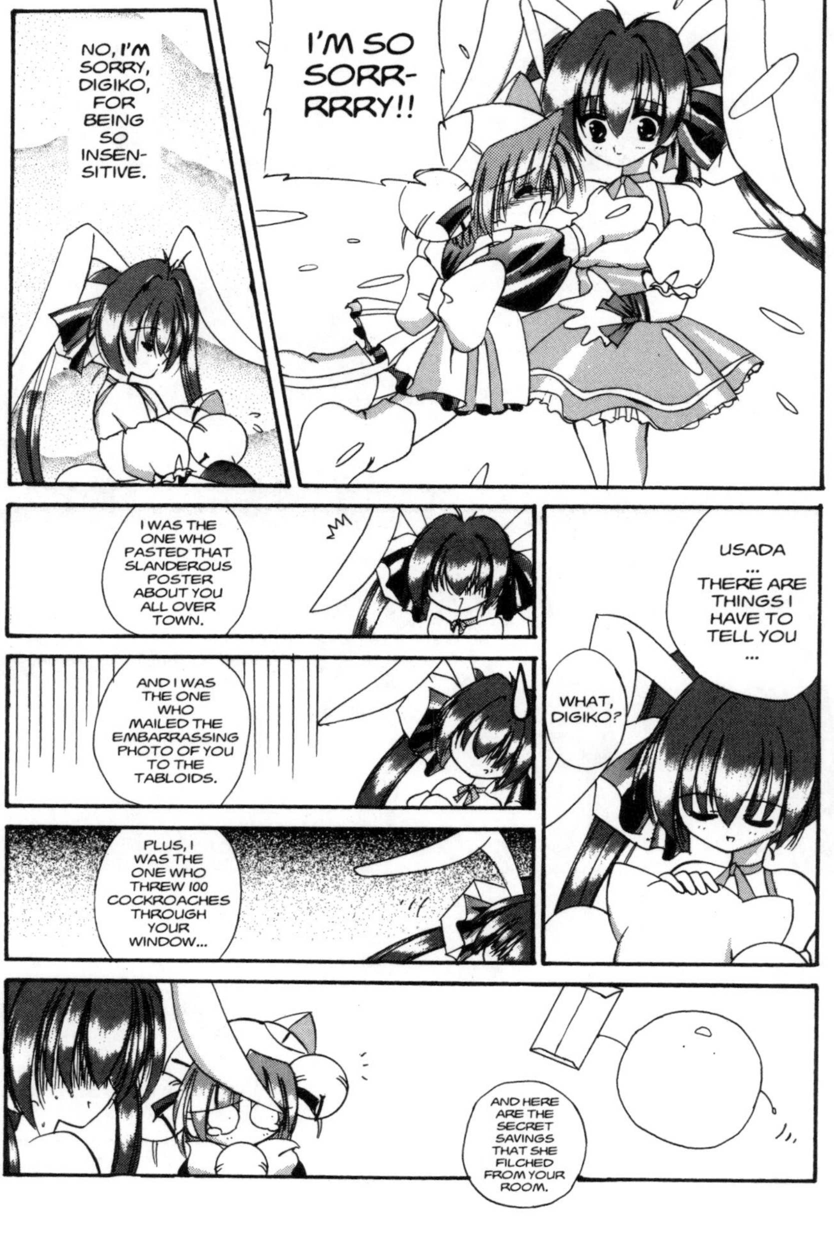
I'M SO SORRR-RRRY!!
NO, I'M SORRY, DIGIKO, FOR BEING SO INSENSITIVE.
USADA ... THERE ARE THINGS I HAVE TO TELL YOU ...
WHAT, DIGIKO?
I WAS THE ONE WHO PASTED THAT SLANDEROUS POSTER ABOUT YOU ALL OVER TOWN.
AND I WAS THE ONE WHO MAILED THE EMBARRASSING PHOTO OF YOU TO THE TABLOIDS.
PLUS, I WAS THE ONE WHO THREW 100 COCKROACHES THROUGH YOUR WINDOW...
AND HERE ARE THE SECRET SAVINGS THAT SHE FILCHED FROM YOUR ROOM.

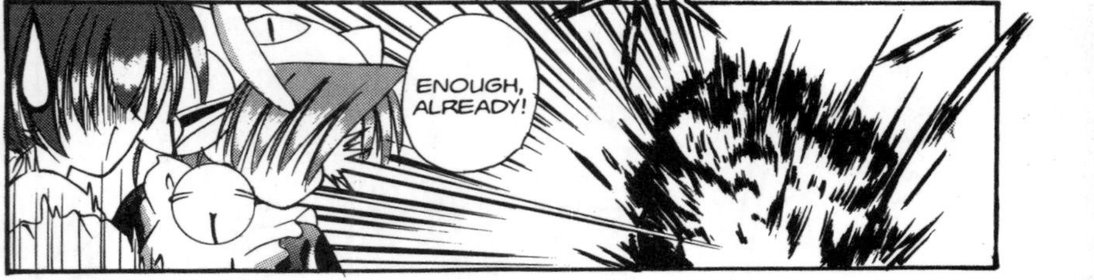
ENOUGH, ALREADY!

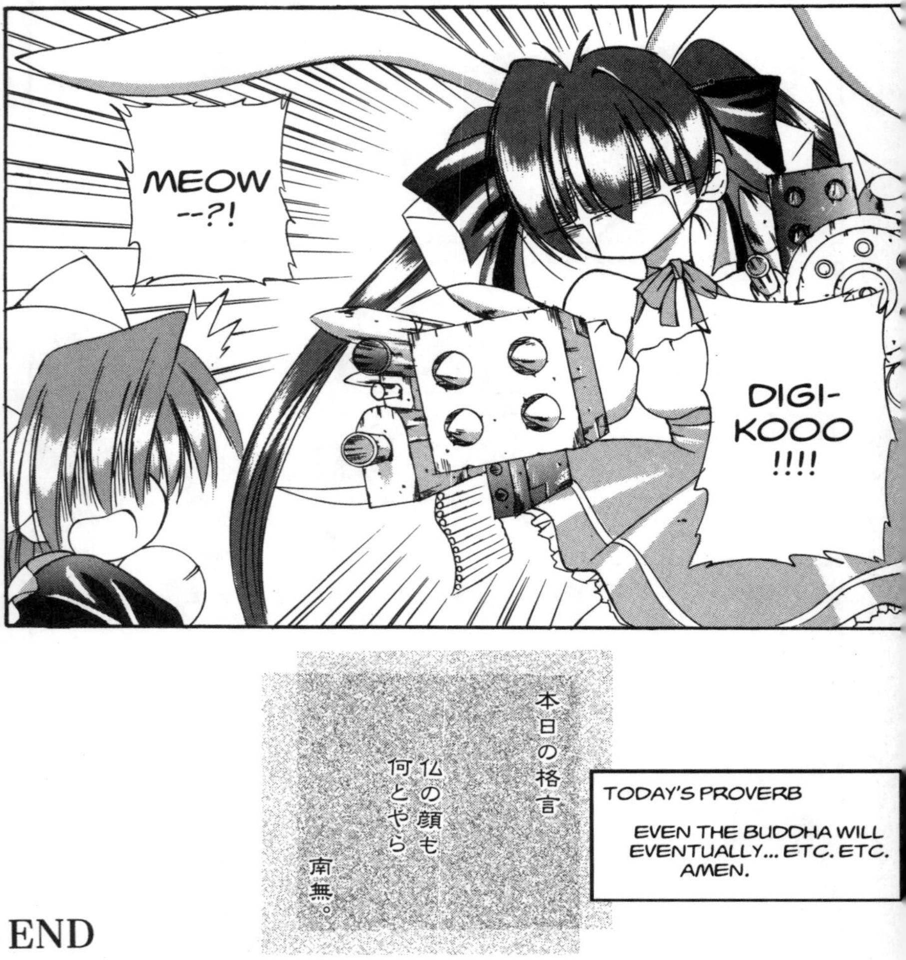
DIGI-KOOO !!!!
MEOW --?!

本日の格言

仏の顔も何とやら

南無。

TODAY'S PROVERB

EVEN THE BUDDHA WILL EVENTUALLY... ETC. ETC. AMEN.

END

A comment about
Di Gi Charat

I'VE ALWAYS LOVED THE THEME OF "THE RIVAL TRYING TO WIN AGAINST THE LEAD CHARACTER." SO, OF COURSE, USADA STRIKES A CHORD WITH ME.

HER BOLDNESS AND DETERMINATION ALWAYS STIRS MY HEART (HEH).

... I GUESS SHE NEVER WILL BEAT DIGIKO, THOUGH...

TAKAHIRO AKIDUKI

TAKAHIRO AKIDUKI

KAPPA:

"EVEN A MAGIC IMP WILL BECOME A CLERK IF IT LOITERS IN A STORE."

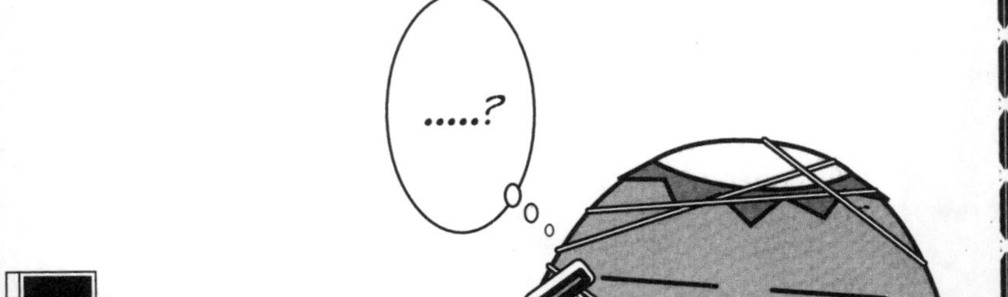
.....?

ILLUSTRATION/KURIMU

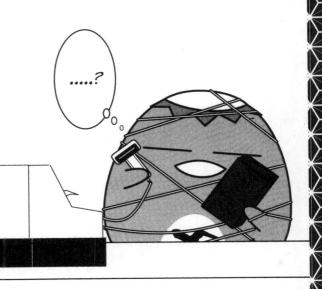

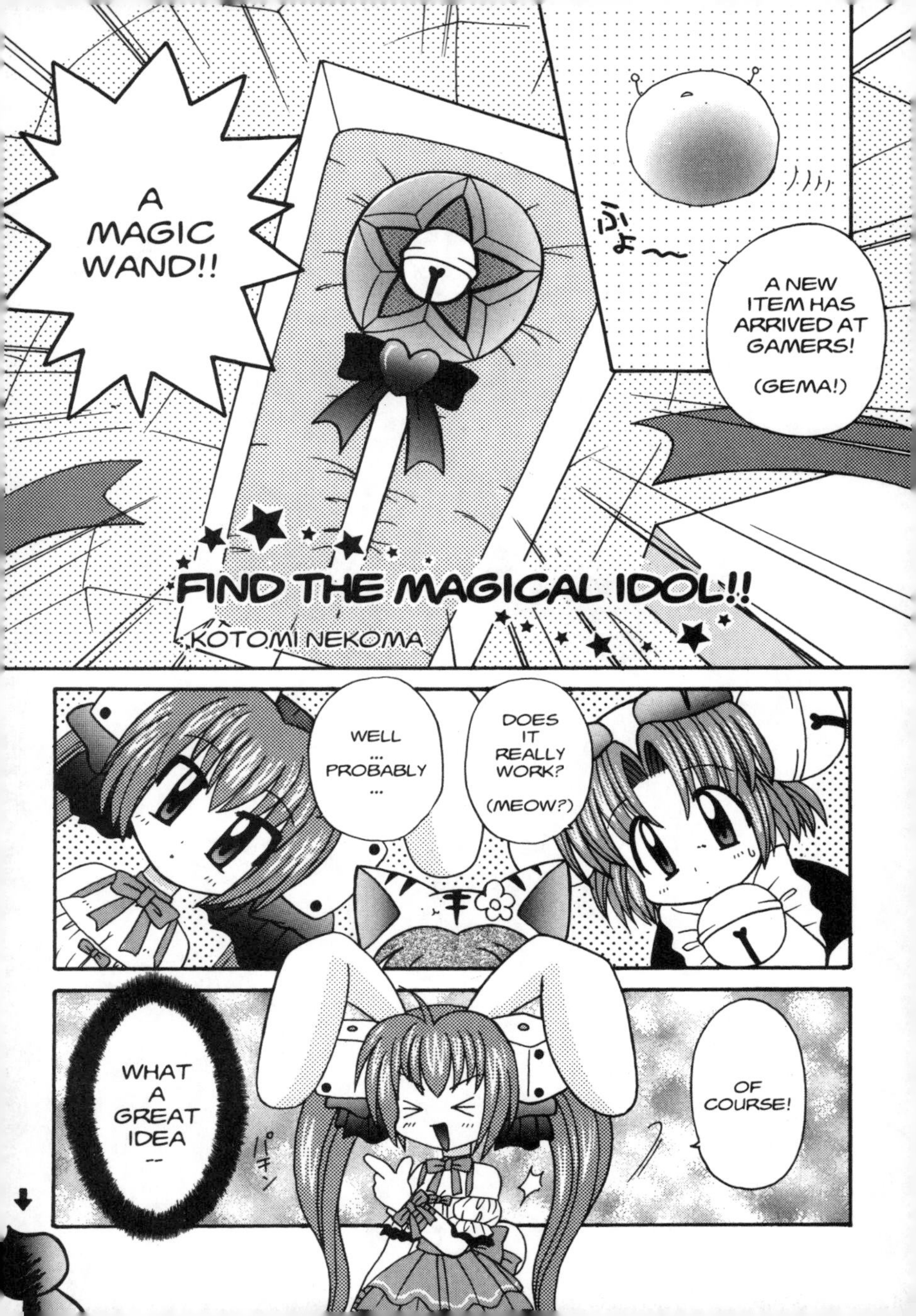
ぷよ～
A NEW ITEM HAS ARRIVED AT GAMERS! (GEMA!)
A MAGIC WAND!!
FIND THE MAGICAL IDOL!!
KOTOMI NEKOMA
DOES IT REALLY WORK? (MEOW?)
WELL ... PROBABLY ...
OF COURSE!
パチン
WHAT A GREAT IDEA --

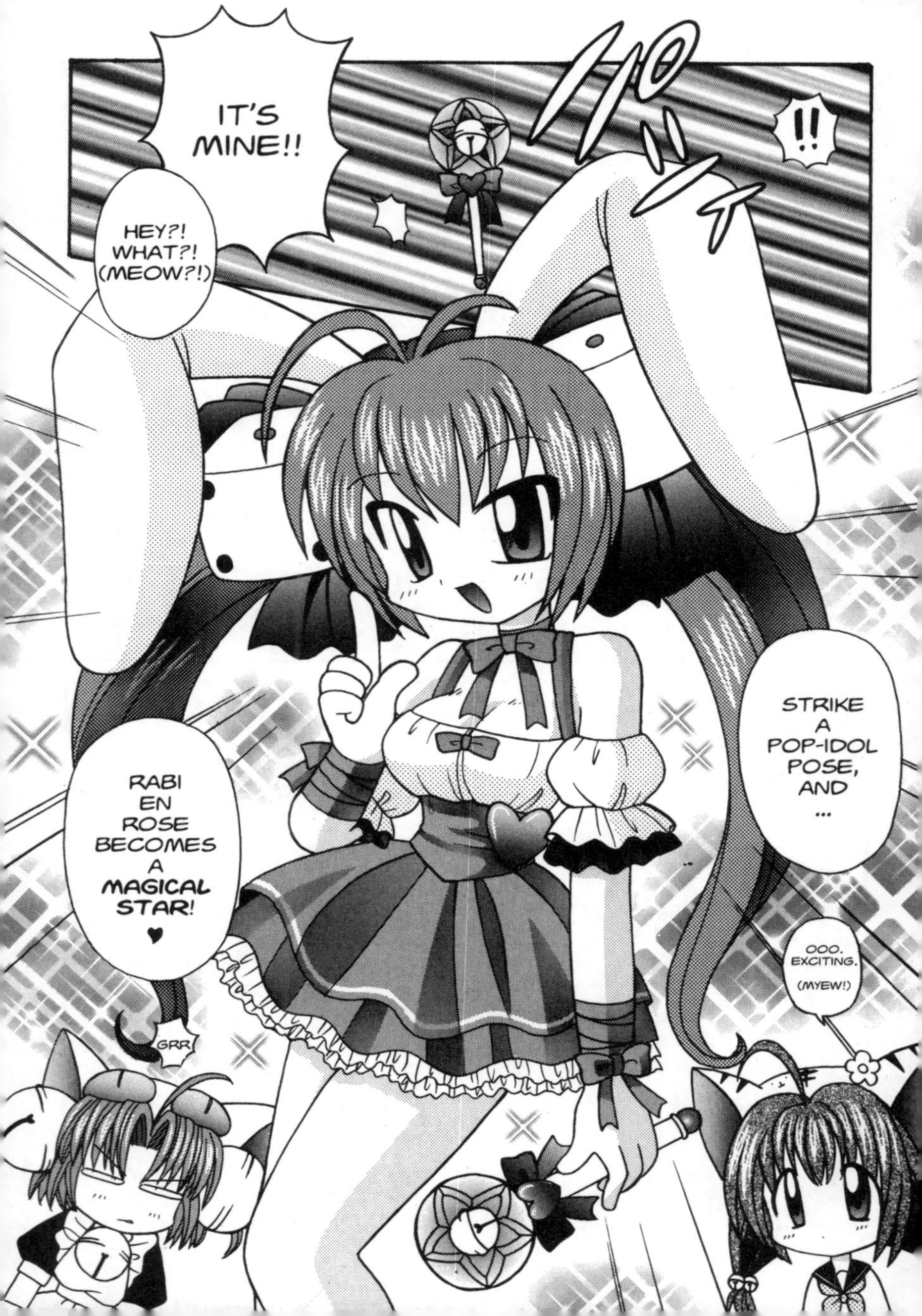
!!
IT'S MINE!!
HEY?! WHAT?! (MEOW?!)
STRIKE A POP-IDOL POSE, AND ...
RABI EN ROSE BECOMES A MAGICAL STAR! ♥
OOO. EXCITING. (MYEW!)
GRR

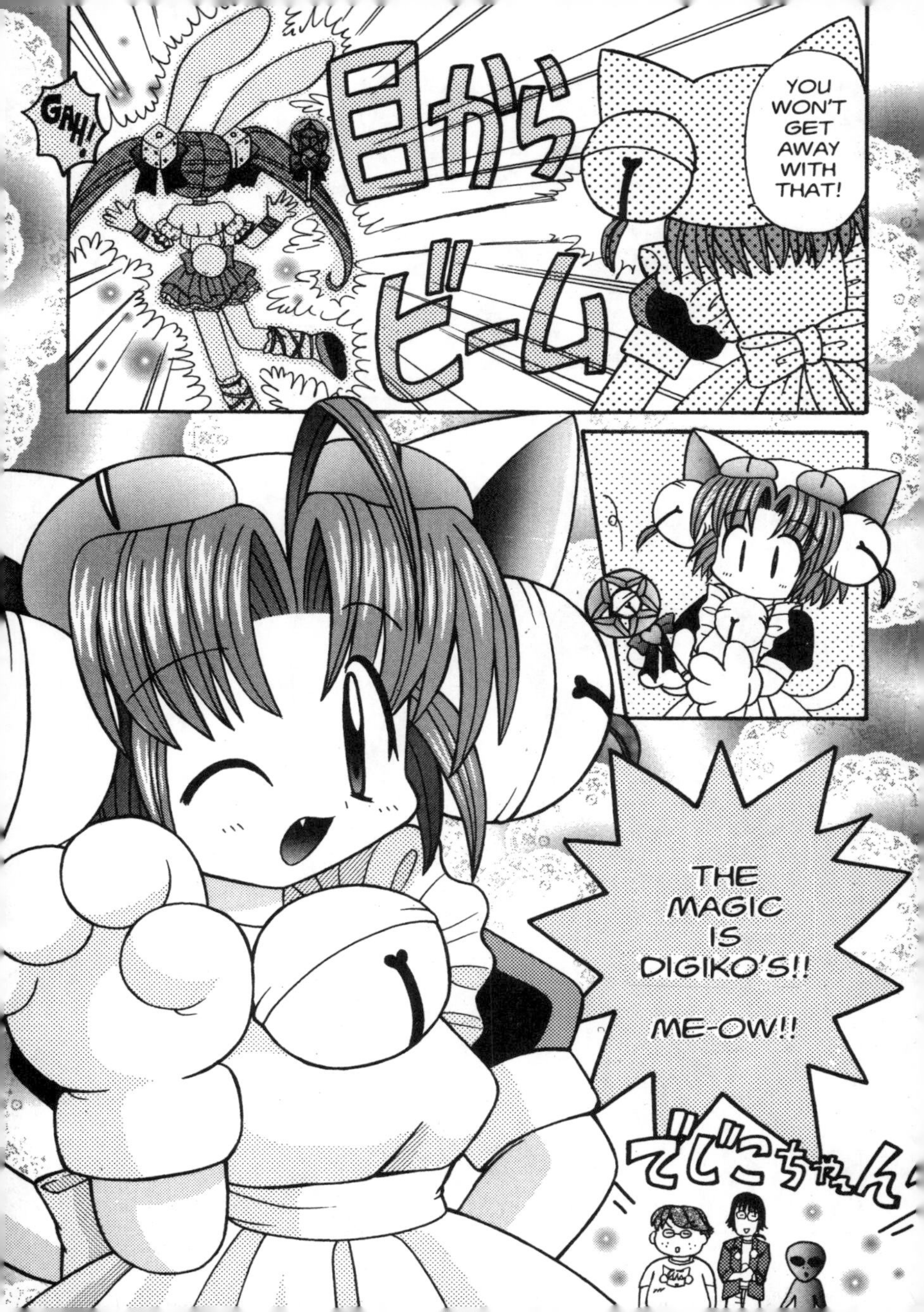
YOU WON'T GET AWAY WITH THAT!
目からビーム
GAH!
THE MAGIC IS DIGIKO'S!!
ME-OW!!
でじこちゃん

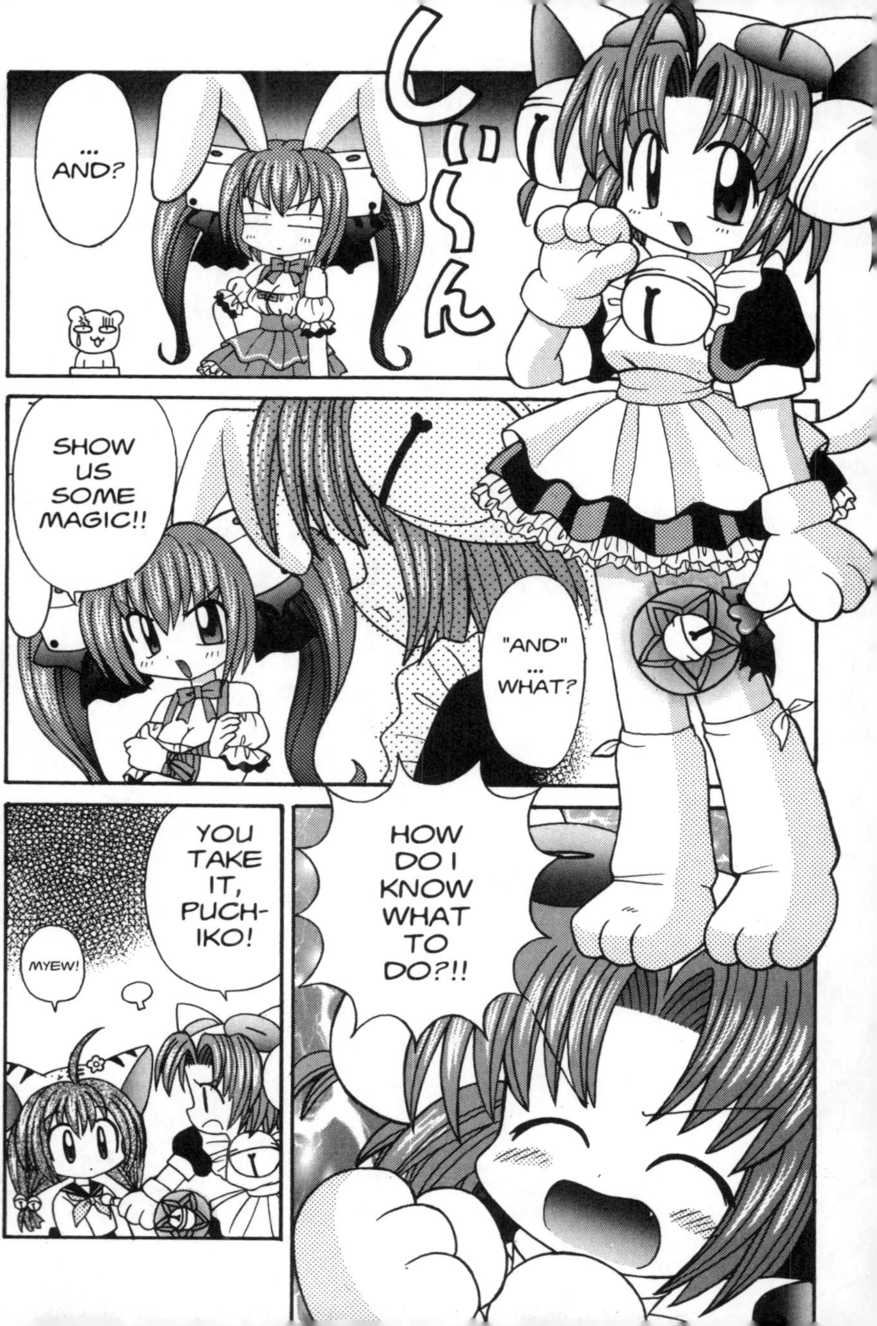
しい〜ん
"AND" ... WHAT?
... AND?
SHOW US SOME MAGIC!!
HOW DO I KNOW WHAT TO DO?!!
YOU TAKE IT, PUCH-IKO!
MYEW!

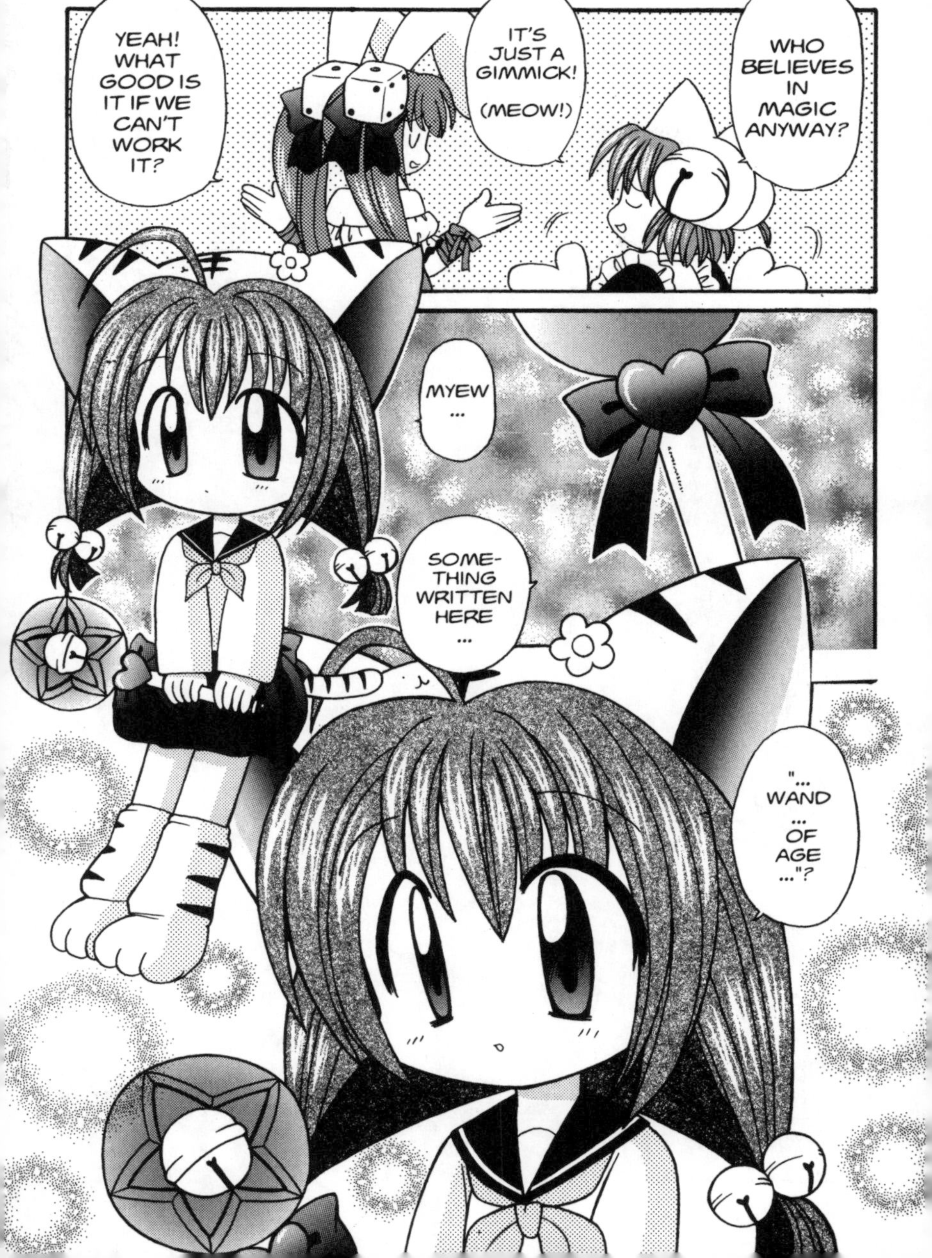
WHO BELIEVES IN MAGIC ANYWAY?
IT'S JUST A GIMMICK!
(MEOW!)
YEAH! WHAT GOOD IS IT IF WE CAN'T WORK IT?
MYEW ...
SOME-THING WRITTEN HERE ...
"... WAND ... OF AGE ..."?

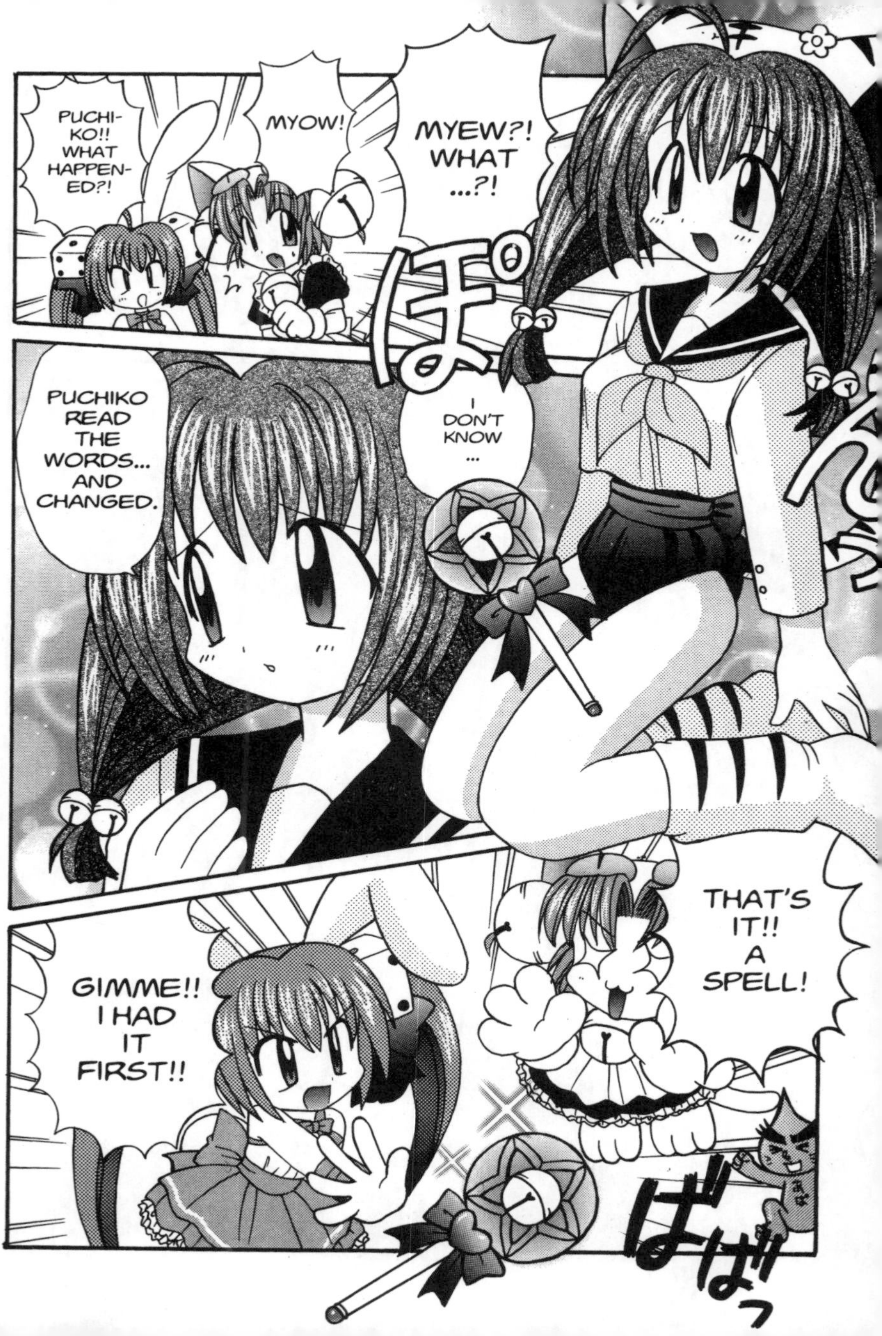
MYEW?! WHAT ...?!
ぽ
I DON'T KNOW ...
MYOW!
PUCHIKO!! WHAT HAPPENED?!
PUCHIKO READ THE WORDS... AND CHANGED.
THAT'S IT!! A SPELL!
GIMME!! I HAD IT FIRST!!
ばばっ

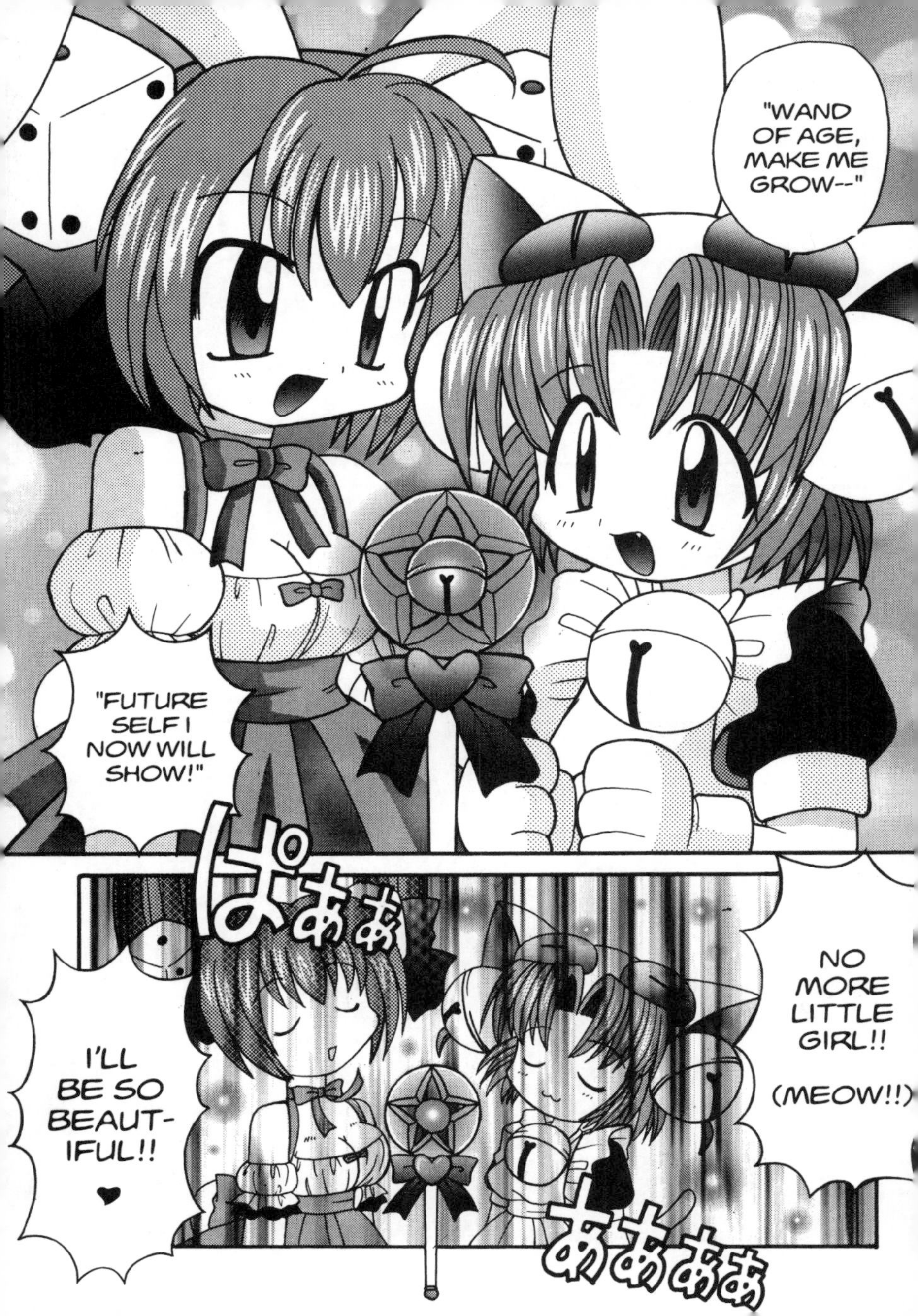
"WAND OF AGE, MAKE ME GROW--"
"FUTURE SELF I NOW WILL SHOW!"
ぱあああ
NO MORE LITTLE GIRL!!
(MEOW!!)
I'LL BE SO BEAUT-IFUL!! ♥
ああああ

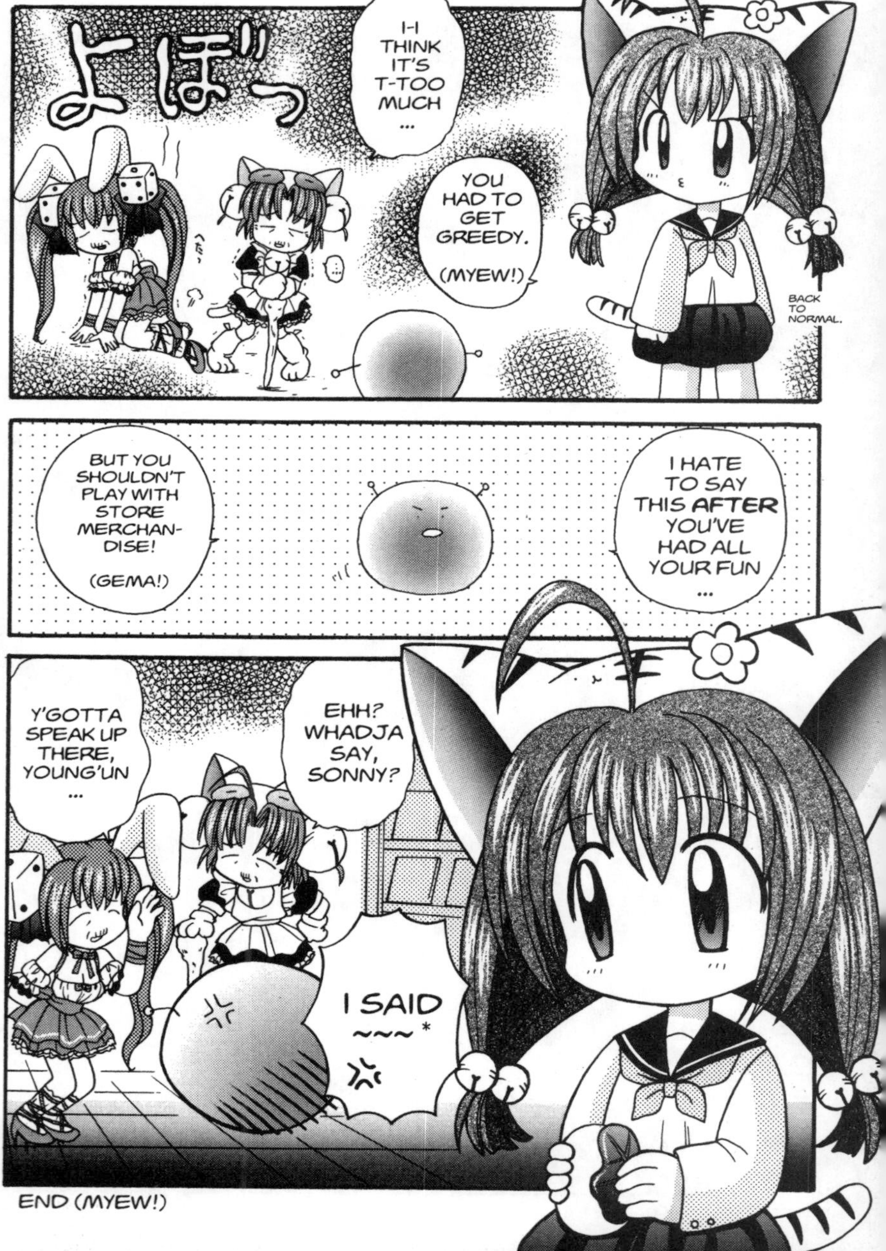
BACK TO NORMAL.
I-I THINK IT'S T-TOO MUCH ...
YOU HAD TO GET GREEDY. (MYEW!)
よぼっ
I HATE TO SAY THIS AFTER YOU'VE HAD ALL YOUR FUN ...
BUT YOU SHOULDN'T PLAY WITH STORE MERCHANDISE! (GEMA!)
EHH? WHADJA SAY, SONNY?
Y'GOTTA SPEAK UP THERE, YOUNG'UN ...
I SAID ~~~ *

END (MYEW!)

A comment about Di Gi Charat

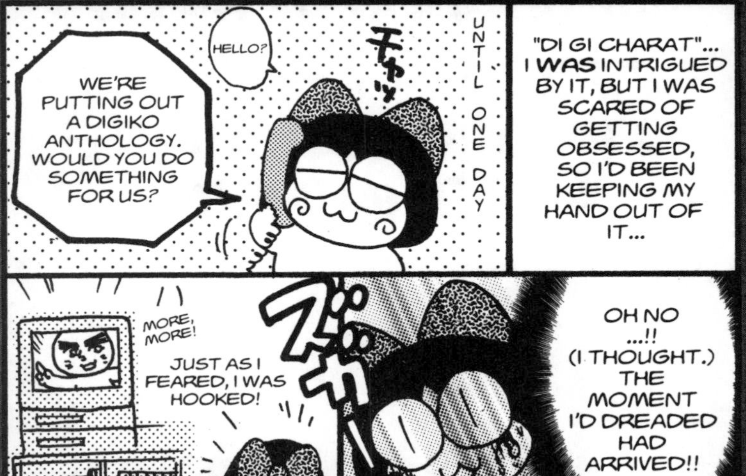
"DI GI CHARAT"... I **WAS** INTRIGUED BY IT, BUT I WAS SCARED OF GETTING OBSESSED, SO I'D BEEN KEEPING MY HAND OUT OF IT...
UNTIL ONE DAY
HELLO?
WE'RE PUTTING OUT A DIGIKO ANTHOLOGY. WOULD YOU DO SOMETHING FOR US?
OH NO ...!! (I THOUGHT.) THE MOMENT I'D DREADED HAD ARRIVED!!
MORE, MORE!
JUST AS I FEARED, I WAS HOOKED!
AND . . .
SOMEHOW I EVEN WANT TO CREATE...
...A FAN MAGAZINE!! (HA!)
I WONDER HOW I'LL FEEL TOMORROW?!
MYEW!

I LOOK FORWARD TO MEETING AGAIN SOME DAY ♥
BY KOTOMI NEKOMA

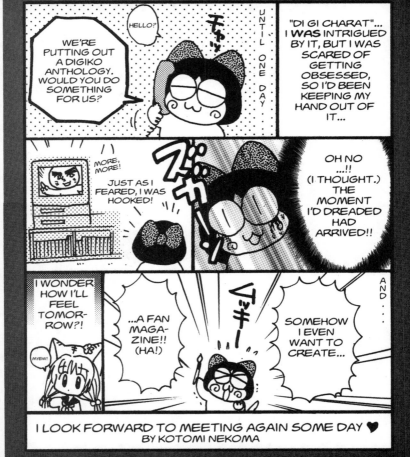

KOTOMI NEKOMA

KAPPA:

"IF ENOUGH IMPS ARE GATHERED, THEY WILL MAKE A MOUNTAIN."

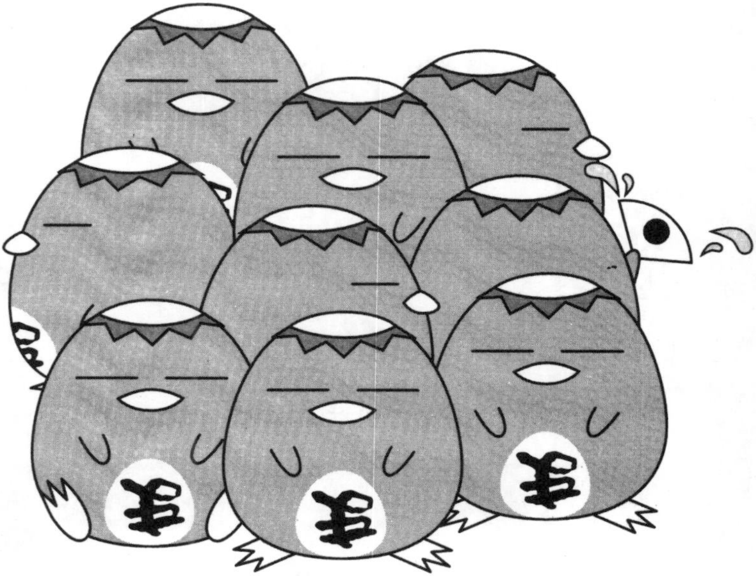

ILLUSTRATION/KURIMU

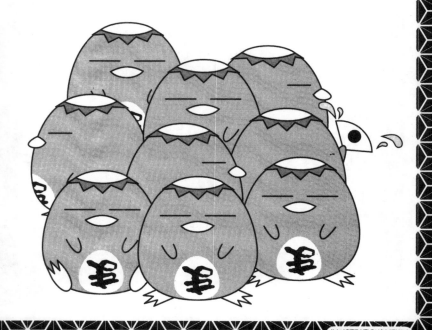

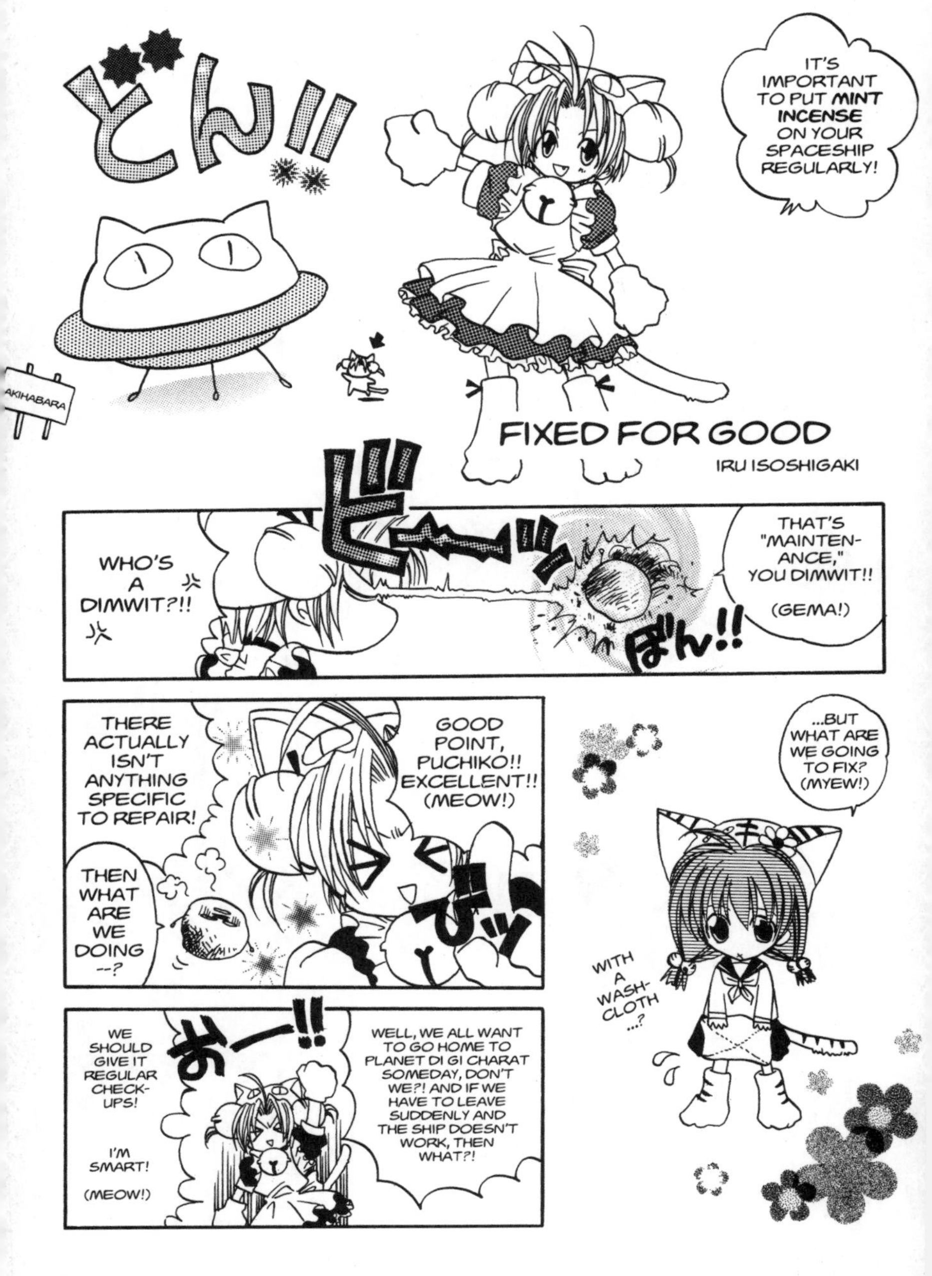
IT'S IMPORTANT TO PUT **MINT INCENSE** ON YOUR SPACESHIP REGULARLY!
どん!!
AKIHABARA
FIXED FOR GOOD
IRU ISOSHIGAKI
THAT'S "MAINTEN-ANCE," YOU DIMWIT!!
(GEMA!)
ビーッ
ぼん!!
WHO'S A DIMWIT?!!
GOOD POINT, PUCHIKO!! EXCELLENT!! (MEOW!)
THERE ACTUALLY ISN'T ANYTHING SPECIFIC TO REPAIR!
ぴッ
THEN WHAT ARE WE DOING --?
WELL, WE ALL WANT TO GO HOME TO PLANET DI GI CHARAT SOMEDAY, DON'T WE?! AND IF WE HAVE TO LEAVE SUDDENLY AND THE SHIP DOESN'T WORK, THEN WHAT?!
おー!!
WE SHOULD GIVE IT REGULAR CHECK-UPS!
I'M SMART!
(MEOW!)
...BUT WHAT ARE WE GOING TO FIX? (MYEW!)
WITH A WASH-CLOTH ...?

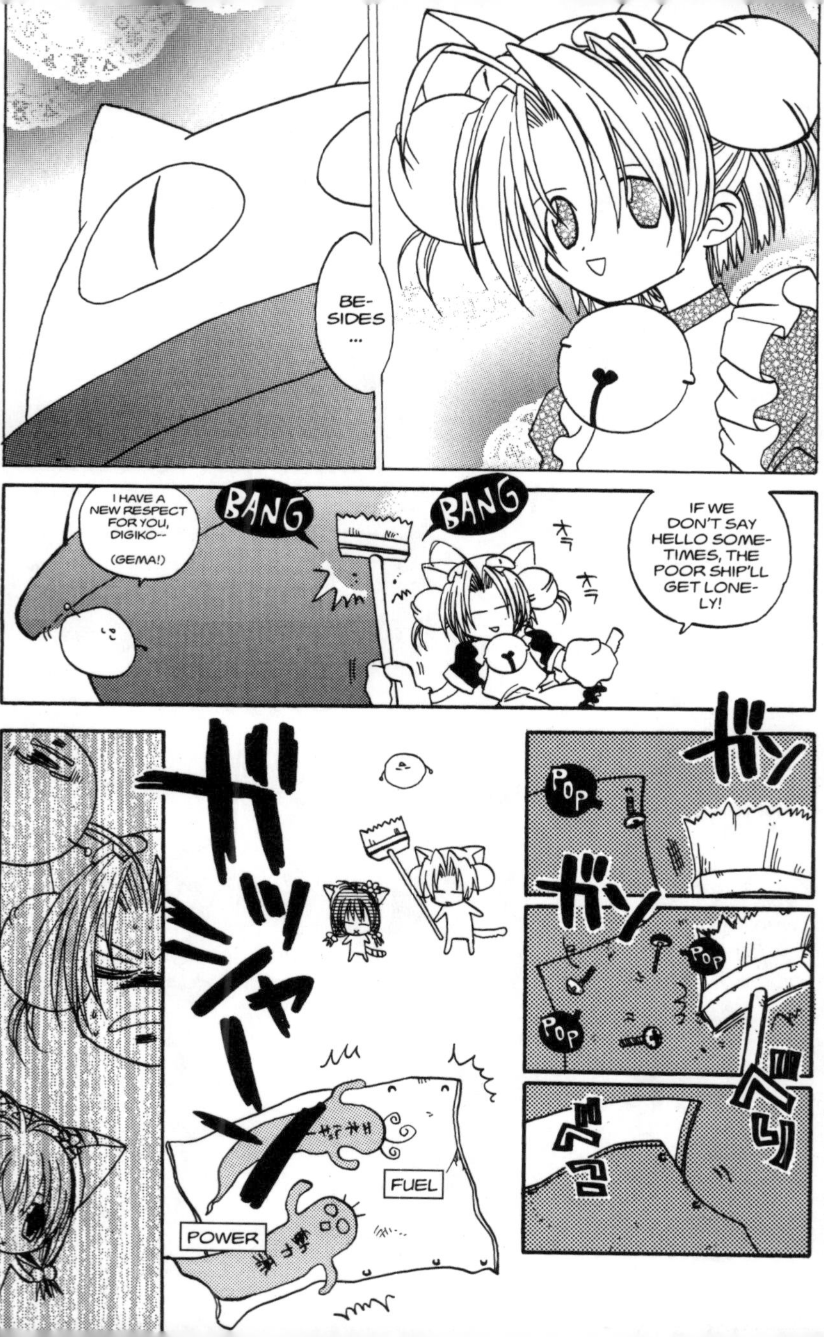
BE-SIDES ...
IF WE DON'T SAY HELLO SOME-TIMES, THE POOR SHIP'LL GET LONE-LY!
BANG
BANG
I HAVE A NEW RESPECT FOR YOU, DIGIKO-- (GEMA!)
バン
POP
バン
POP
POP
ガッシャーン
FUEL
POWER

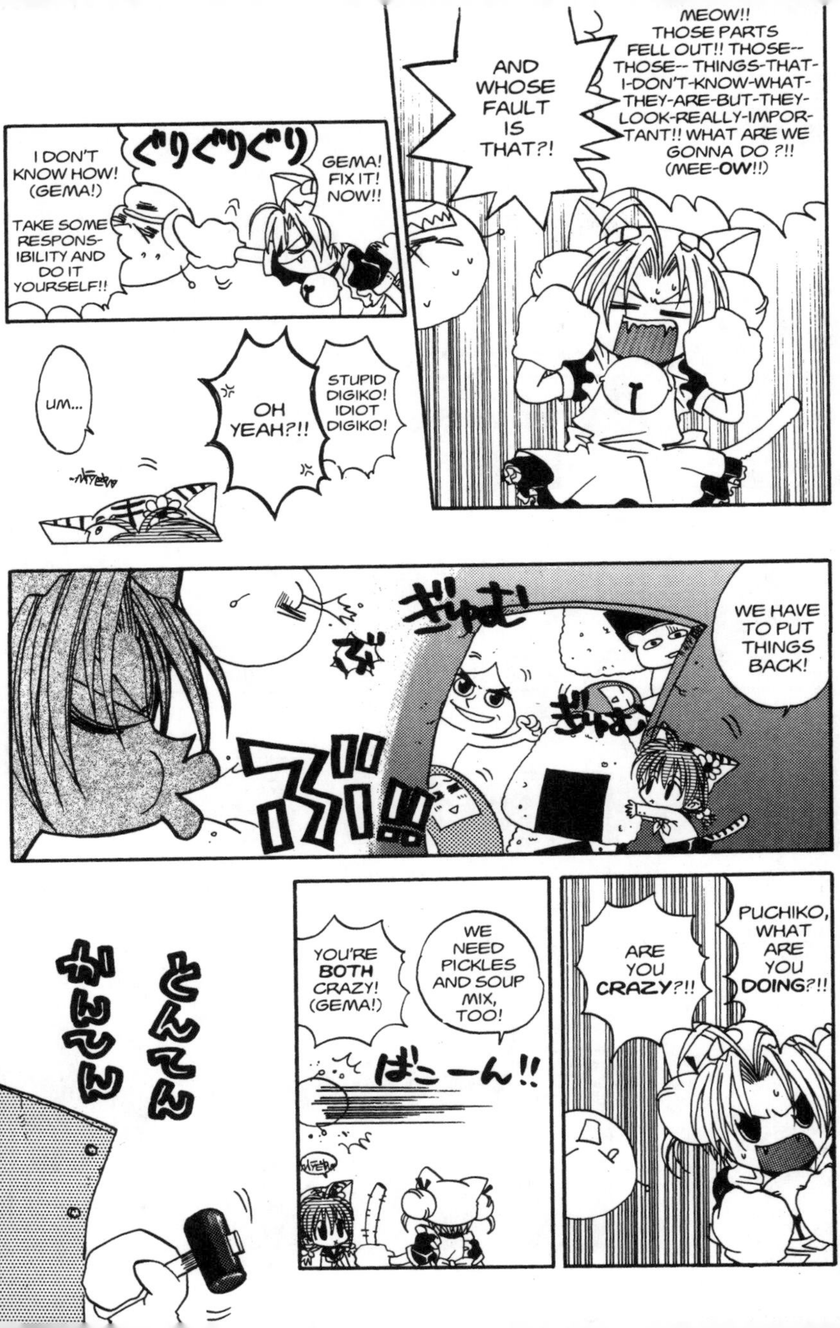
MEOW!! THOSE PARTS FELL OUT!! THOSE-- THOSE-- THINGS-THAT-I-DON'T-KNOW-WHAT-THEY-ARE-BUT-THEY-LOOK-REALLY-IMPORTANT!! WHAT ARE WE GONNA DO ?!! (MEE-OW!!)
AND WHOSE FAULT IS THAT?!
GEMA! FIX IT! NOW!!
ぐりぐりぐり
I DON'T KNOW HOW! (GEMA!)
TAKE SOME RESPONSIBILITY AND DO IT YOURSELF!!
STUPID DIGIKO! IDIOT DIGIKO!
OH YEAH?!!
UM...
WE HAVE TO PUT THINGS BACK!
ぎゅむ!
ぶ
ぎゅむ
ぶ!!
PUCHIKO, WHAT ARE YOU DOING?!!
ARE YOU CRAZY?!!
WE NEED PICKLES AND SOUP MIX, TOO!
YOU'RE BOTH CRAZY! (GEMA!)
ばこーん!!
とんてん
かんてん

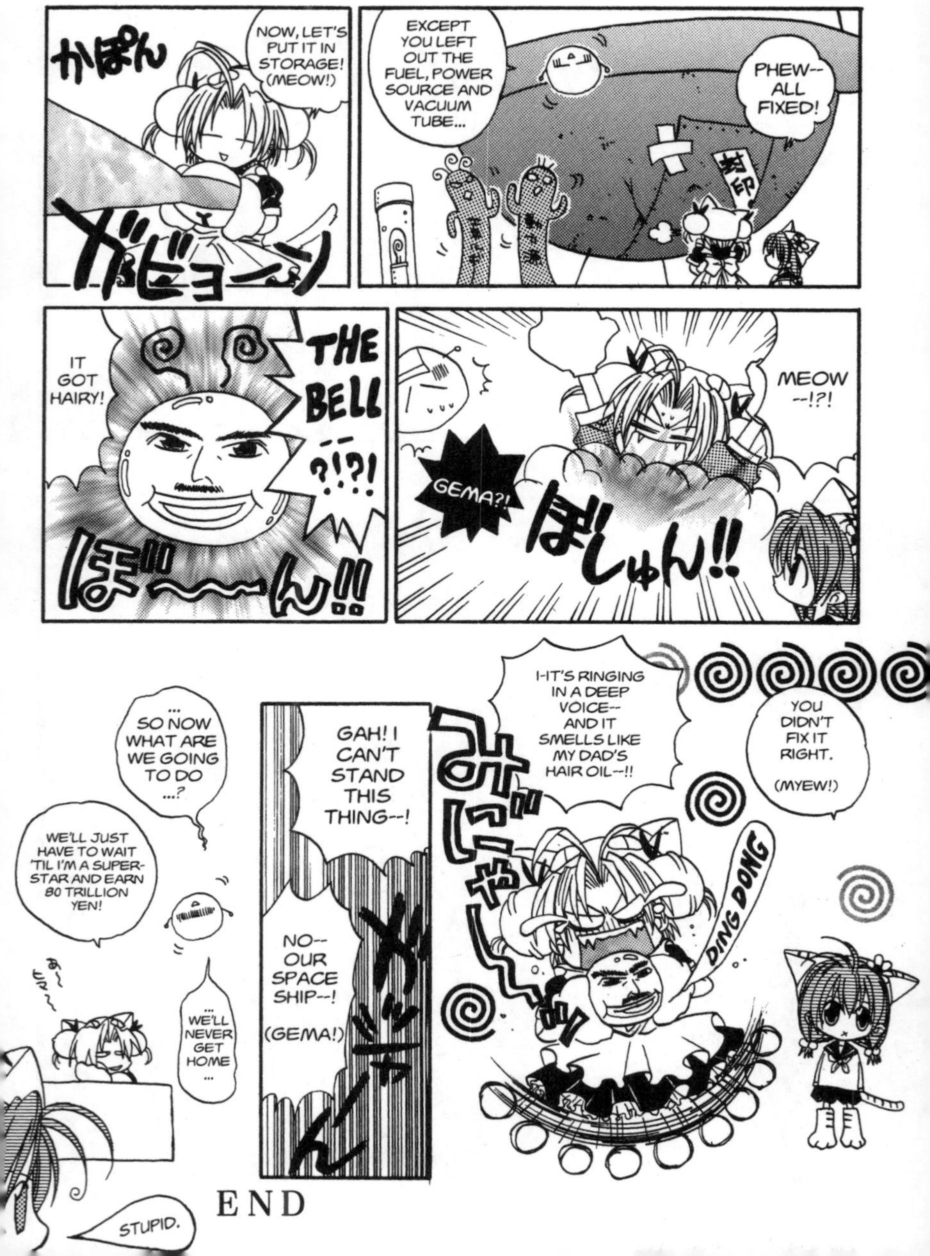
PHEW-- ALL FIXED!
封印
EXCEPT YOU LEFT OUT THE FUEL, POWER SOURCE AND VACUUM TUBE...
NOW, LET'S PUT IT IN STORAGE! (MEOW!)
かぽん
MEOW --!?!
GEMA?!
ぼしゅん!!
THE BELL --?!?!
IT GOT HAIRY!
YOU DIDN'T FIX IT RIGHT. (MYEW!)
I-IT'S RINGING IN A DEEP VOICE-- AND IT SMELLS LIKE MY DAD'S HAIR OIL--!!
DING DONG
GAH! I CAN'T STAND THIS THING--!
NO-- OUR SPACE SHIP--! (GEMA!)
... SO NOW WHAT ARE WE GOING TO DO ...?
WE'LL JUST HAVE TO WAIT 'TIL I'M A SUPER-STAR AND EARN 80 TRILLION YEN!
... WE'LL NEVER GET HOME ...
STUPID.
END

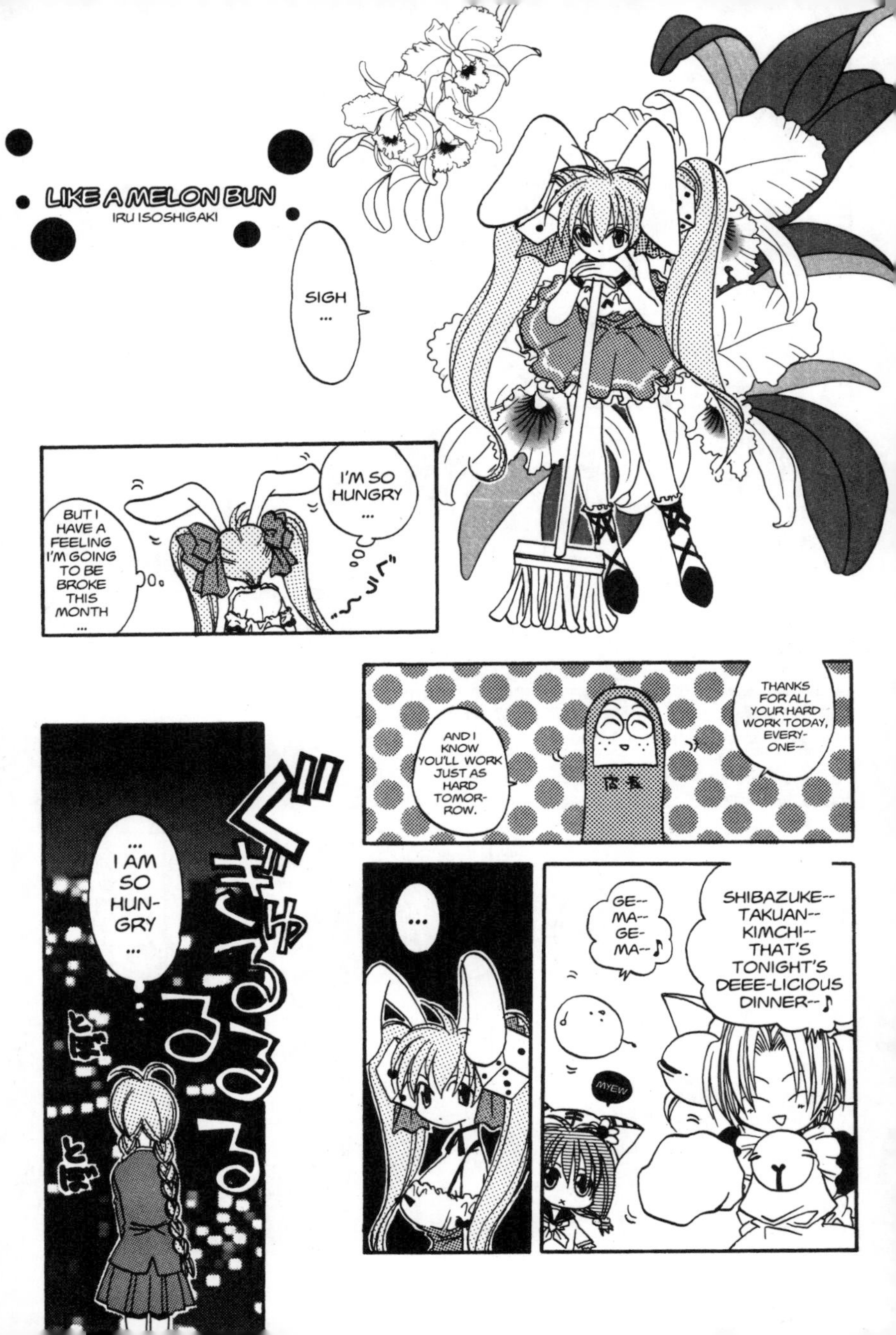
LIKE A MELON BUN
IRU ISOSHIGAKI
SIGH ...
I'M SO HUNGRY ...
BUT I HAVE A FEELING I'M GOING TO BE BROKE THIS MONTH ...
THANKS FOR ALL YOUR HARD WORK TODAY, EVERY-ONE--
AND I KNOW YOU'LL WORK JUST AS HARD TOMOR-ROW.
SHIBAZUKE-- TAKUAN-- KIMCHI-- THAT'S TONIGHT'S DEEE-LICIOUS DINNER--♪
GE-- MA-- GE-MA--♪
MYEW
...
... I AM SO HUN-GRY ...

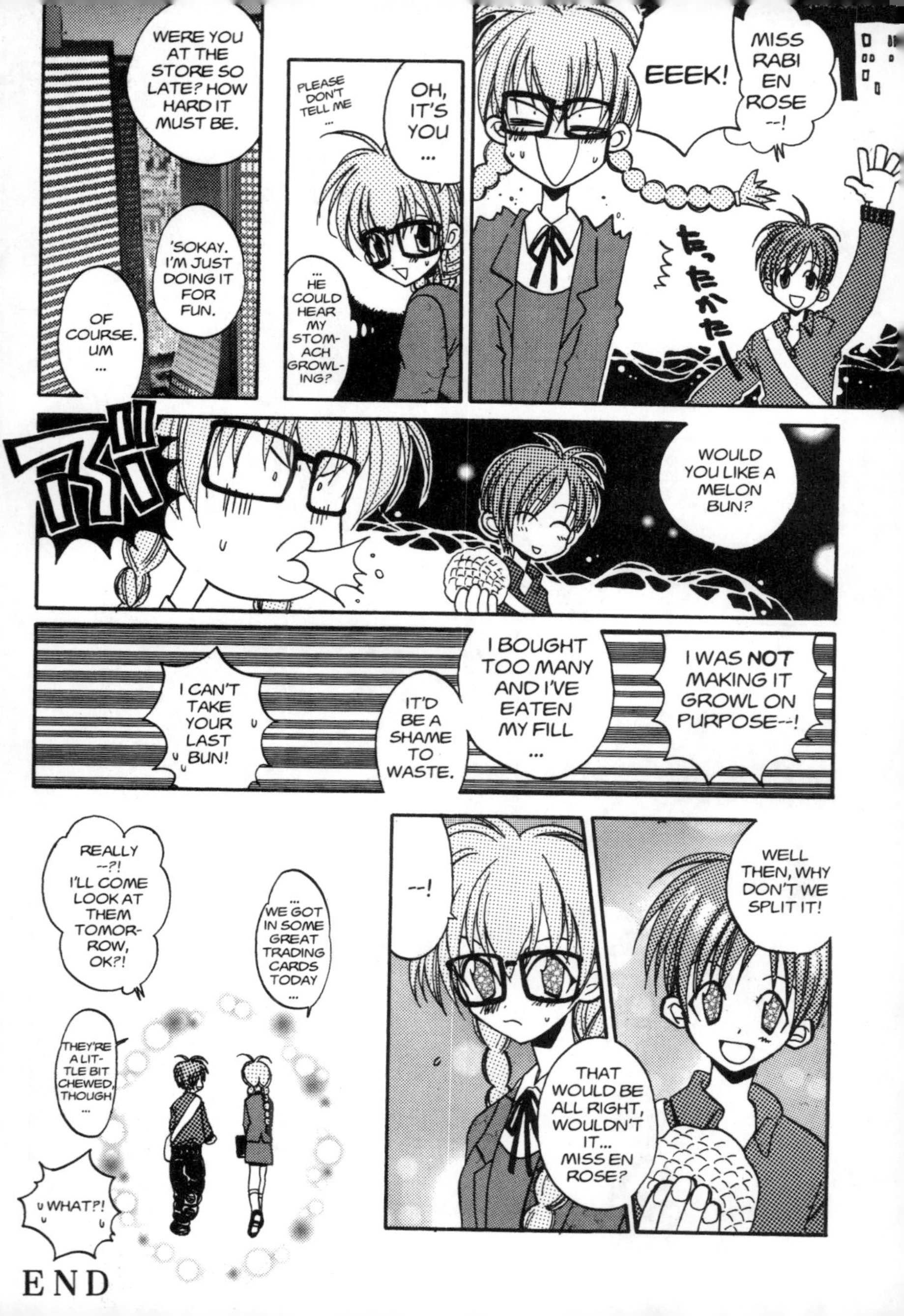
MISS RABI EN ROSE --!
EEEK!
たったかたー
OH, IT'S YOU ...
PLEASE DON'T TELL ME ...
... HE COULD HEAR MY STOMACH GROWLING?
WERE YOU AT THE STORE SO LATE? HOW HARD IT MUST BE.
'SOKAY. I'M JUST DOING IT FOR FUN.
OF COURSE. UM ...
WOULD YOU LIKE A MELON BUN?
I WAS **NOT** MAKING IT GROWL ON PURPOSE--!
I BOUGHT TOO MANY AND I'VE EATEN MY FILL ...
IT'D BE A SHAME TO WASTE.
I CAN'T TAKE YOUR LAST BUN!
WELL THEN, WHY DON'T WE SPLIT IT!
--!
THAT WOULD BE ALL RIGHT, WOULDN'T IT... MISS EN ROSE?
... WE GOT IN SOME GREAT TRADING CARDS TODAY ...
REALLY --?! I'LL COME LOOK AT THEM TOMORROW, OK?!
THEY'RE A LITTLE BIT CHEWED, THOUGH ...
WHAT?!
END

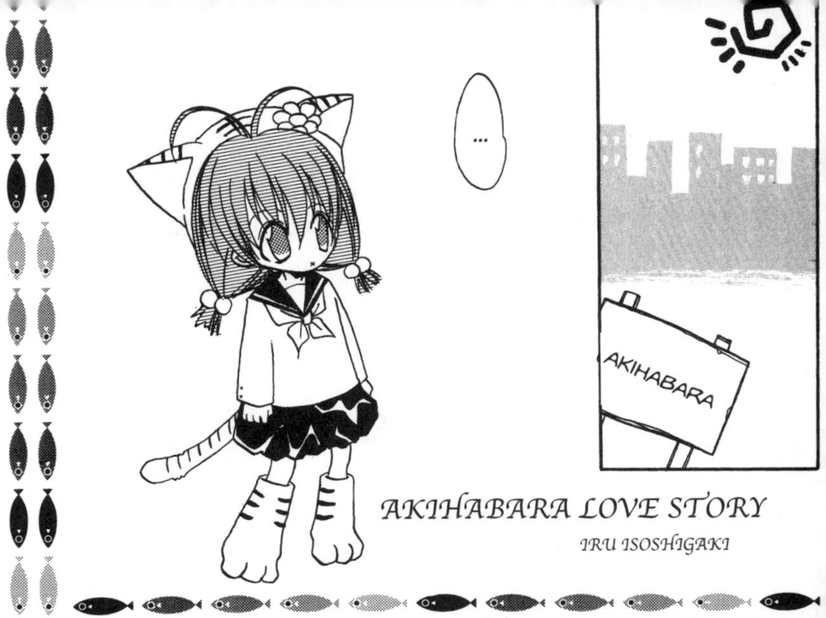
AKIHABARA
...

AKIHABARA LOVE STORY

IRU ISOSHIGAKI

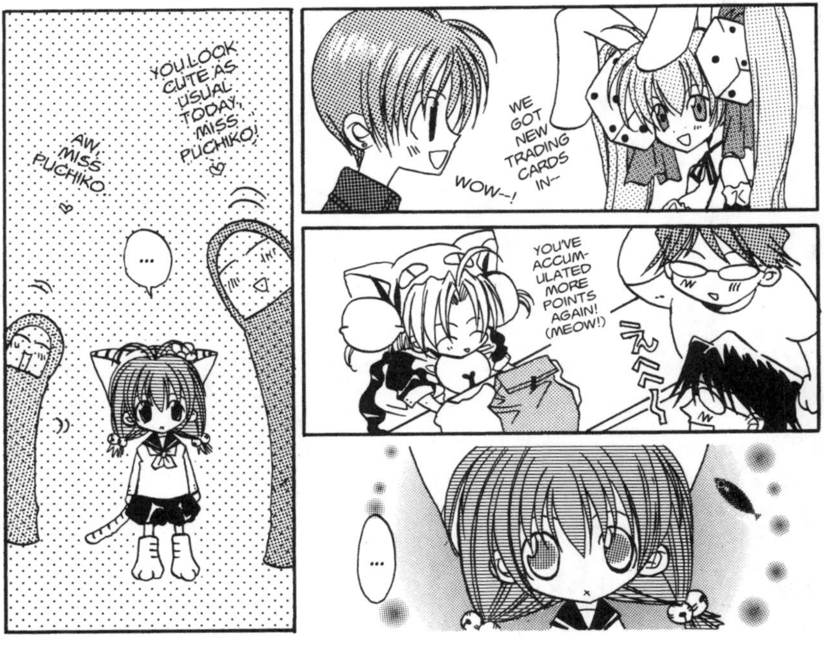
WE GOT NEW TRADING CARDS IN--
WOW--!
YOU'VE ACCUMULATED MORE POINTS AGAIN! (MEOW!)
...
YOU LOOK CUTE AS USUAL TODAY, MISS PUCHIKO!
AW, MISS PUCHIKO
...

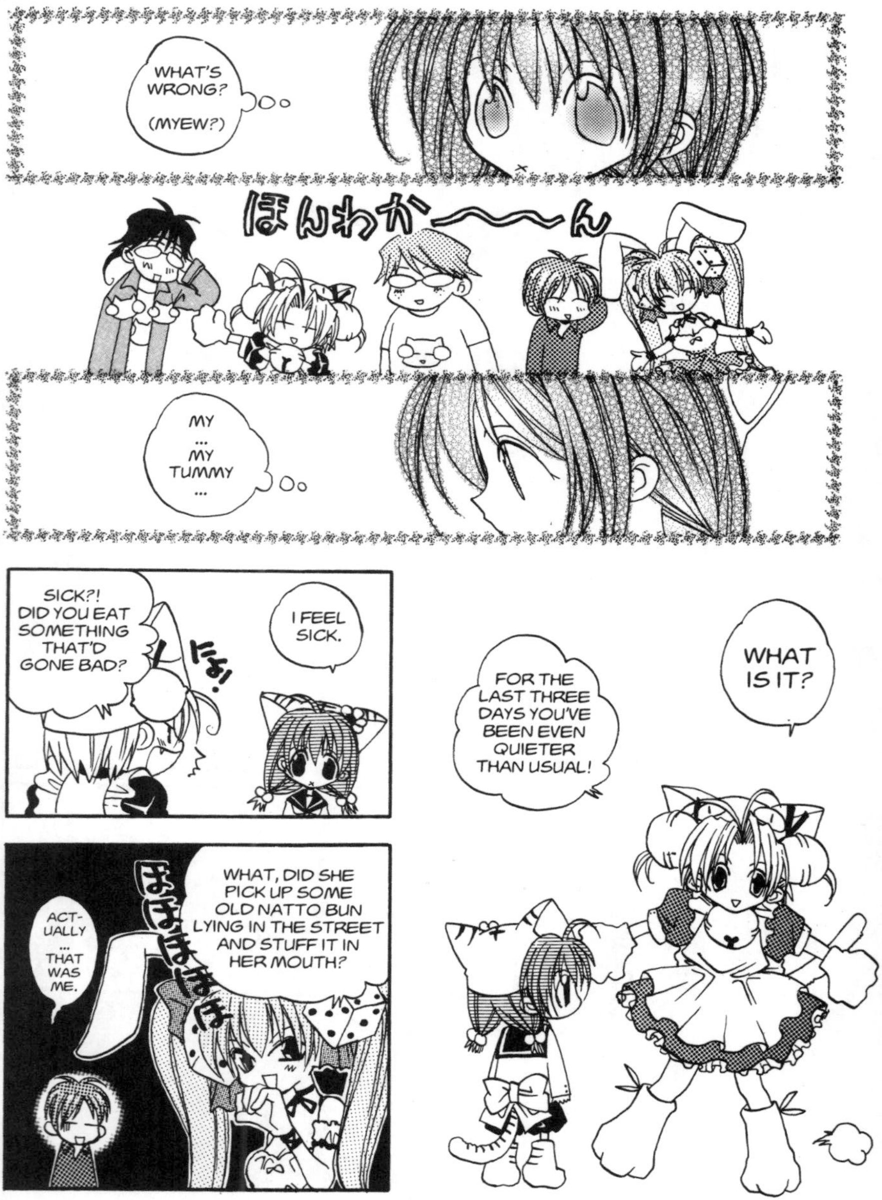
WHAT'S WRONG?
(MYEW?)
ほんわか〜〜ん
MY ... MY TUMMY ...
WHAT IS IT?
FOR THE LAST THREE DAYS YOU'VE BEEN EVEN QUIETER THAN USUAL!
I FEEL SICK.
SICK?! DID YOU EAT SOMETHING THAT'D GONE BAD?
WHAT, DID SHE PICK UP SOME OLD NATTO BUN LYING IN THE STREET AND STUFF IT IN HER MOUTH?
ほほほほほほ
ACT-UALLY ... THAT WAS ME.

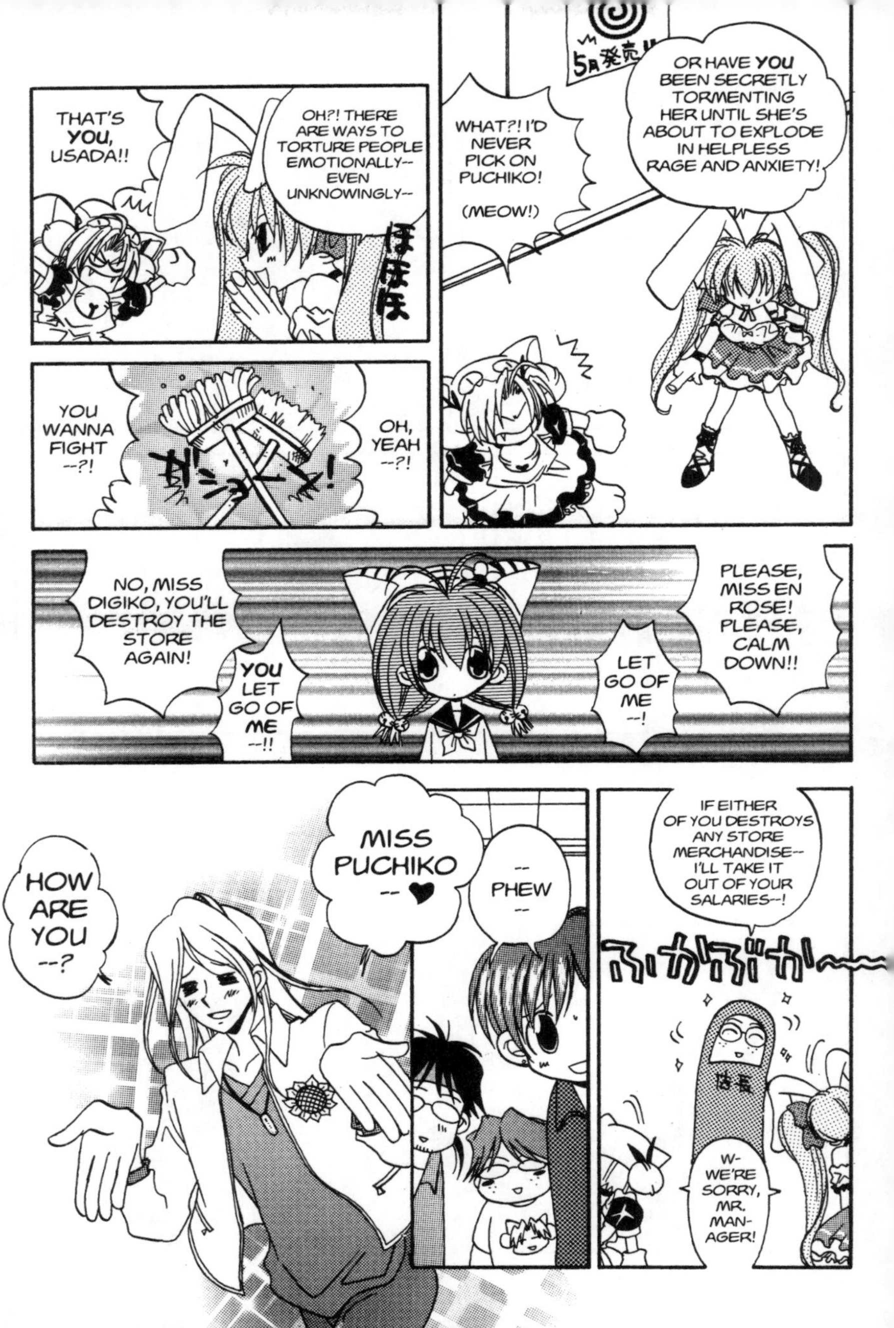
5月発売!!
OR HAVE **YOU** BEEN SECRETLY TORMENTING HER UNTIL SHE'S ABOUT TO EXPLODE IN HELPLESS RAGE AND ANXIETY!
WHAT?! I'D NEVER PICK ON PUCHIKO!
(MEOW!)
OH?! THERE ARE WAYS TO TORTURE PEOPLE EMOTIONALLY-- EVEN UNKNOWINGLY--
ほほほ
THAT'S **YOU**, USADA!!
OH, YEAH --?!
YOU WANNA FIGHT --?!
PLEASE, MISS EN ROSE! PLEASE, CALM DOWN!!
LET GO OF ME --!
NO, MISS DIGIKO, YOU'LL DESTROY THE STORE AGAIN!
YOU LET GO OF **ME** --!!
IF EITHER OF YOU DESTROYS ANY STORE MERCHANDISE-- I'LL TAKE IT OUT OF YOUR SALARIES--!
ふかぶか~~
W-WE'RE SORRY, MR. MAN-AGER!
-- PHEW --
MISS PUCHIKO -- ♥
HOW ARE YOU --?

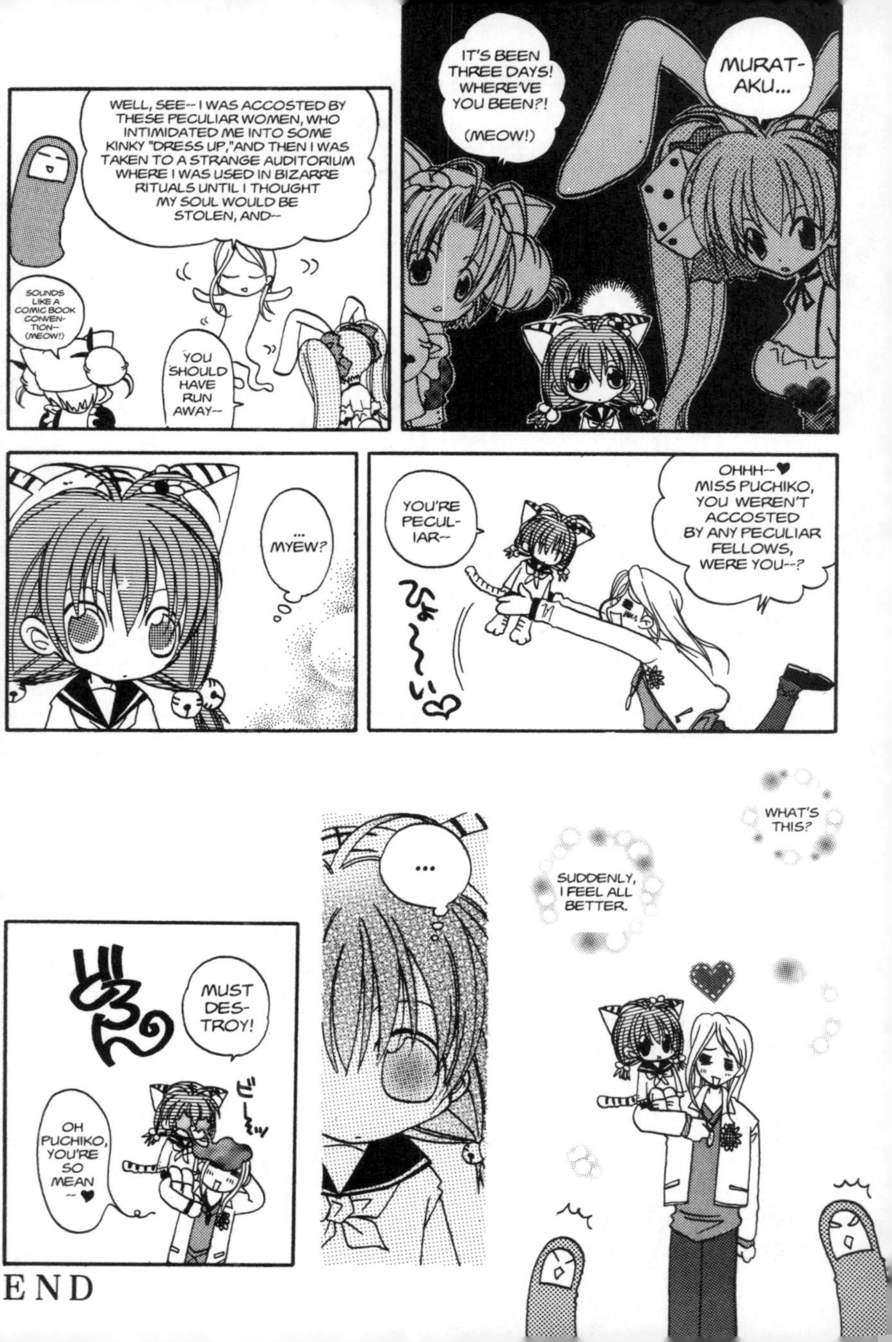
MURAT-AKU...
IT'S BEEN THREE DAYS! WHERE'VE YOU BEEN?! (MEOW!)
WELL, SEE-- I WAS ACCOSTED BY THESE PECULIAR WOMEN, WHO INTIMIDATED ME INTO SOME KINKY "DRESS UP," AND THEN I WAS TAKEN TO A STRANGE AUDITORIUM WHERE I WAS USED IN BIZARRE RITUALS UNTIL I THOUGHT MY SOUL WOULD BE STOLEN, AND--
YOU SHOULD HAVE RUN AWAY--
SOUNDS LIKE A COMIC BOOK CONVENTION-- (MEOW!)
OHHH--♥ MISS PUCHIKO, YOU WEREN'T ACCOSTED BY ANY PECULIAR FELLOWS, WERE YOU--?
YOU'RE PECULIAR--
... MYEW?
WHAT'S THIS?
SUDDENLY, I FEEL ALL BETTER.
...
MUST DES-TROY!
OH PUCHIKO, YOU'RE SO MEAN --♥
END

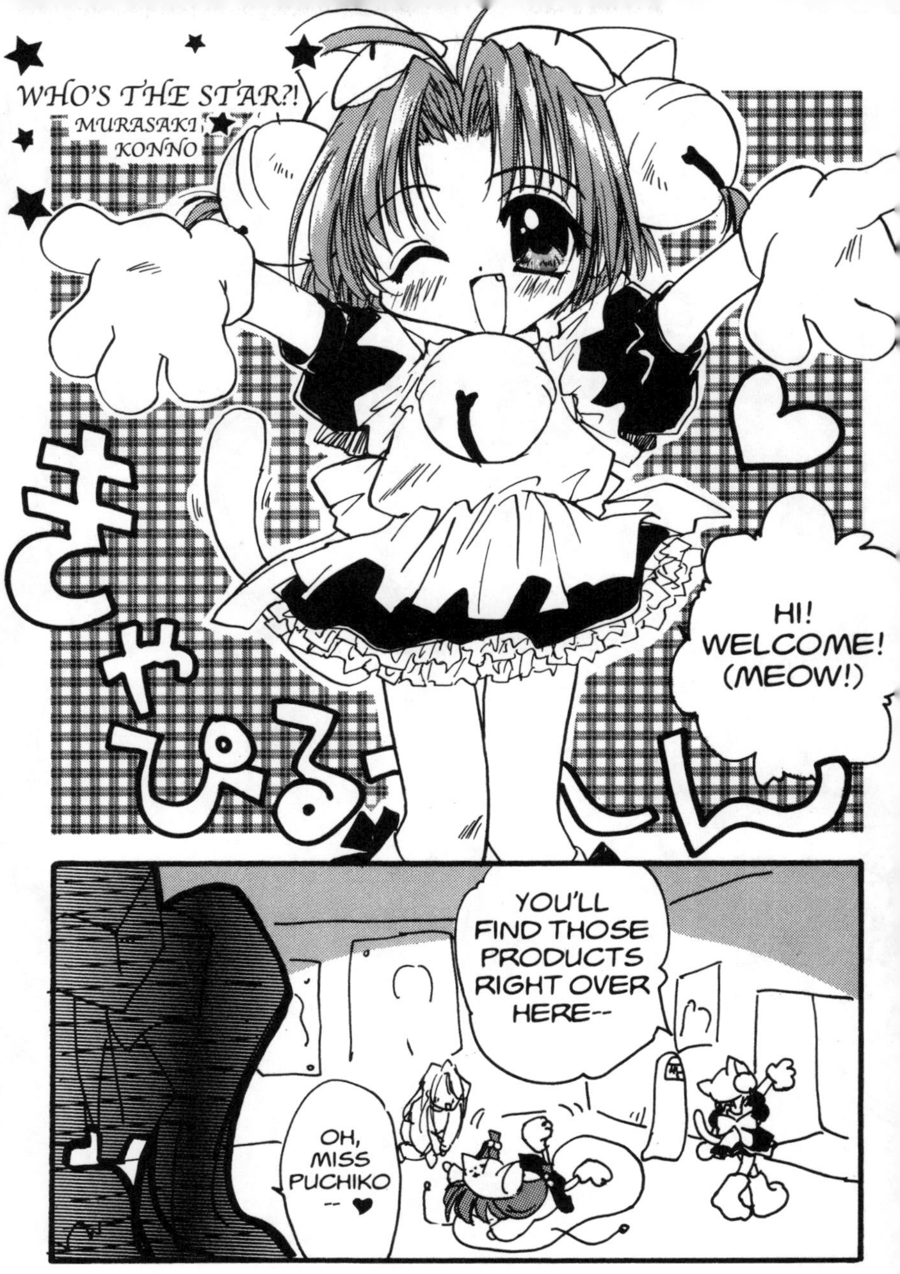
WHO'S THE STAR?!
MURASAKI KONNO
きゃぴるーん
HI! WELCOME! (MEOW!)
YOU'LL FIND THOSE PRODUCTS RIGHT OVER HERE--
OH, MISS PUCHIKO -- ♥

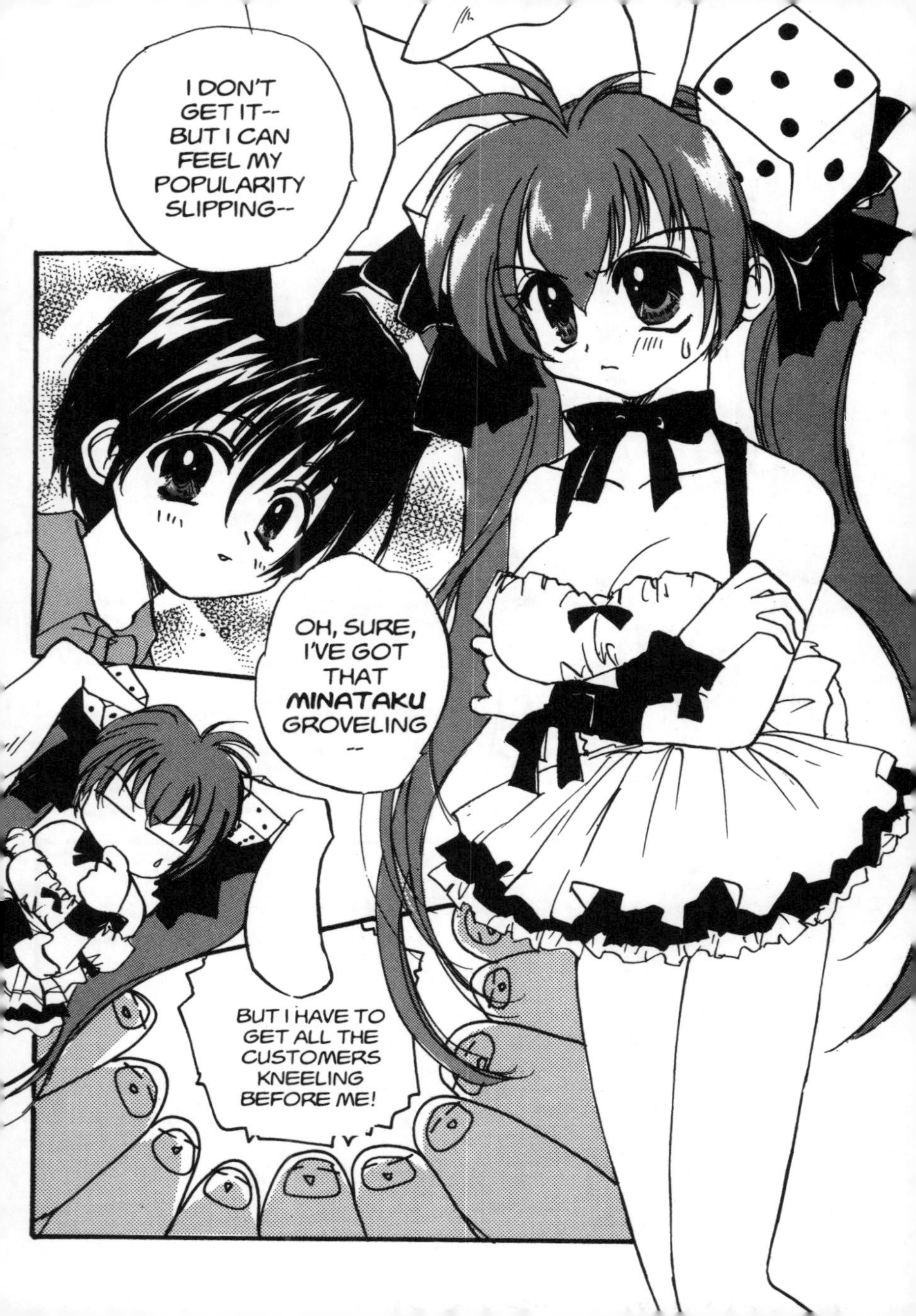
I DON'T GET IT-- BUT I CAN FEEL MY POPULARITY SLIPPING--
OH, SURE, I'VE GOT THAT **MINATAKU** GROVELING --
BUT I HAVE TO GET ALL THE CUSTOMERS KNEELING BEFORE ME!

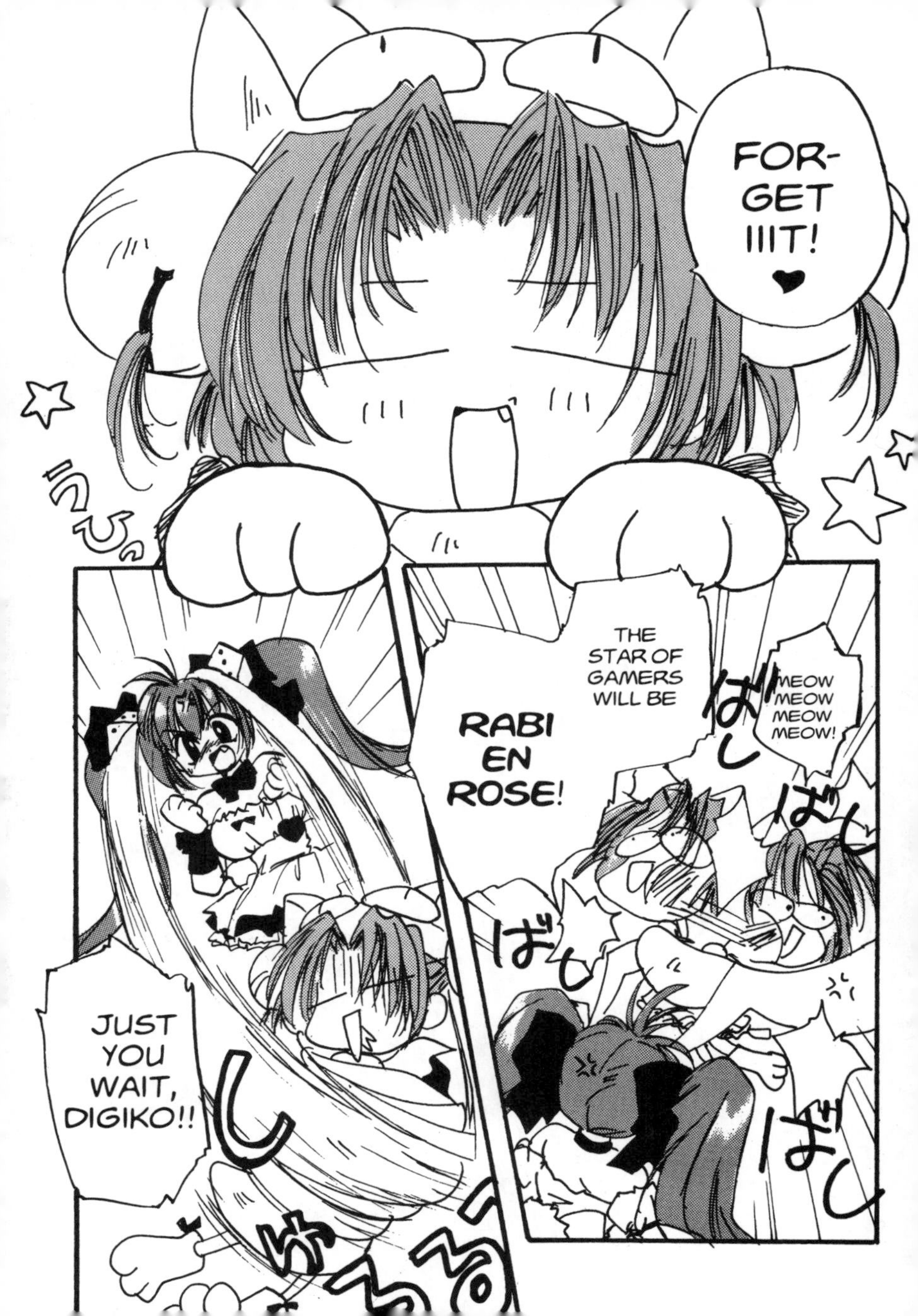

FOR-GET IIIT! ♥
うひっ
THE STAR OF GAMERS WILL BE
RABI EN ROSE!
MEOW MEOW MEOW MEOW!
ばし
ばし
ばし
ばし
JUST YOU WAIT, DIGIKO!!

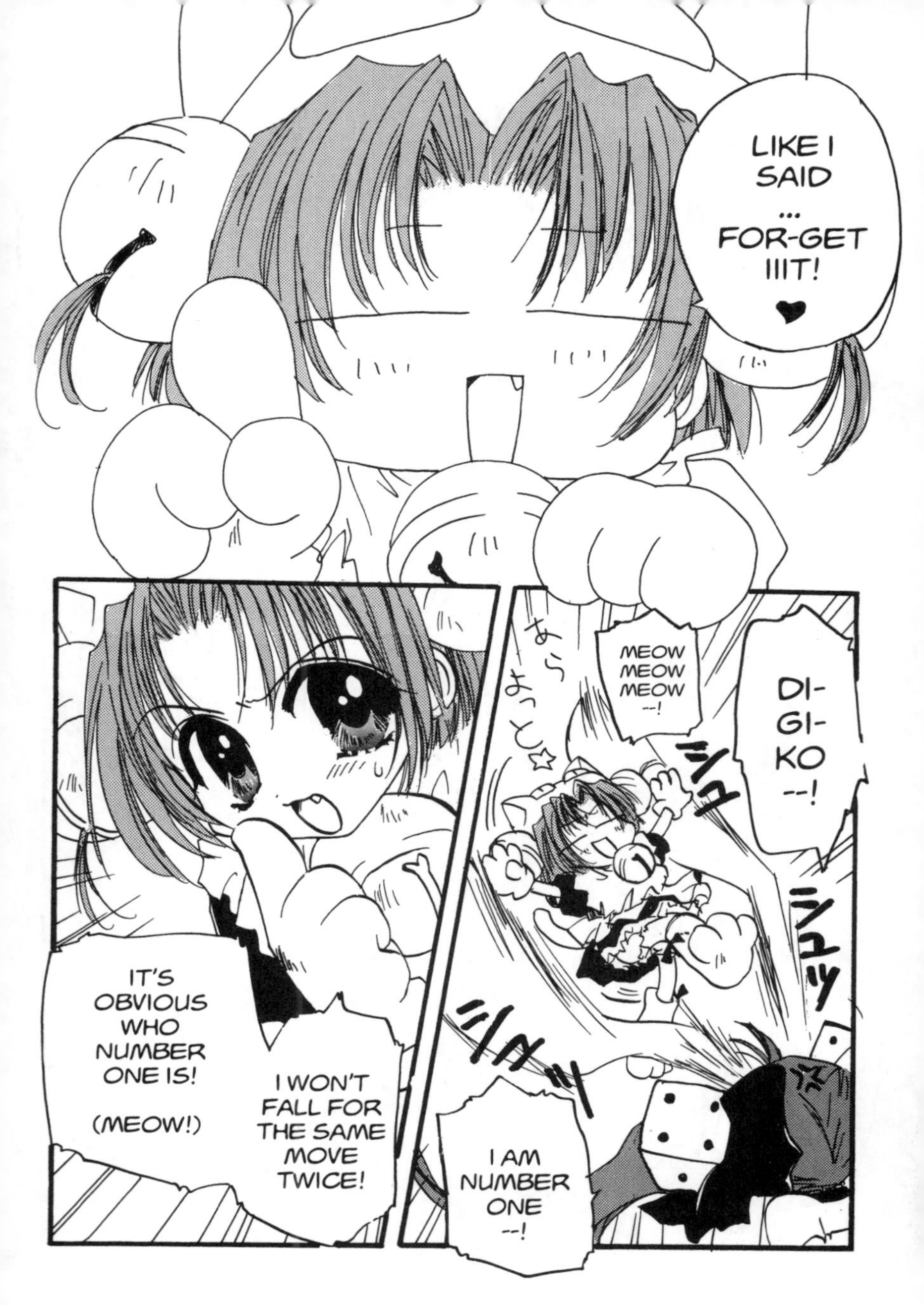
LIKE I SAID ... FOR-GET IIIT! ♥
あらよっと☆
MEOW MEOW MEOW --!
DI-GI-KO --!
I AM NUMBER ONE --!
I WON'T FALL FOR THE SAME MOVE TWICE!
IT'S OBVIOUS WHO NUMBER ONE IS!
(MEOW!)

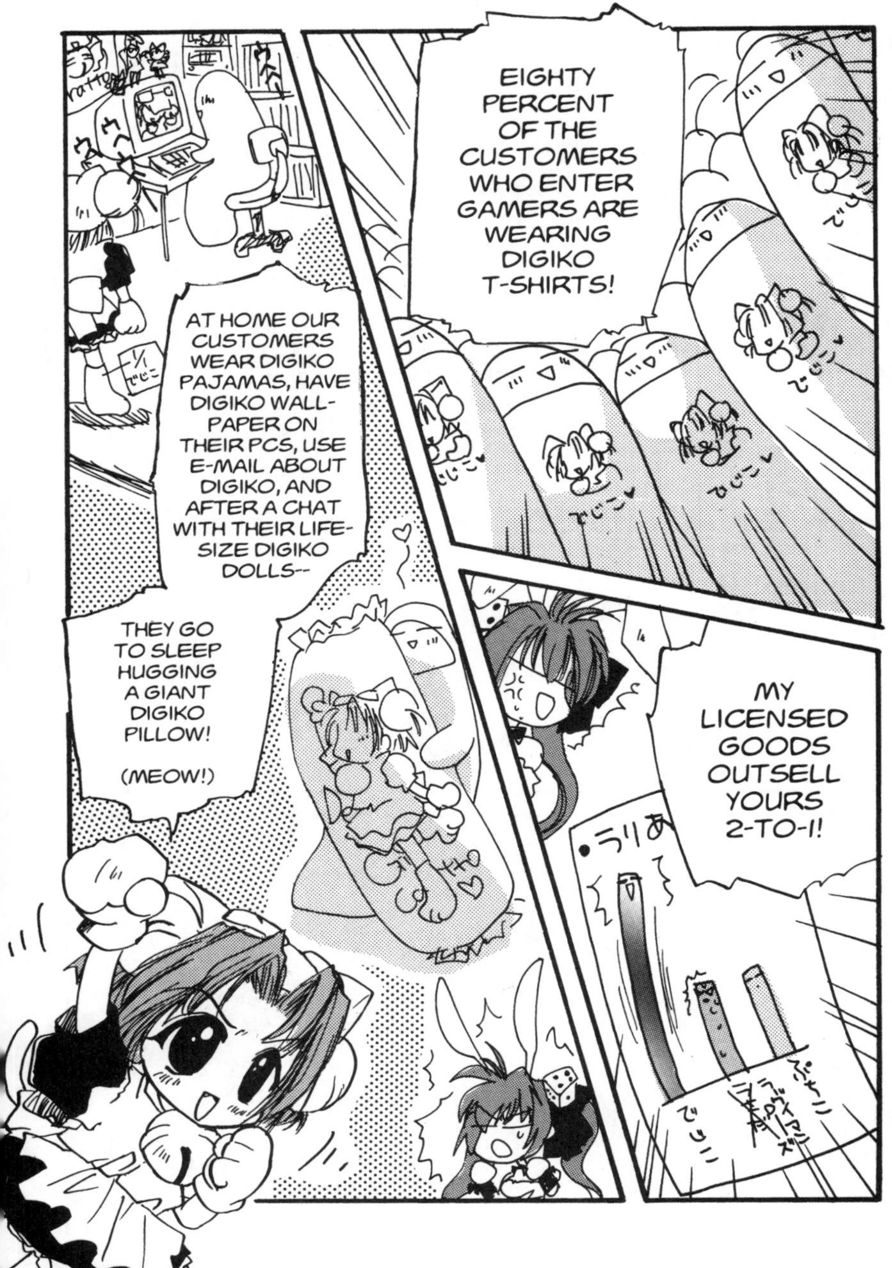
EIGHTY PERCENT OF THE CUSTOMERS WHO ENTER GAMERS ARE WEARING DIGIKO T-SHIRTS!
AT HOME OUR CUSTOMERS WEAR DIGIKO PAJAMAS, HAVE DIGIKO WALL-PAPER ON THEIR PCS, USE E-MAIL ABOUT DIGIKO, AND AFTER A CHAT WITH THEIR LIFE-SIZE DIGIKO DOLLS--
THEY GO TO SLEEP HUGGING A GIANT DIGIKO PILLOW!
(MEOW!)
MY LICENSED GOODS OUTSELL YOURS 2-TO-1!

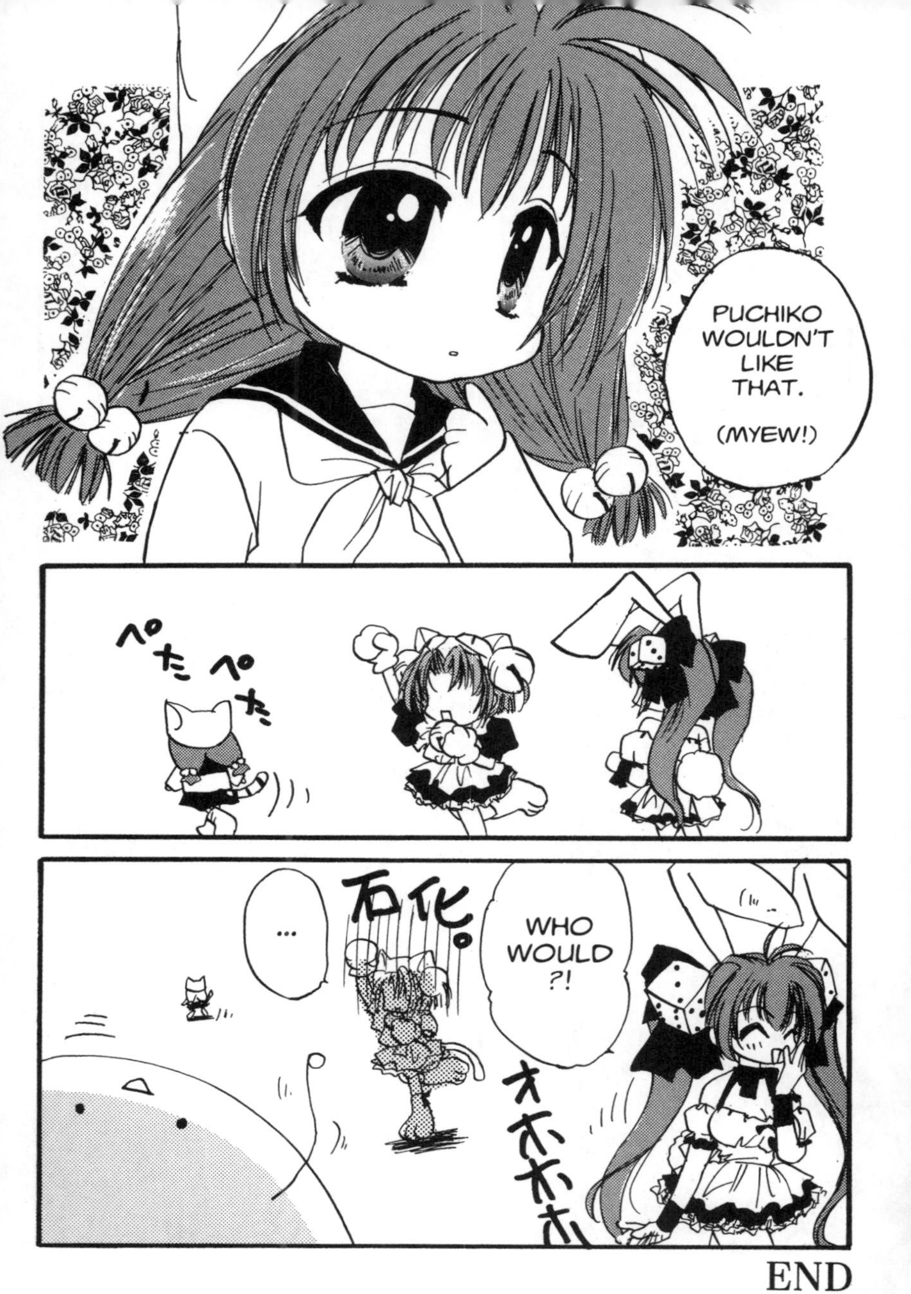
PUCHIKO WOULDN'T LIKE THAT.
(MYEW!)
ぺた ぺた ぺた
WHO WOULD ?!
オホホホ
石化。
...

END

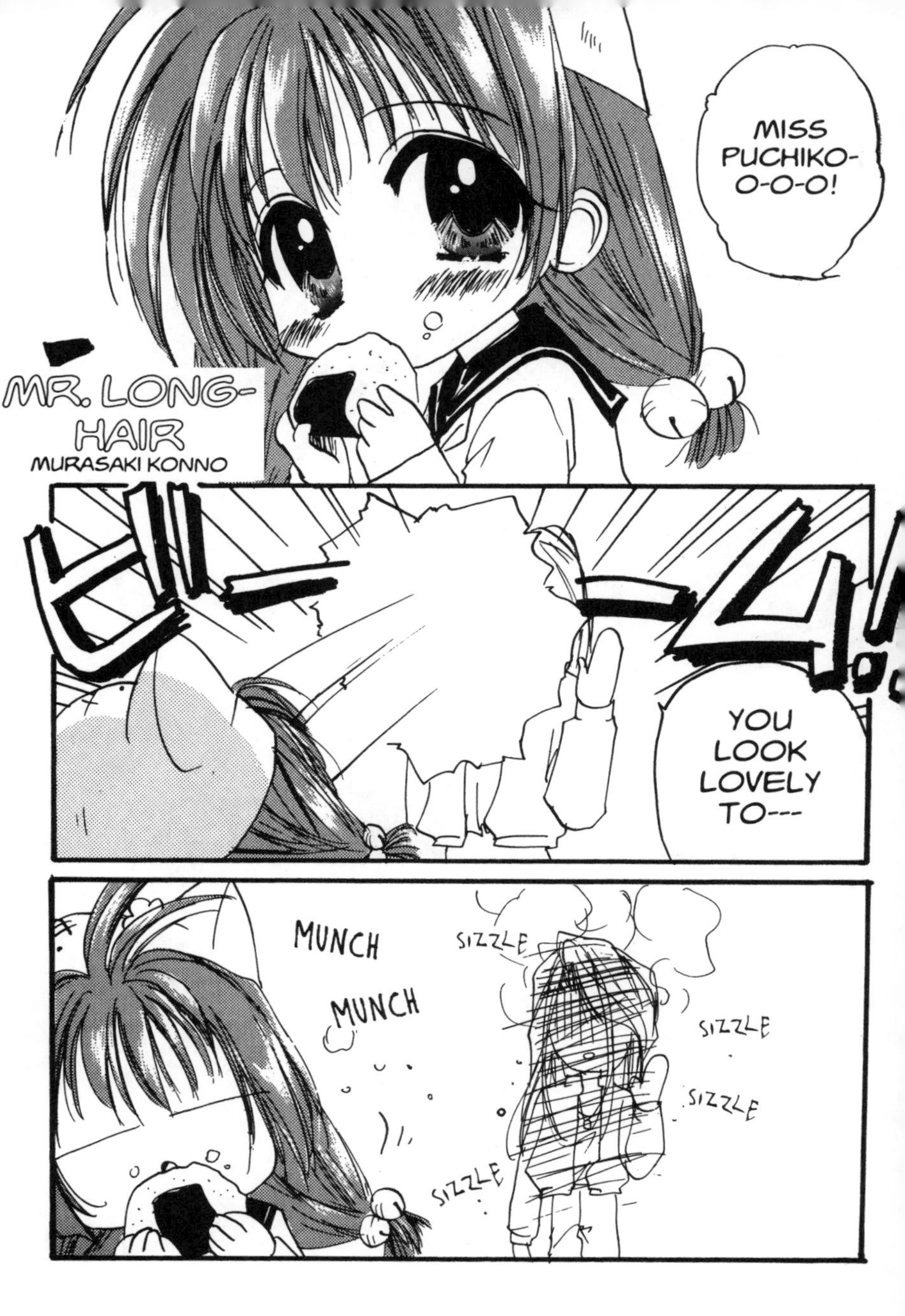
MISS PUCHIKO-O-O-O!
MR. LONG-HAIR
MURASAKI KONNO
ビーーム!
YOU LOOK LOVELY TO---
SIZZLE
SIZZLE
SIZZLE
SIZZLE
MUNCH
MUNCH

NOW, MISS PUCHIKO... HA HA HA HA HA... IS THAT ANY WAY TO SAY HELLO...?

MUNCH
MUNCH
MUNCH

MUNCH
MUNCH
MUNCH

...

SIZZLE
SIZZLE
SIZZLE

END

A comment abou
Di Gi Charat

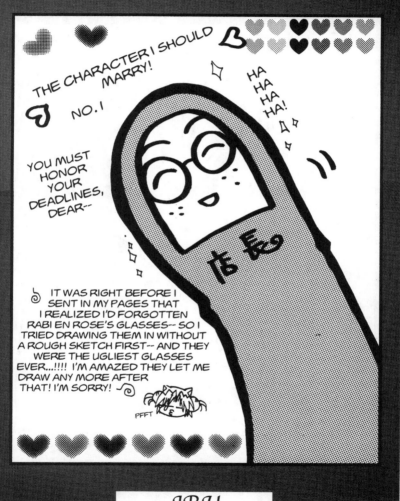

THE CHARACTER I SHOULD MARRY!
NO. 1
HA HA HA HA!
YOU MUST HONOR YOUR DEADLINES, DEAR--
店長
IT WAS RIGHT BEFORE I SENT IN MY PAGES THAT I REALIZED I'D FORGOTTEN RABI EN ROSE'S GLASSES-- SO I TRIED DRAWING THEM IN WITHOUT A ROUGH SKETCH FIRST-- AND THEY WERE THE UGLIEST GLASSES EVER...!!!! I'M AMAZED THEY LET ME DRAW ANY MORE AFTER THAT! I'M SORRY!
PFFT

IRU ISOSHIGAKI

A comment about Di Gi Charat

I LOVE PUCHIKO. SCHOOL UNIFORMS ARE FUN TO DRAW.

MURASAKI KONNO

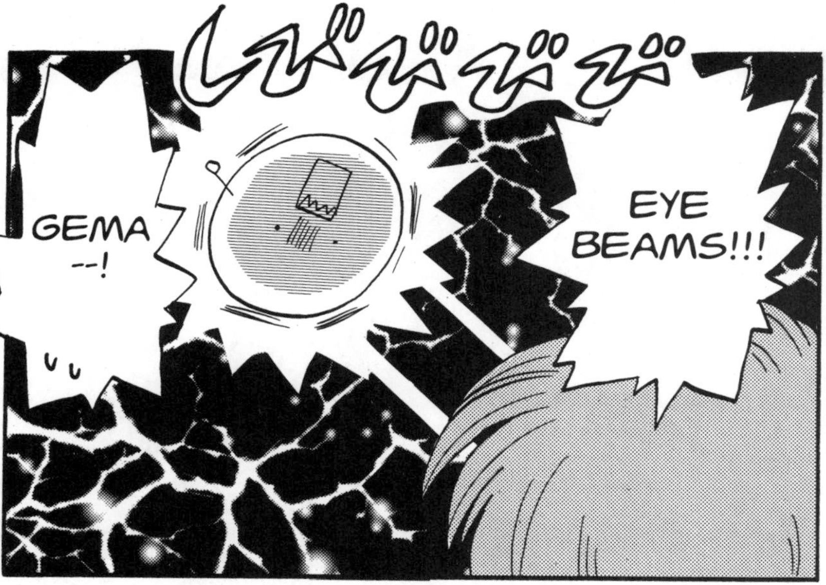
しびびびび
EYE BEAMS!!!
GEMA --!

THE TALE OF GEMA

STRIKE-HEISUKE

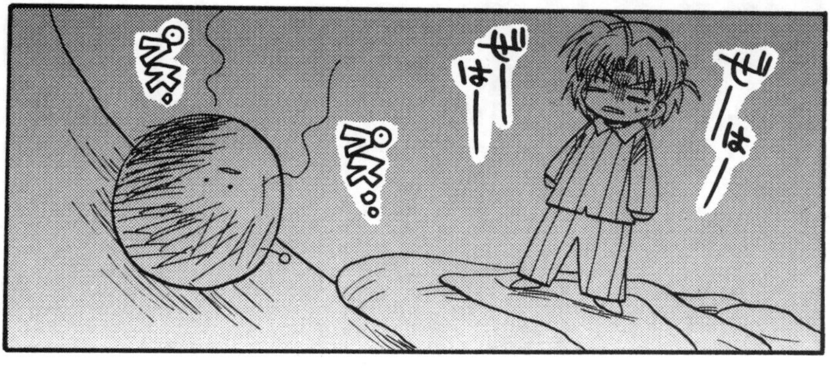
ぜーはー
ぜーはー
ぷス。。
ぷス。

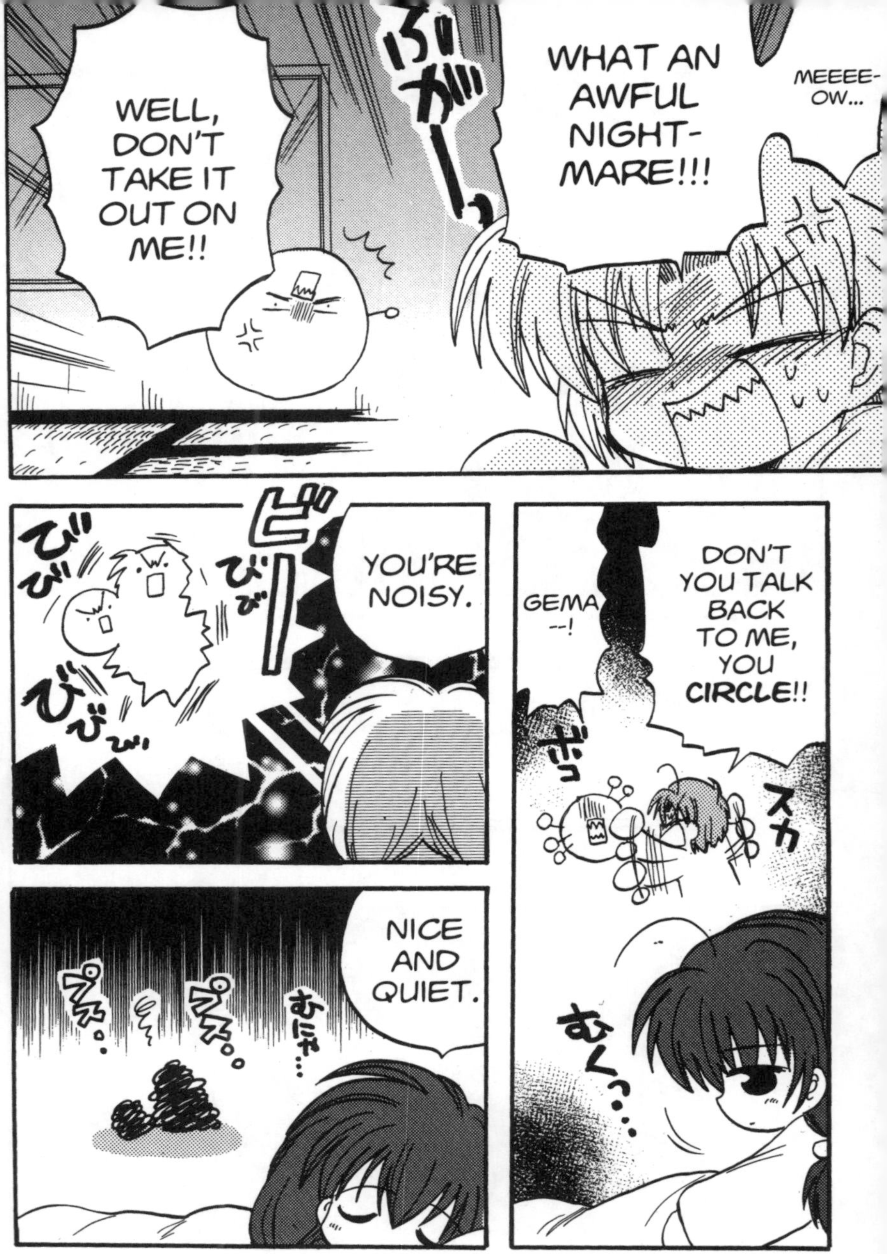
MEEEE-OW...
WHAT AN AWFUL NIGHT-MARE!!!
ふがーっ
WELL, DON'T TAKE IT OUT ON ME!!
DON'T YOU TALK BACK TO ME, YOU **CIRCLE**!!
GEMA--!
ボコ
スカ
ビー
YOU'RE NOISY.
びびび
びびび
びびびび
むくっ...
NICE AND QUIET.
むにゃ...
ぷふ。
ぷふ。

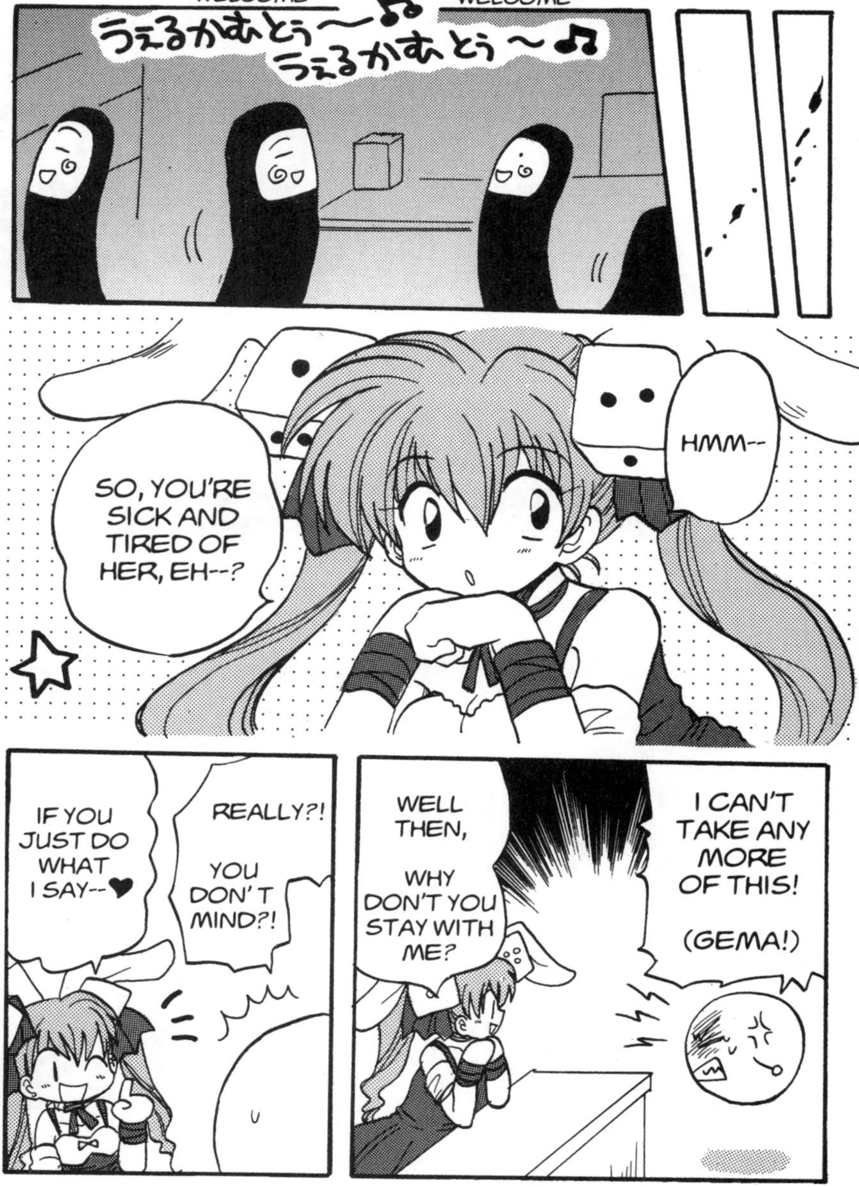
WELCOME--
WELCOME--
うぇるかむとぅ〜♫
うぇるかむとぅ〜♫
HMM--
SO, YOU'RE SICK AND TIRED OF HER, EH--?
I CAN'T TAKE ANY MORE OF THIS!
(GEMA!)
WELL THEN,
WHY DON'T YOU STAY WITH ME?
REALLY?!
YOU DON'T MIND?!
IF YOU JUST DO WHAT I SAY--❤

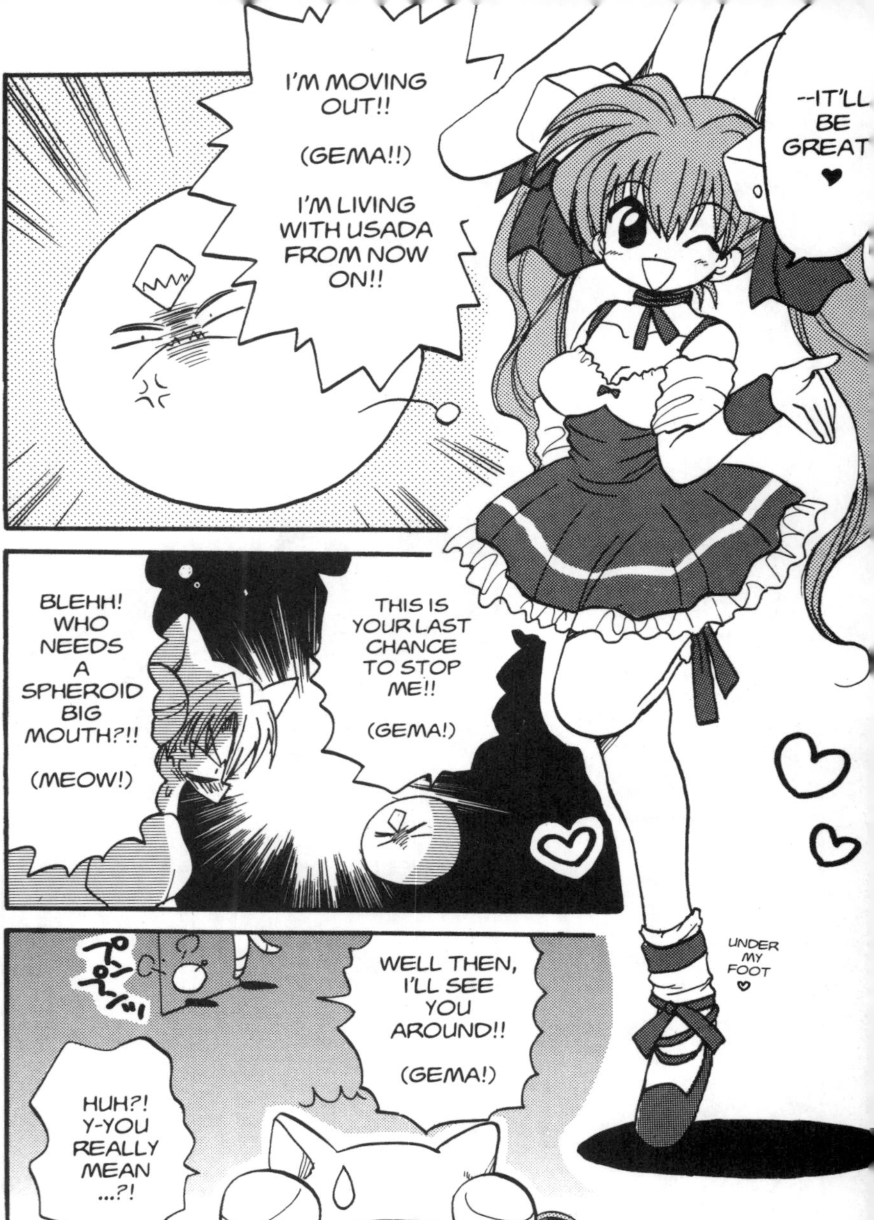
I'M MOVING OUT!! (GEMA!!) I'M LIVING WITH USADA FROM NOW ON!!
--IT'LL BE GREAT ♥
THIS IS YOUR LAST CHANCE TO STOP ME!! (GEMA!)
BLEHH! WHO NEEDS A SPHEROID BIG MOUTH?!! (MEOW!)
UNDER MY FOOT ♡
WELL THEN, I'LL SEE YOU AROUND!! (GEMA!)
HUH?! Y-YOU REALLY MEAN ...?!

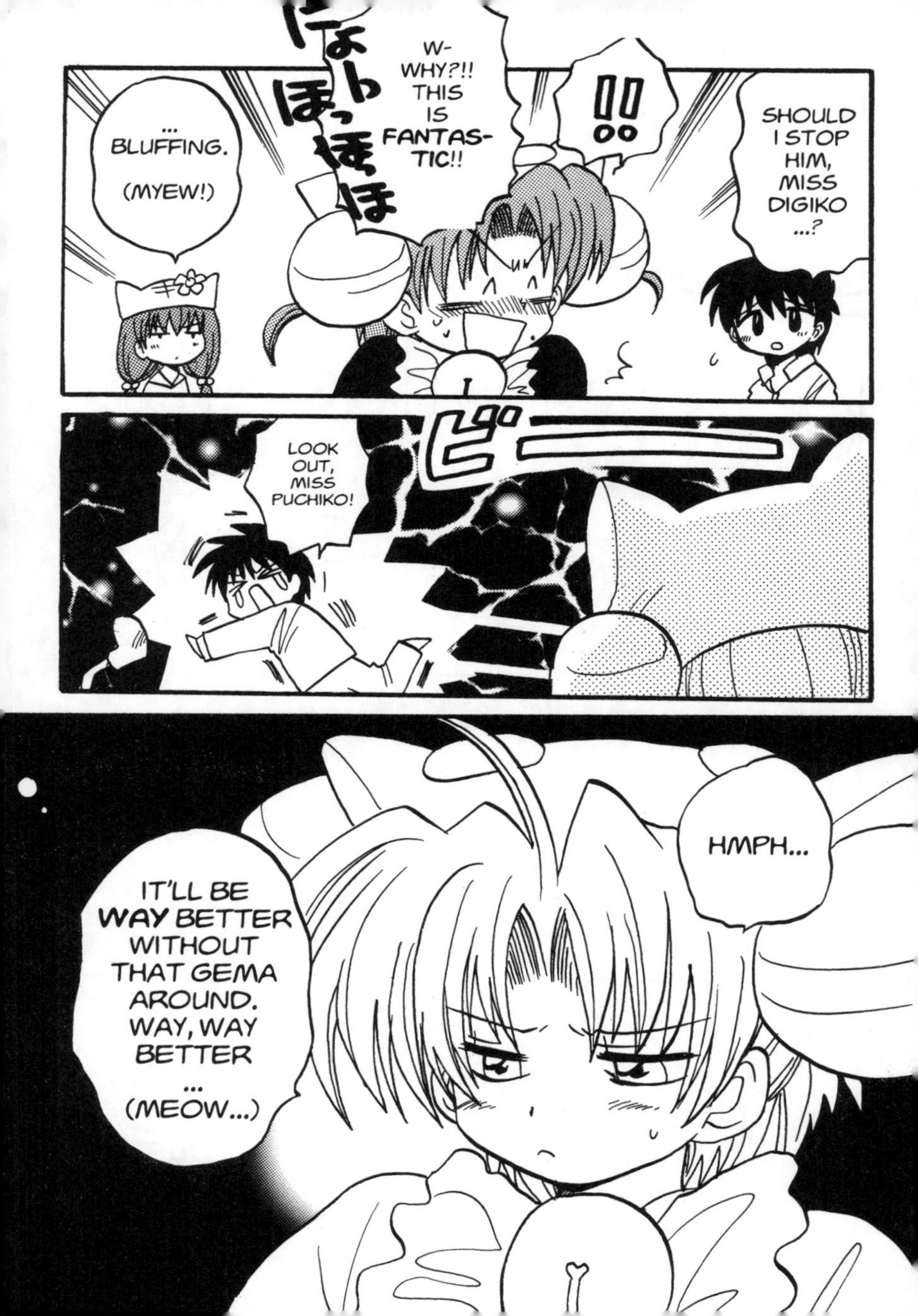

SHOULD I STOP HIM, MISS DIGIKO ...?
!!
W-WHY?!! THIS IS FANTASTIC!!
... BLUFFING.
(MYEW!)
LOOK OUT, MISS PUCHIKO!
HMPH...
IT'LL BE **WAY** BETTER WITHOUT THAT GEMA AROUND. WAY, WAY BETTER ... (MEOW...)

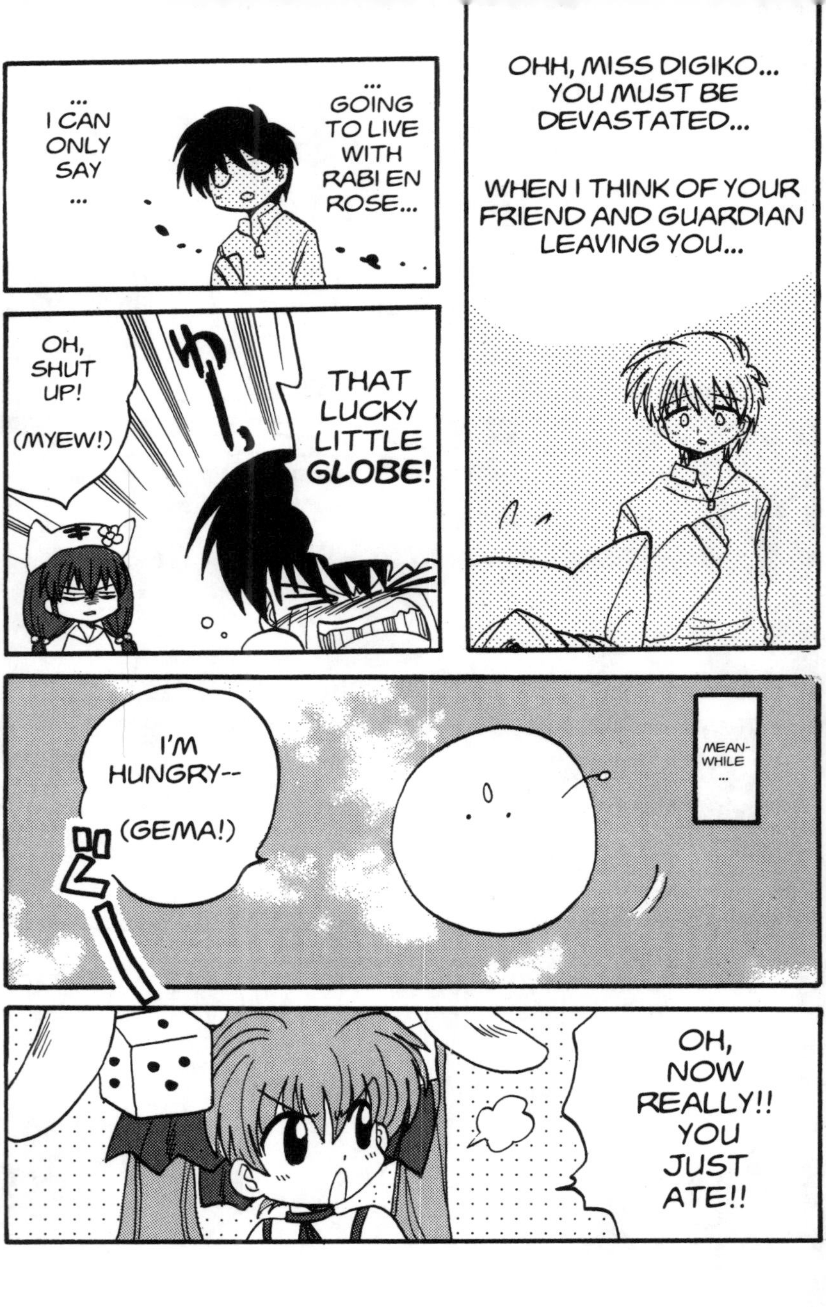
OHH, MISS DIGIKO... YOU MUST BE DEVASTATED...
WHEN I THINK OF YOUR FRIEND AND GUARDIAN LEAVING YOU...
... GOING TO LIVE WITH RABI EN ROSE...
... I CAN ONLY SAY ...
THAT LUCKY LITTLE GLOBE!
OH, SHUT UP! (MYEW!)
MEAN-WHILE ...
I'M HUNGRY-- (GEMA!)
OH, NOW REALLY!! YOU JUST ATE!!

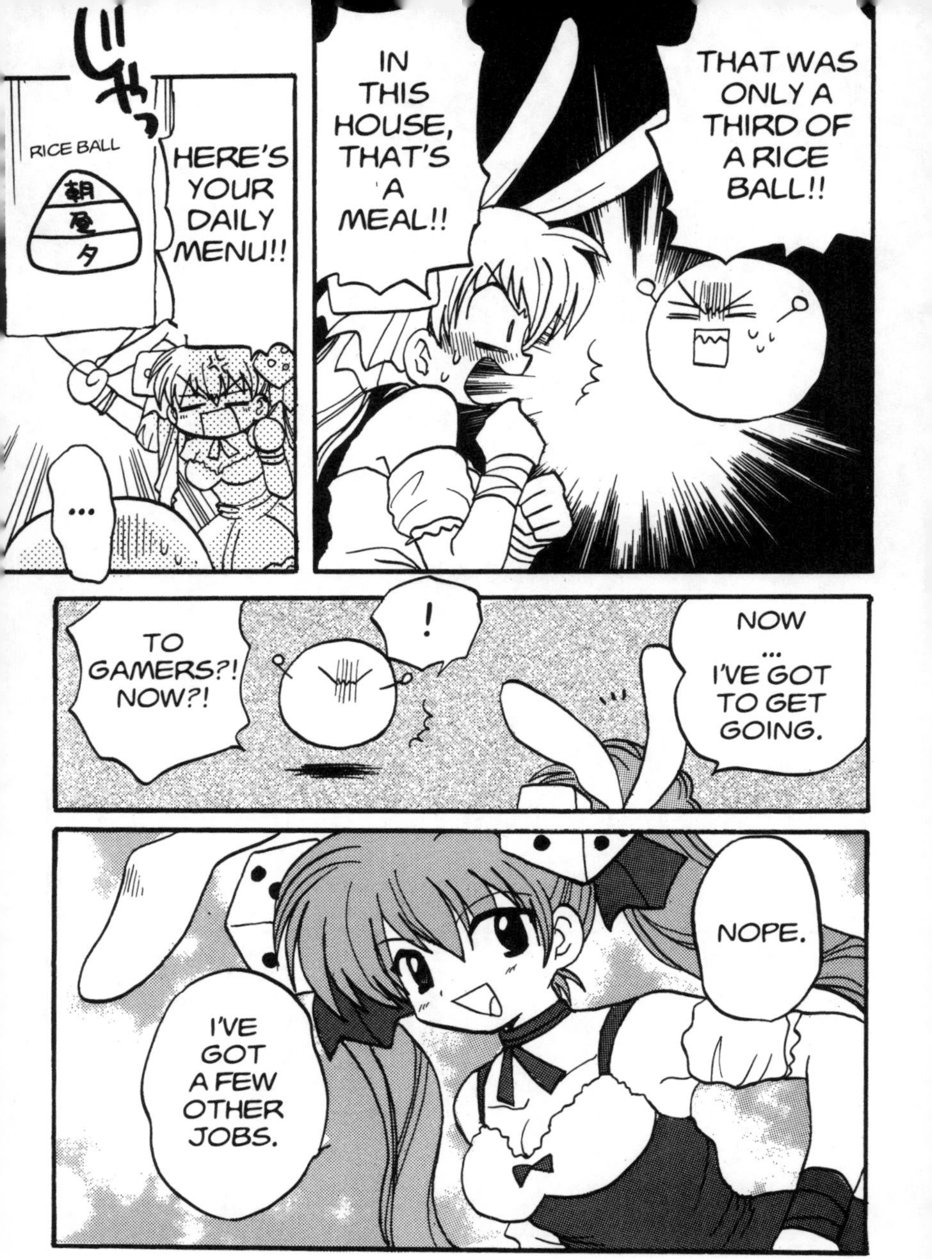
THAT WAS ONLY A THIRD OF A RICE BALL!!
IN THIS HOUSE, THAT'S A MEAL!!
じゃっ
HERE'S YOUR DAILY MENU!!
RICE BALL
朝
昼
夕
...
NOW ... I'VE GOT TO GET GOING.
!
TO GAMERS?! NOW?!
NOPE.
I'VE GOT A FEW OTHER JOBS.

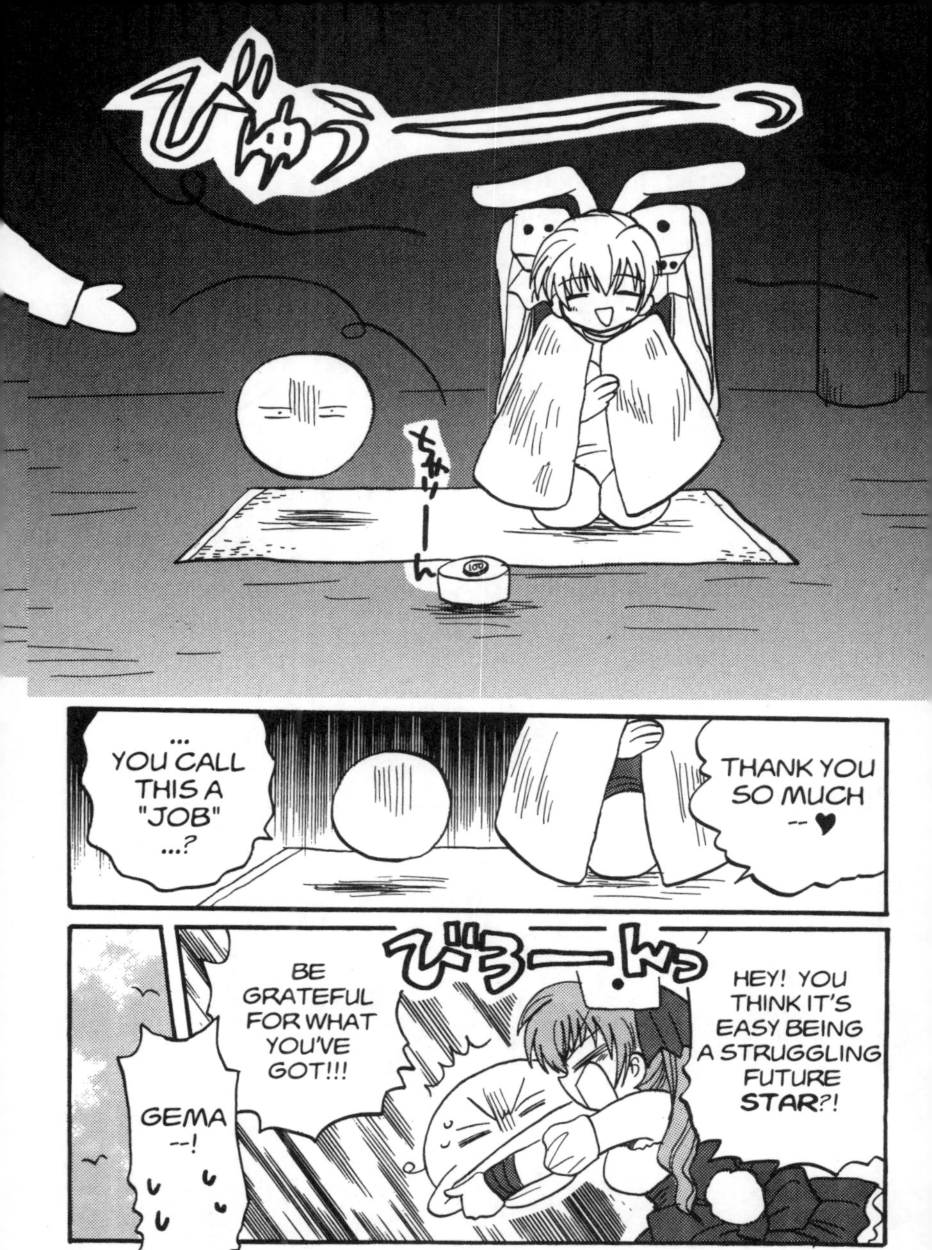
ひゅっ
ちゃりーん
THANK YOU SO MUCH --♥
... YOU CALL THIS A "JOB" ...?
びろーんっ
HEY! YOU THINK IT'S EASY BEING A STRUGGLING FUTURE STAR?!
BE GRATEFUL FOR WHAT YOU'VE GOT!!!
GEMA --!

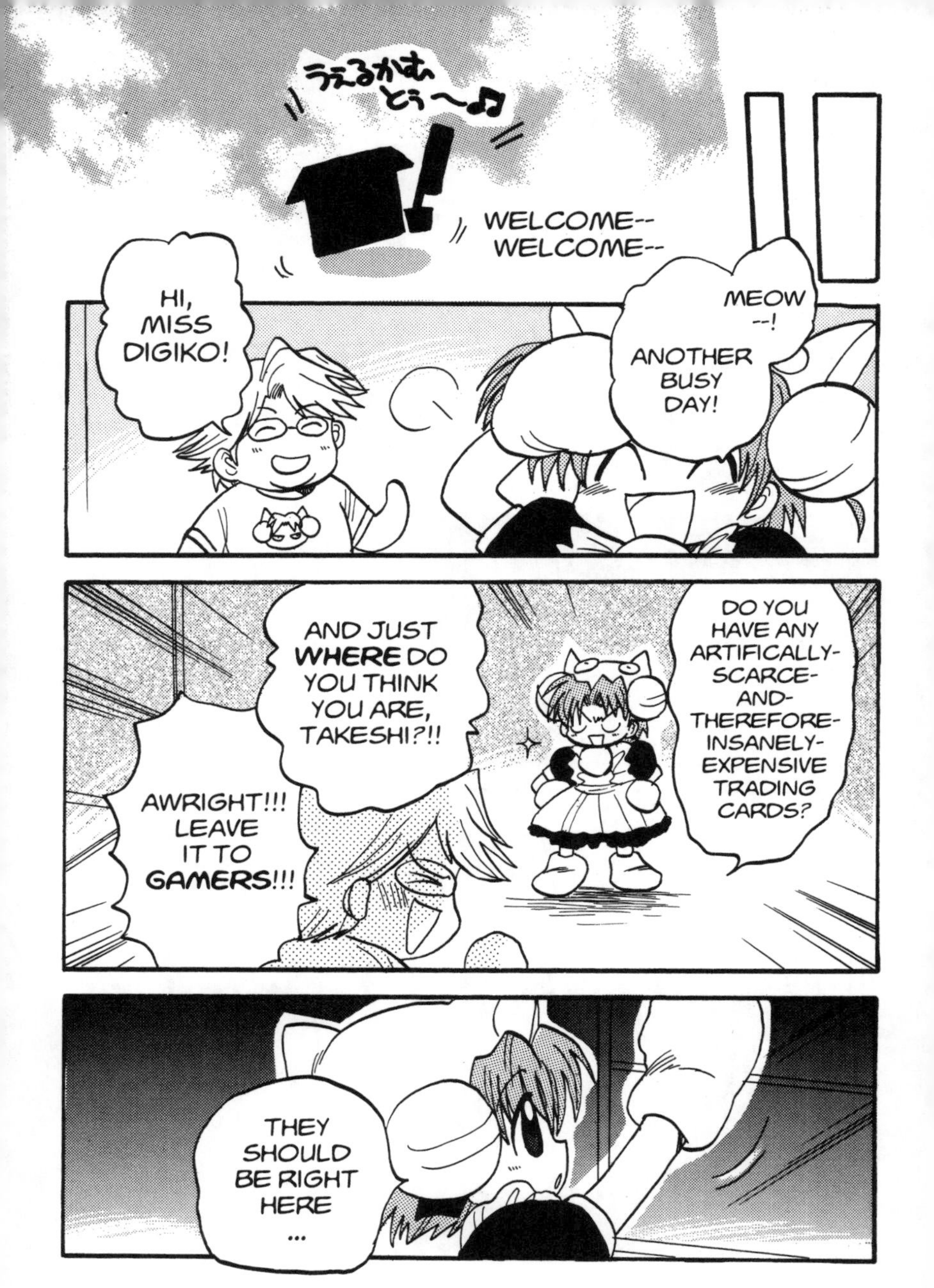
うぇるかむ とぅ～♪♫
WELCOME-- WELCOME--
MEOW --! ANOTHER BUSY DAY!
HI, MISS DIGIKO!
DO YOU HAVE ANY ARTIFICALLY-SCARCE-AND-THEREFORE-INSANELY-EXPENSIVE TRADING CARDS?
AND JUST WHERE DO YOU THINK YOU ARE, TAKESHI?!!
AWRIGHT!!! LEAVE IT TO GAMERS!!!
THEY SHOULD BE RIGHT HERE ...

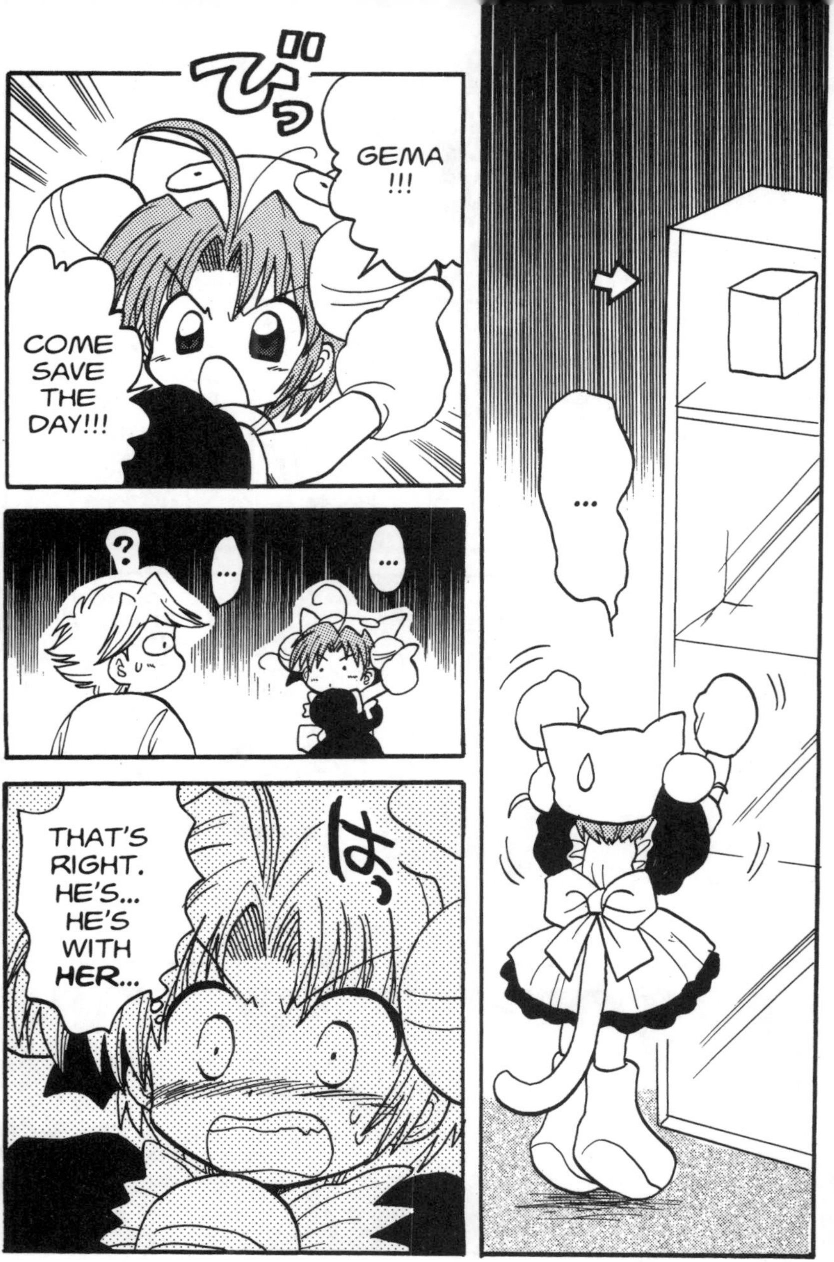
...
びっ
GEMA !!!
COME SAVE THE DAY!!!
?
...
...
THAT'S RIGHT. HE'S... HE'S WITH HER...
はっ

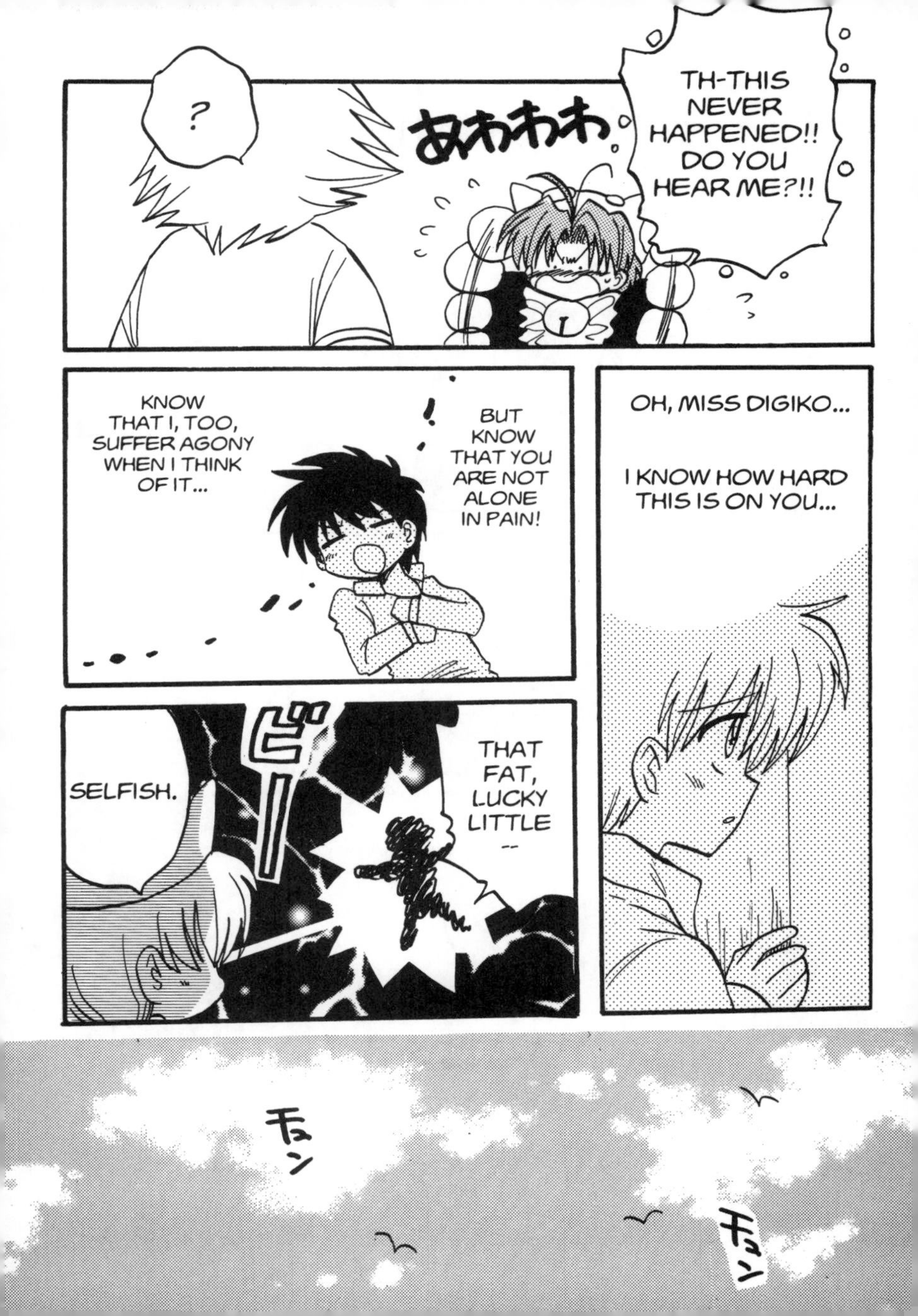
TH-THIS NEVER HAPPENED!! DO YOU HEAR ME?!!
あわわわ
?
OH, MISS DIGIKO...
I KNOW HOW HARD THIS IS ON YOU...
!
BUT KNOW THAT YOU ARE NOT ALONE IN PAIN!
KNOW THAT I, TOO, SUFFER AGONY WHEN I THINK OF IT...
THAT FAT, LUCKY LITTLE --
ビー
SELFISH.
キュン
キュン

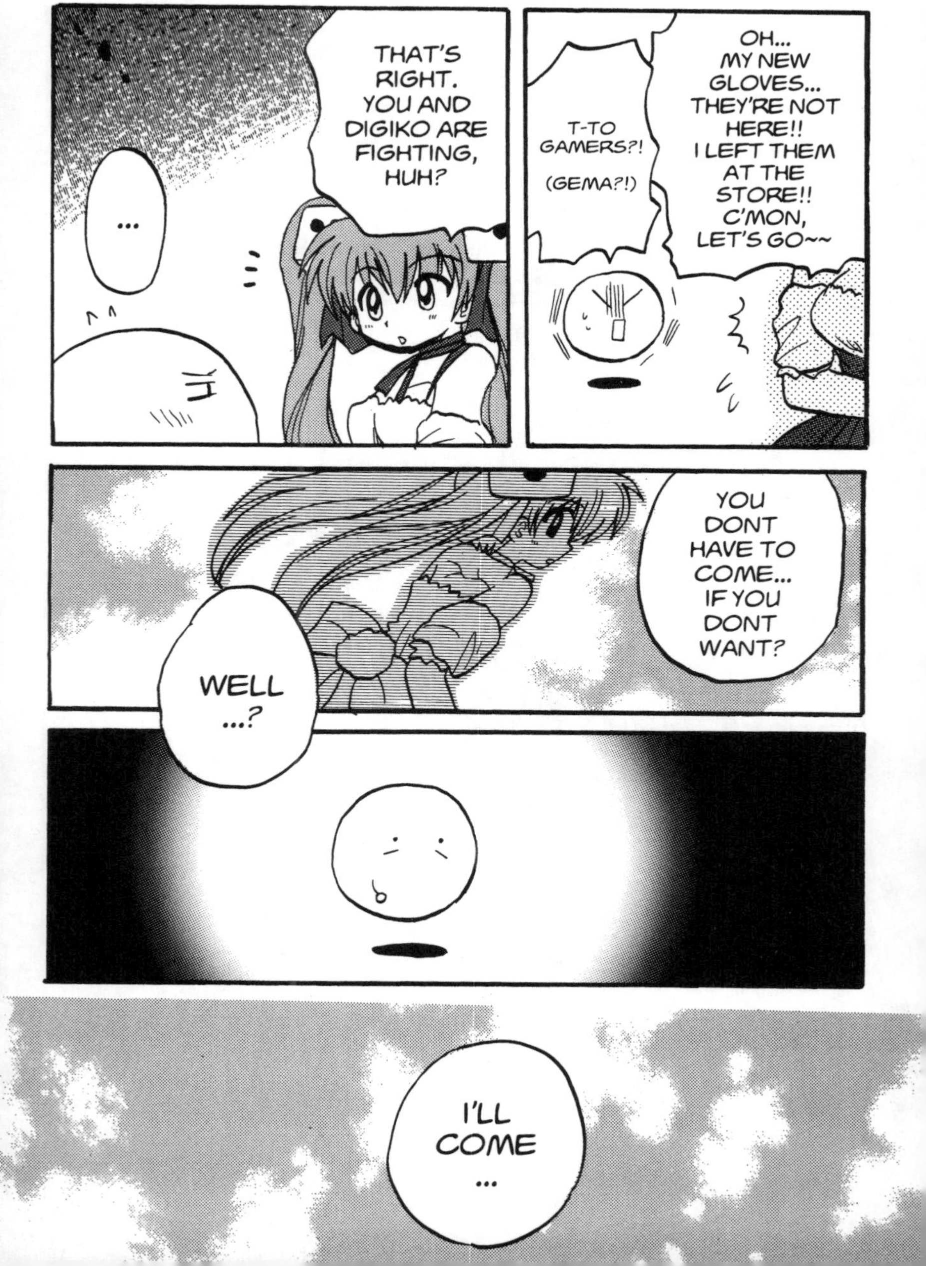
OH... MY NEW GLOVES... THEY'RE NOT HERE!! I LEFT THEM AT THE STORE!! C'MON, LET'S GO~~
T-TO GAMERS?!
(GEMA?!)
THAT'S RIGHT. YOU AND DIGIKO ARE FIGHTING, HUH?
...
YOU DONT HAVE TO COME... IF YOU DONT WANT?
WELL ...?
I'LL COME ...

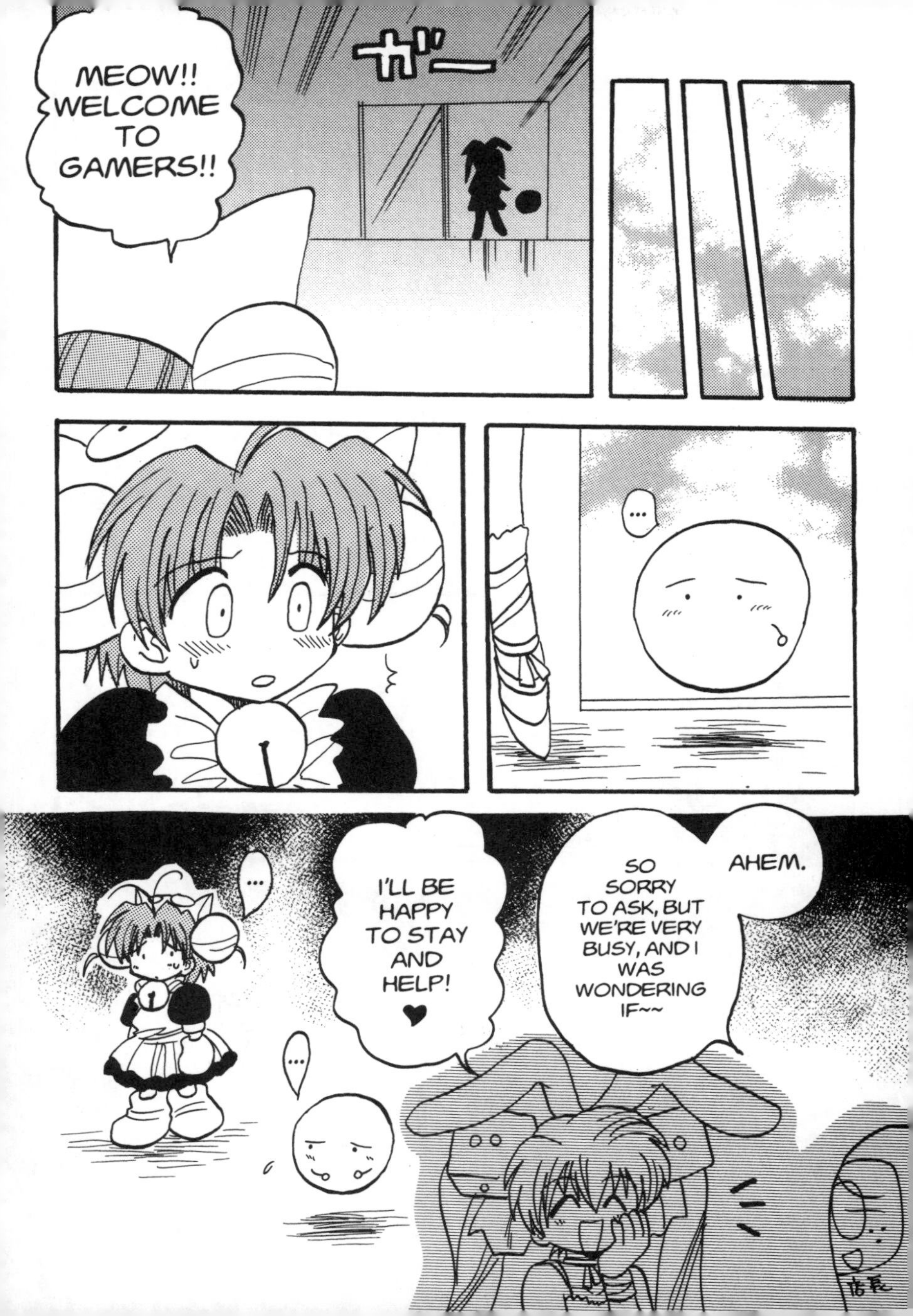
ガー
MEOW!! WELCOME TO GAMERS!!
...
AHEM.
SO SORRY TO ASK, BUT WE'RE VERY BUSY, AND I WAS WONDERING IF~~
I'LL BE HAPPY TO STAY AND HELP! ♥
...
...

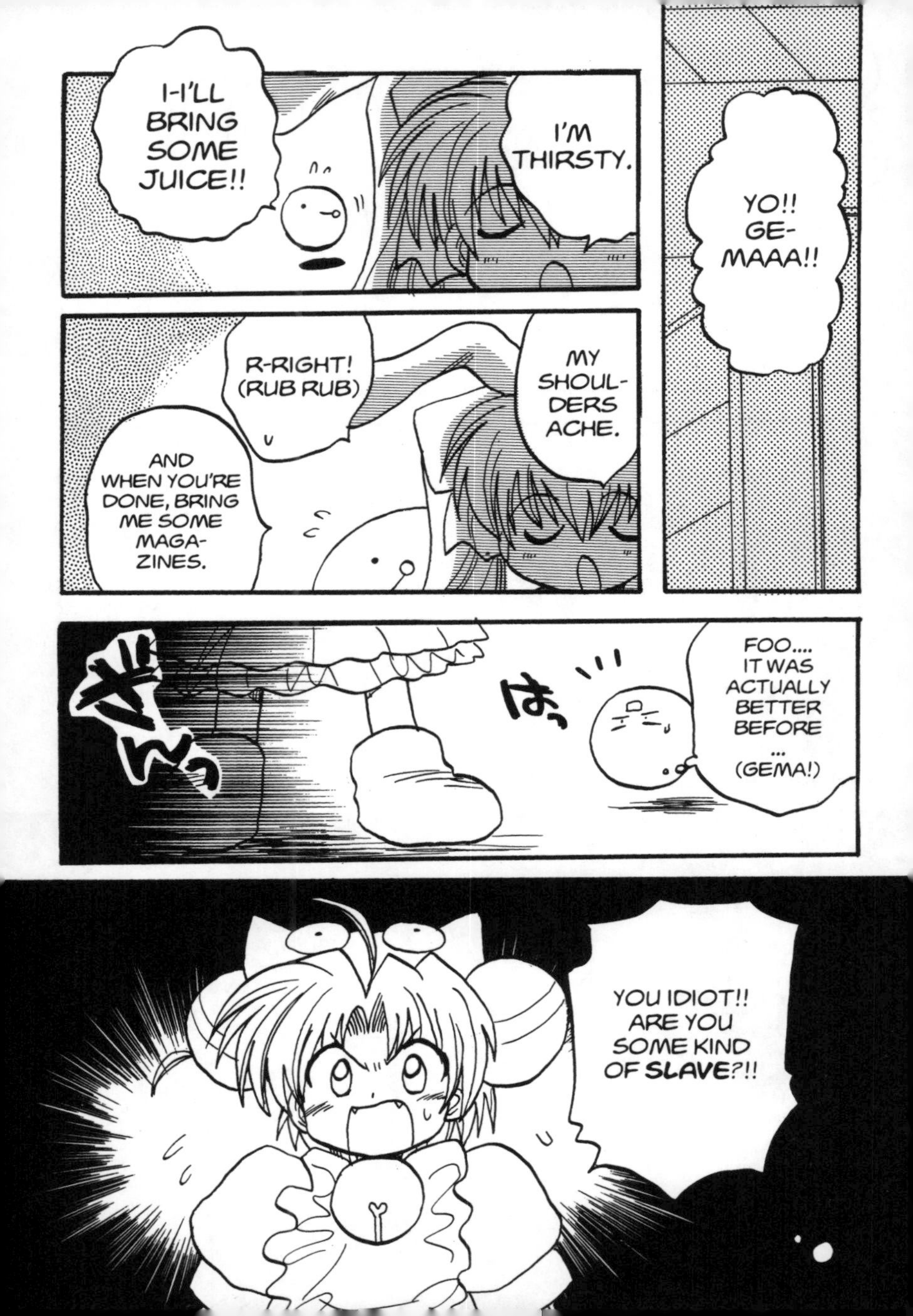
YO!! GE-MAAA!!
I'M THIRSTY.
I-I'LL BRING SOME JUICE!!
MY SHOULDERS ACHE.
R-RIGHT! (RUB RUB)
AND WHEN YOU'RE DONE, BRING ME SOME MAGAZINES.
FOO.... IT WAS ACTUALLY BETTER BEFORE ... (GEMA!)
はっ
YOU IDIOT!! ARE YOU SOME KIND OF **SLAVE**?!!

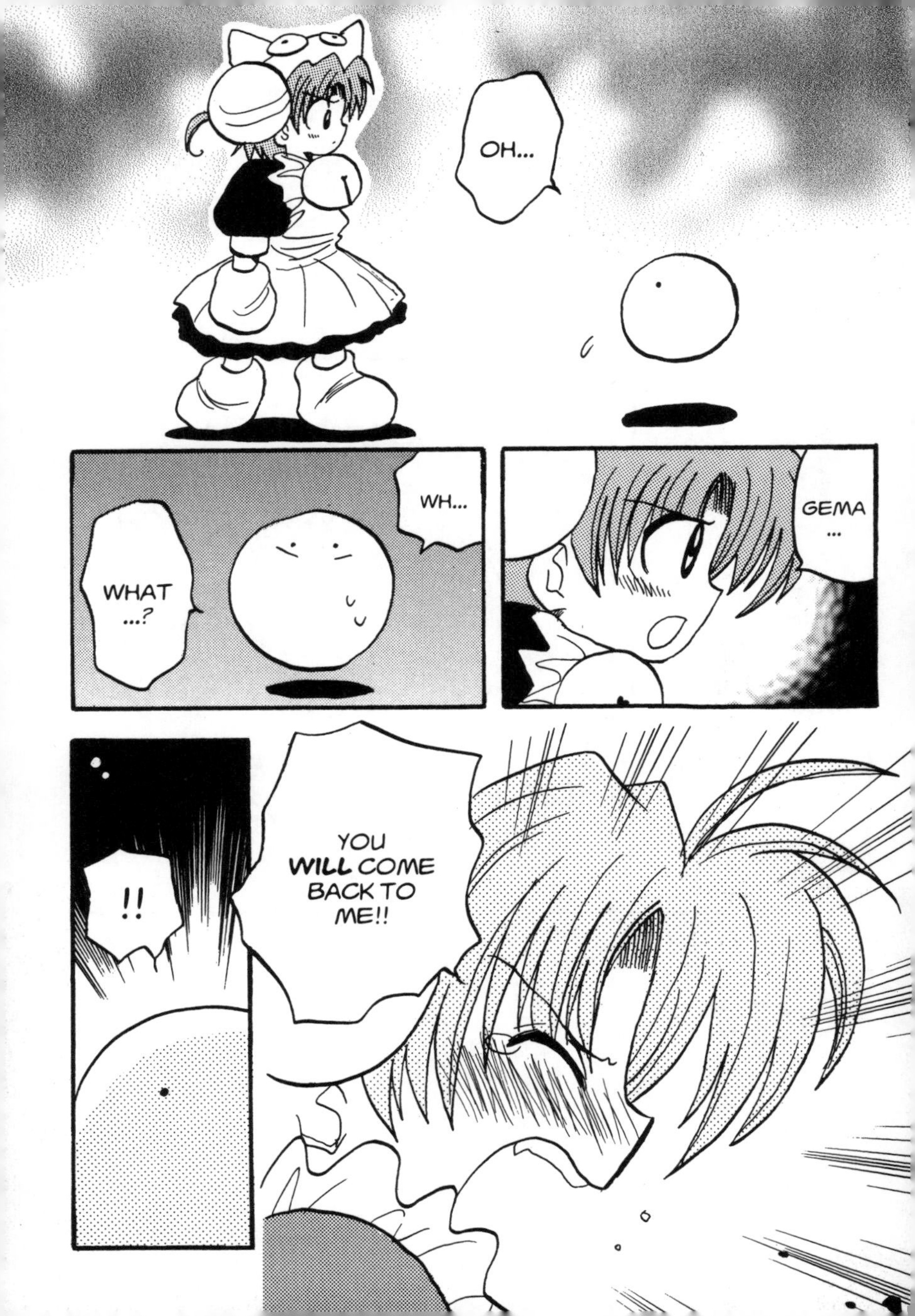
OH...
GEMA ...
WH...
WHAT ...?
YOU WILL COME BACK TO ME!!
!!

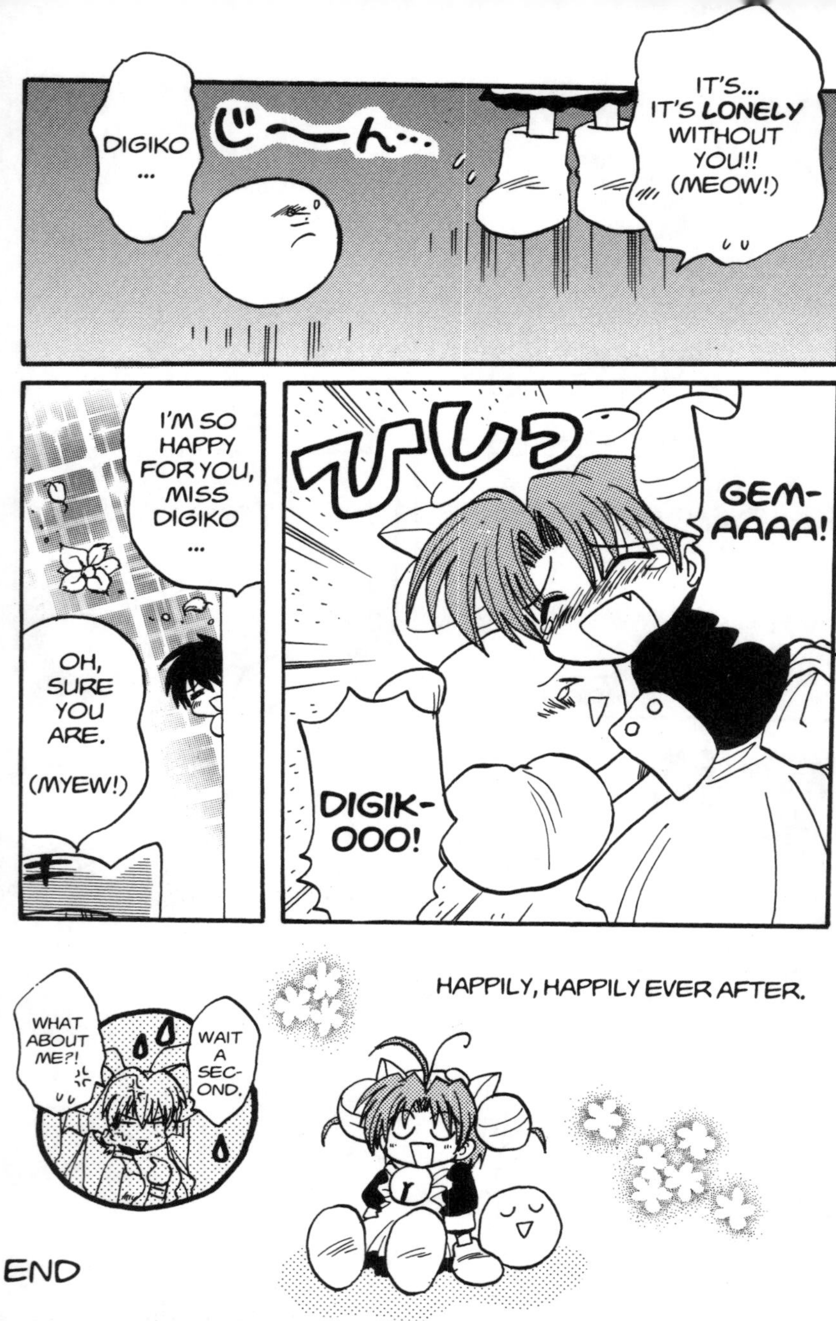
IT'S... IT'S **LONELY** WITHOUT YOU!! (MEOW!)
じ〜ん…
DIGIKO ...
ひしっ
GEM-AAAA!
DIGIK-OOO!
I'M SO HAPPY FOR YOU, MISS DIGIKO ...
OH, SURE YOU ARE. (MYEW!)
HAPPILY, HAPPILY EVER AFTER.
WAIT A SEC-OND.
WHAT ABOUT ME?!
END

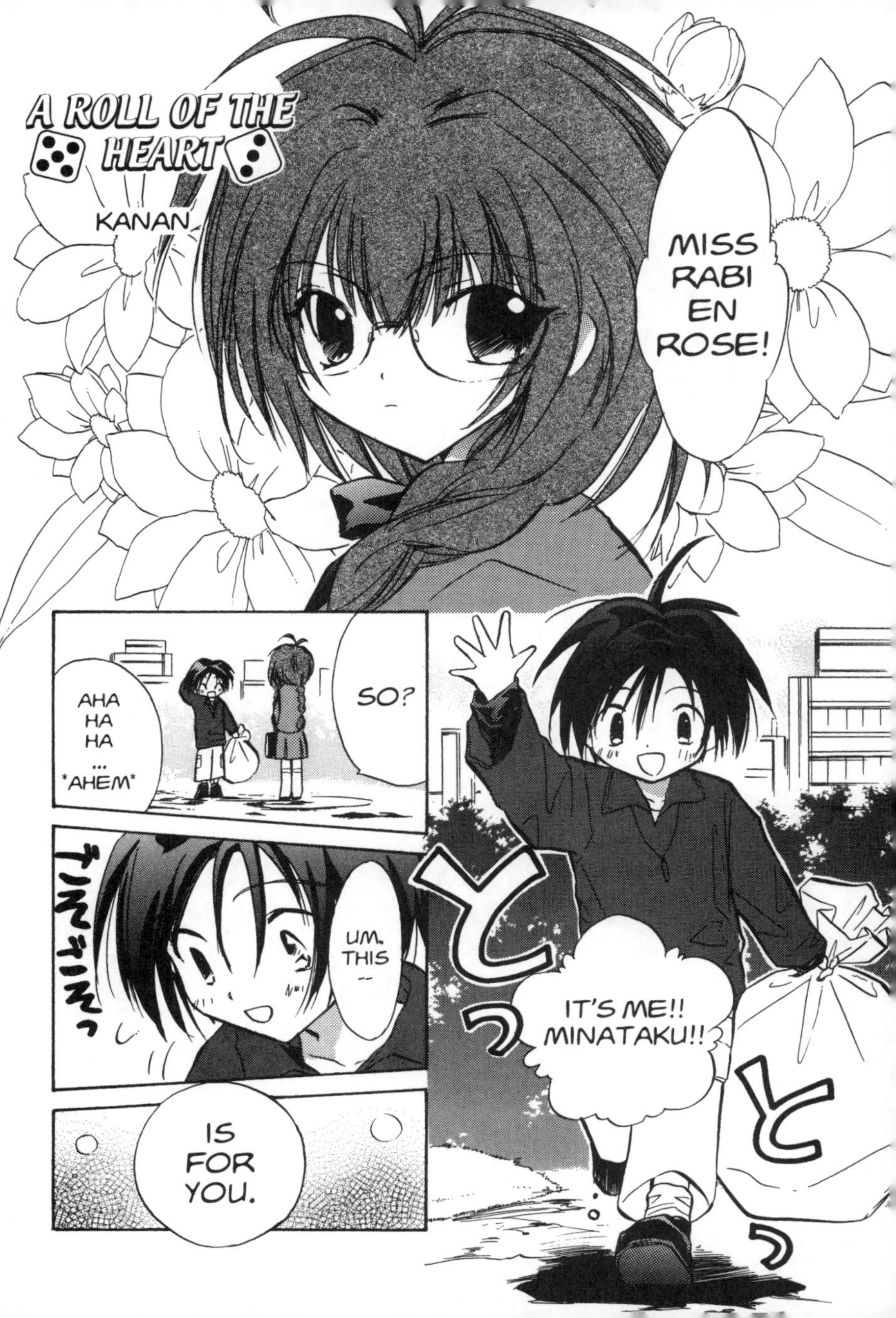
A ROLL OF THE HEART
KANAN
MISS RABI EN ROSE!
IT'S ME!! MINATAKU!!
とっとっ
とっとっ
SO?
AHA HA HA ... *AHEM*
TIN TIN
UM. THIS --
IS FOR YOU.

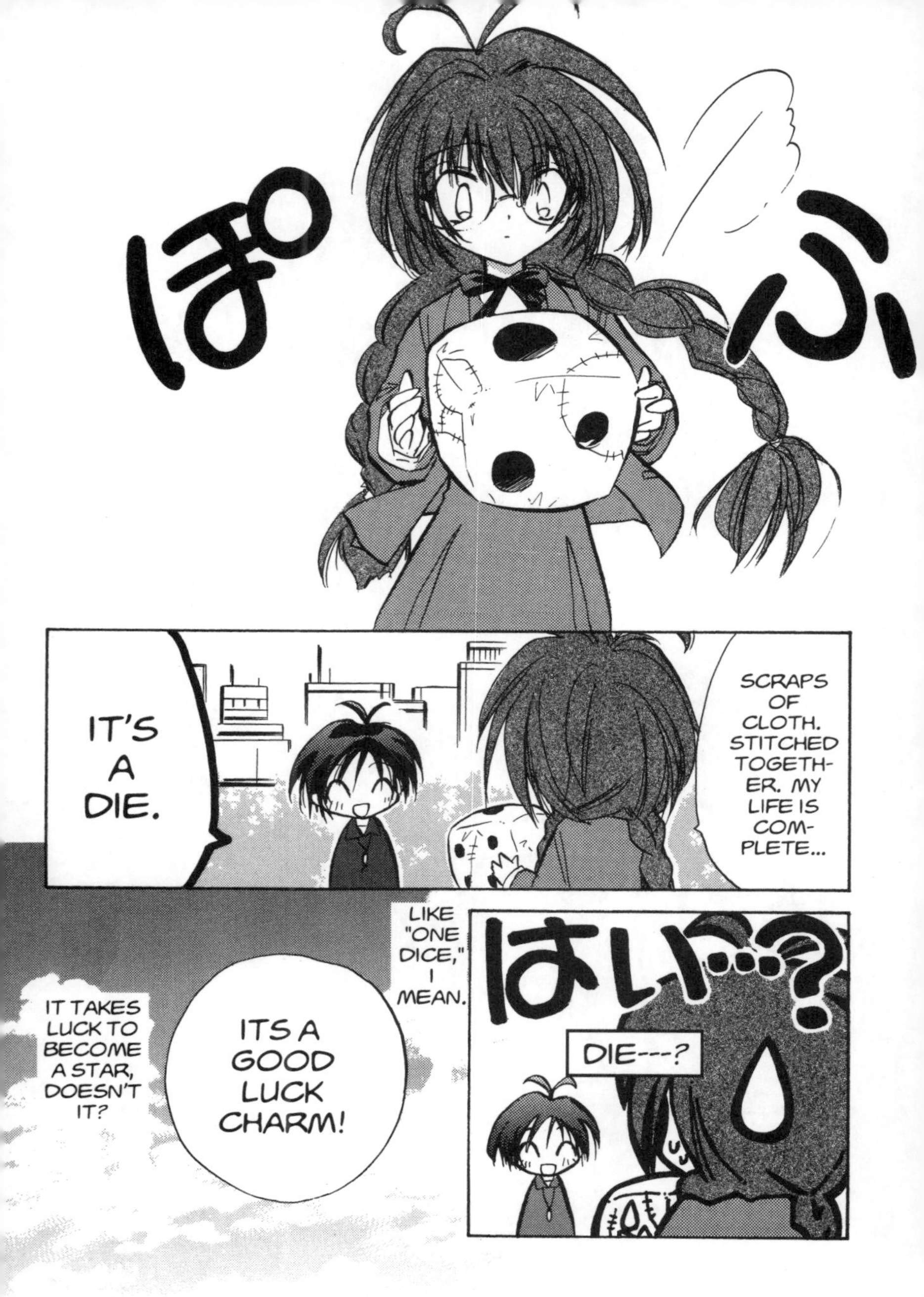
ぽふ
SCRAPS OF CLOTH. STITCHED TOGETHER. MY LIFE IS COMPLETE...
IT'S A DIE.
はい…?
DIE---?
LIKE "ONE DICE," I MEAN.
ITS A GOOD LUCK CHARM!
IT TAKES LUCK TO BECOME A STAR, DOESN'T IT?

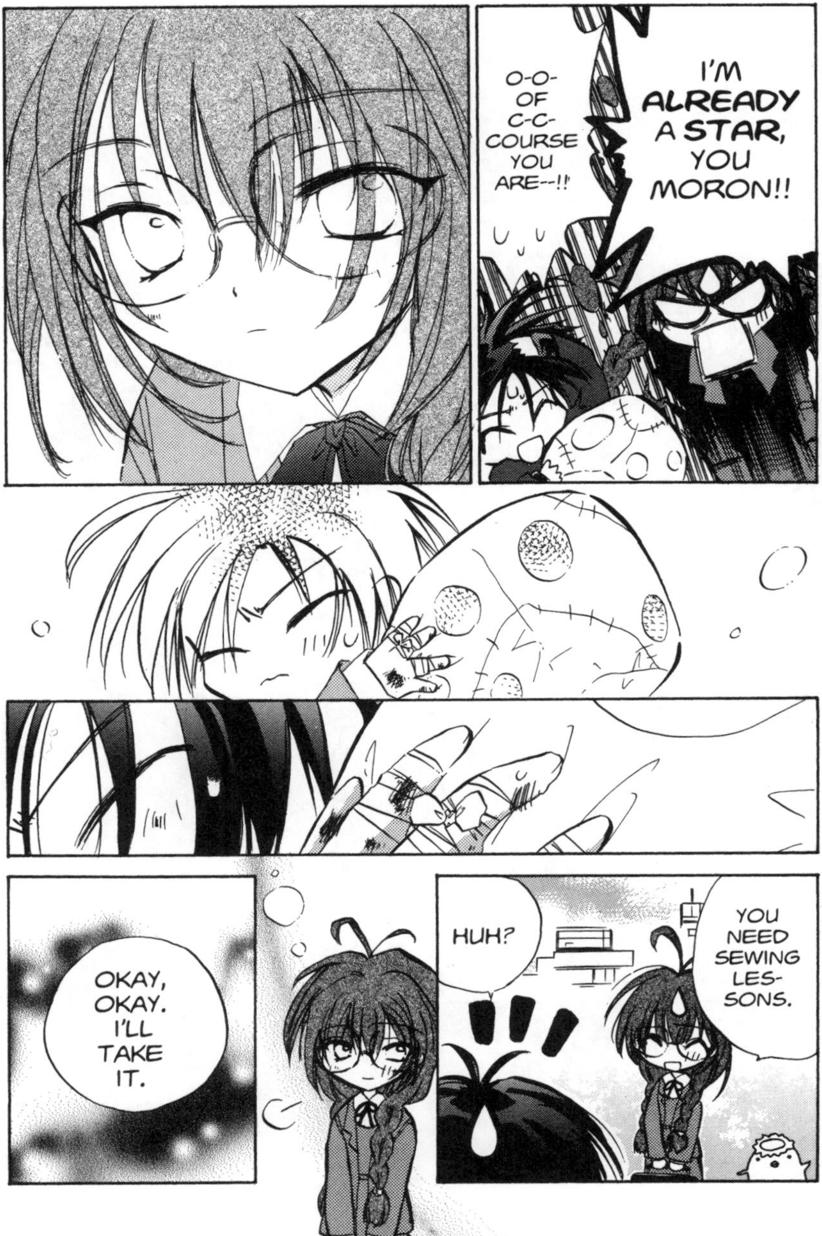
I'M ALREADY A STAR, YOU MORON!!
O-O-OF C-C-COURSE YOU ARE--!!
YOU NEED SEWING LES-SONS.
HUH?
OKAY, OKAY. I'LL TAKE IT.

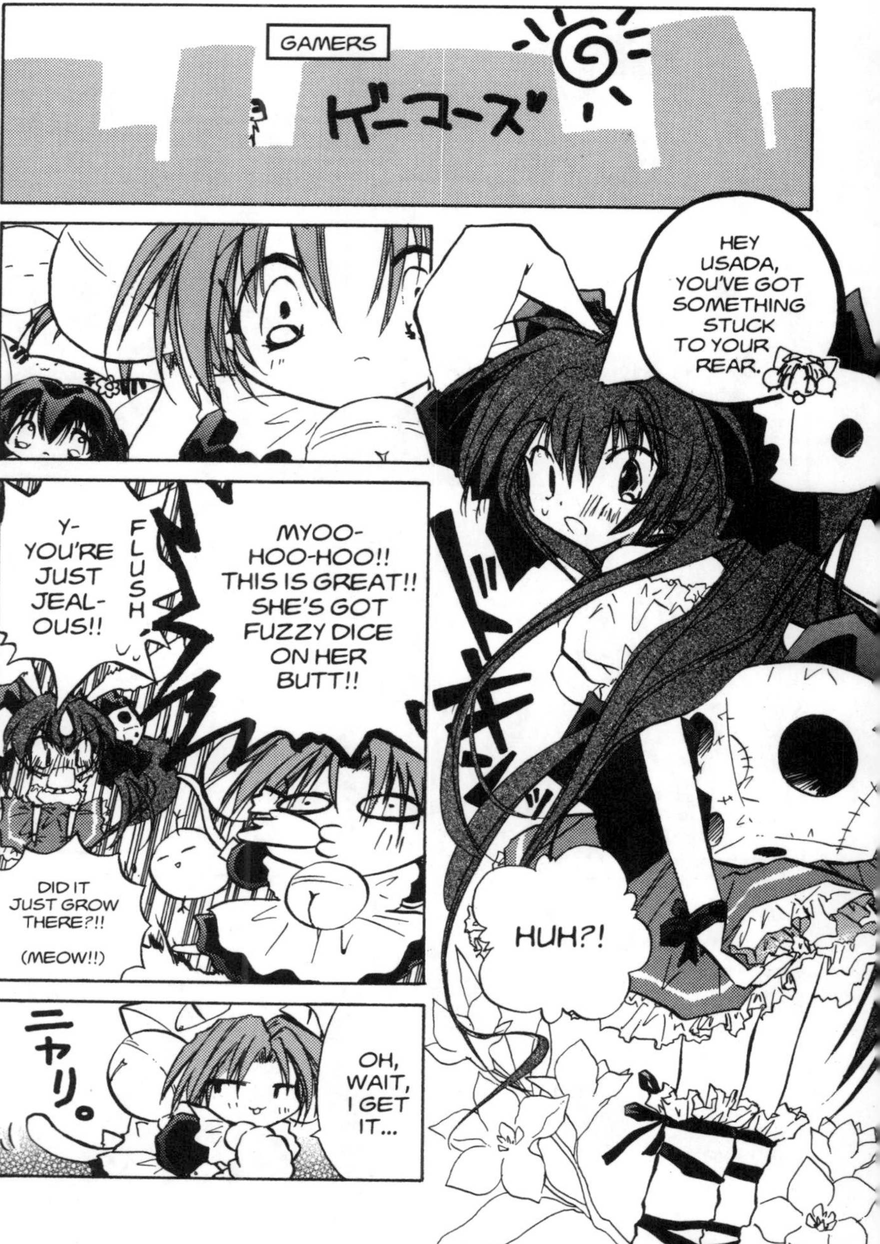
GAMERS
ゲーマーズ
HEY USADA, YOU'VE GOT SOMETHING STUCK TO YOUR REAR.
ドキンッ
HUH?!
MYOO-HOO-HOO!! THIS IS GREAT!! SHE'S GOT FUZZY DICE ON HER BUTT!!
FLUSH
Y-YOU'RE JUST JEALOUS!!
DID IT JUST GROW THERE?!!
(MEOW!!)
OH, WAIT, I GET IT...
ニヤリ。

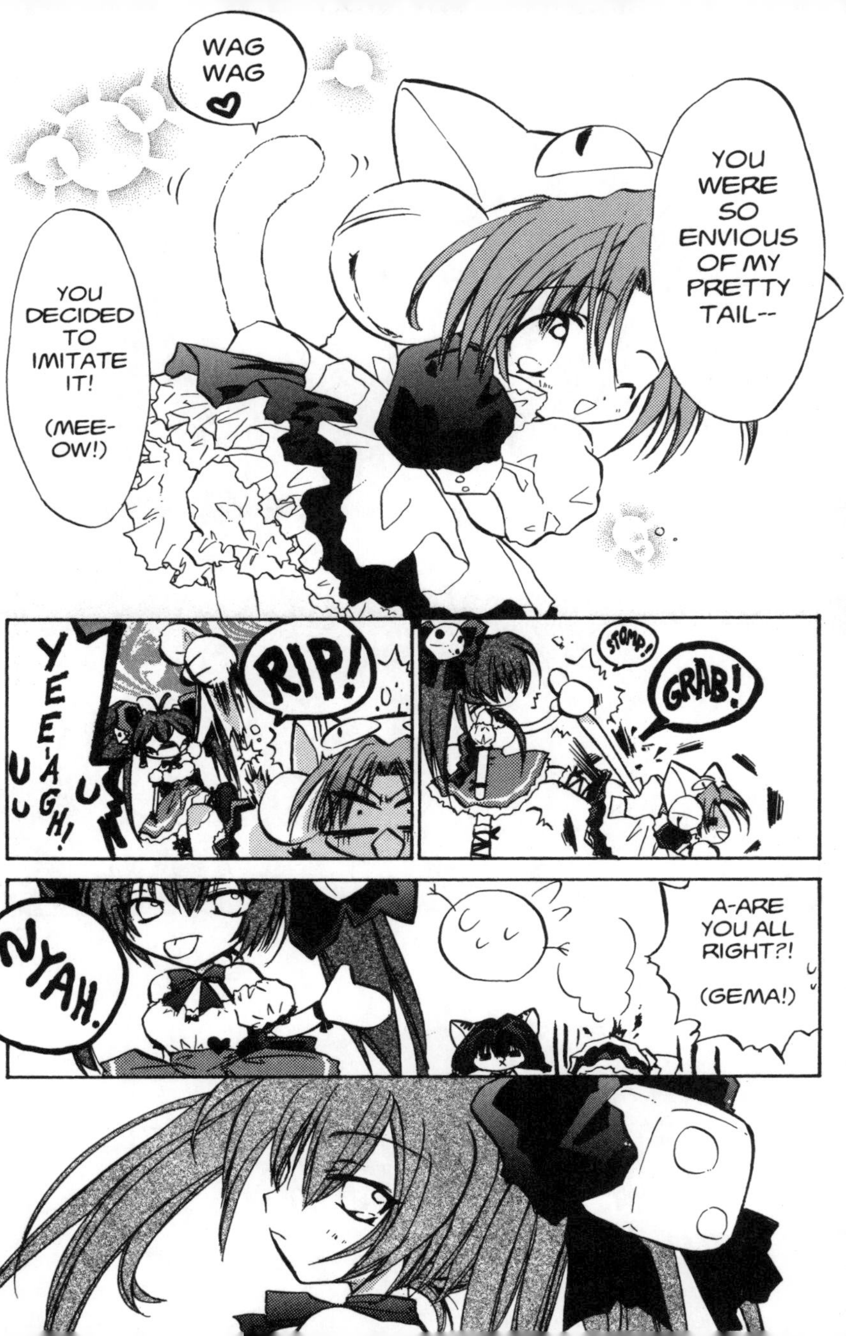
WAG WAG ♥
YOU WERE SO ENVIOUS OF MY PRETTY TAIL--
YOU DECIDED TO IMITATE IT!
(MEE-OW!)
STOMP!
GRAB!
RIP!
YEEE-AGH!
UUUN
A-ARE YOU ALL RIGHT?!
(GEMA!)
NYAH.

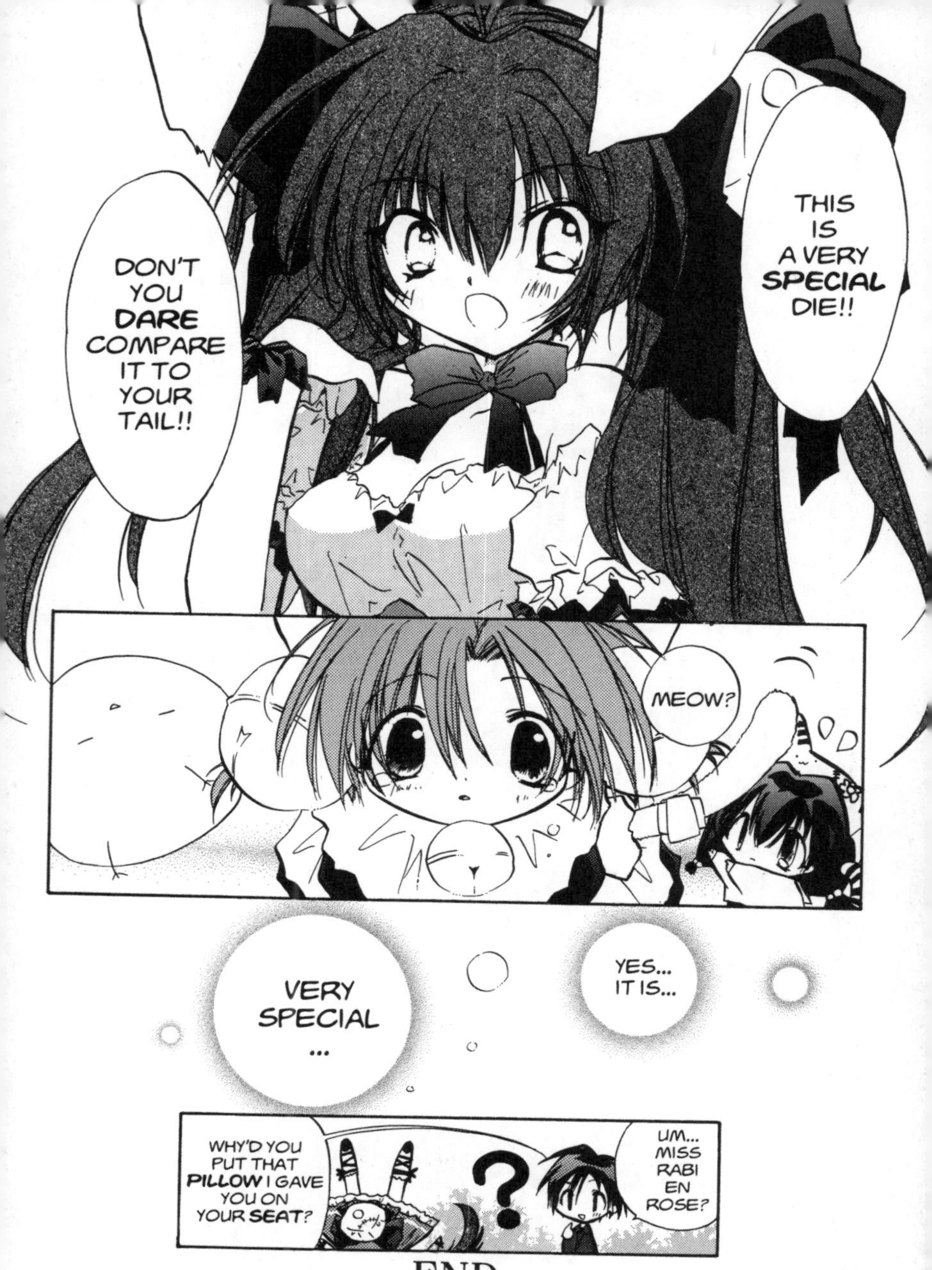
THIS IS A VERY SPECIAL DIE!!
DON'T YOU DARE COMPARE IT TO YOUR TAIL!!
MEOW?
YES... IT IS...
VERY SPECIAL ...
UM... MISS RABI EN ROSE?
WHY'D YOU PUT THAT PILLOW I GAVE YOU ON YOUR SEAT?

END

A comment about Di Gi Charat

THANK YOU FOR ASKING ME TO PARTICIPATE! ♡

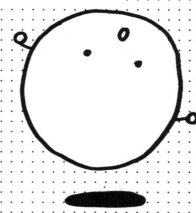

I LIKE USADA THE BEST. ♡
HER PERSONALITY AND HER HAIR ARE SO RIGHT FOR EACH OTHER! ♡ SHE'S SO ADORABLE-- ♡
BUT IF WE'RE TALKING ABOUT THE *ANIME* VOICE ACTORS, THEN I LIKE GEMA BEST.
THOSE WHO UNDERSTAND WILL UNDERSTAND... (HA!)
I'VE BEEN A FAN FOR OVER SIX YEARS!

WAS THERE A REAL-LIFE MODEL FOR DIGIKO...? WHO COULD IT BE

OOOo--??

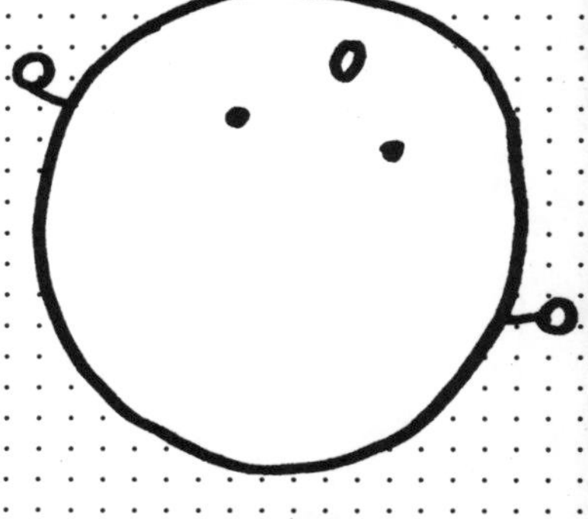

STRIKE-HEISUKE

STRIKE-HEISUKE

A comment about Di Gi Charat

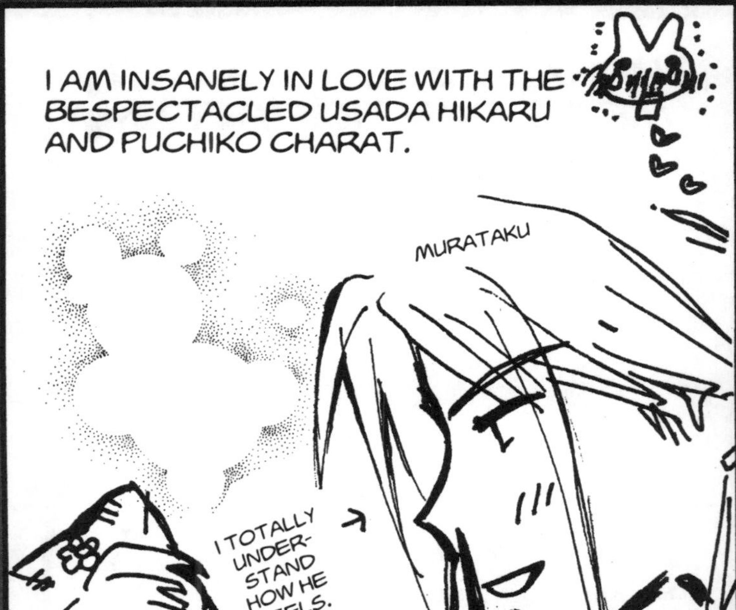
I AM INSANELY IN LOVE WITH THE BESPECTACLED USADA HIKARU AND PUCHIKO CHARAT.
MURATAKU
I TOTALLY UNDER-STAND HOW HE FEELS.
KANAN

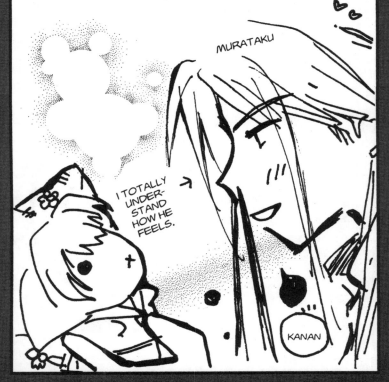

KANAN

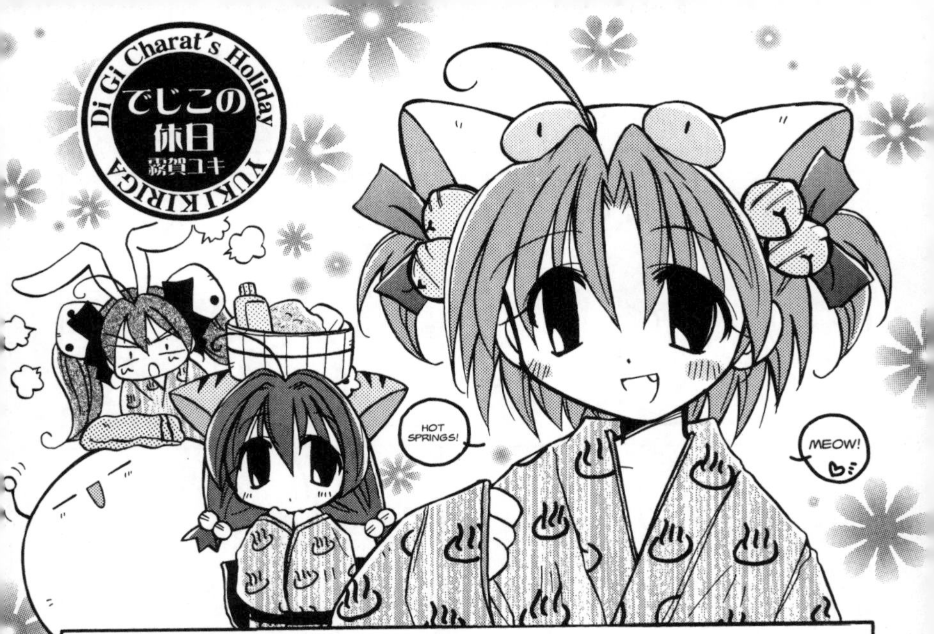
Di Gi Charat's Holiday
でじこの休日
霧賀ユキ
YUKI KIRIGA
HOT SPRINGS!
MEOW!

EVERYBODY NEEDS VACATION!!!

PANELS FOR THIS STORY START ON THE RIGHT AND GO DOWN THE PAGE.

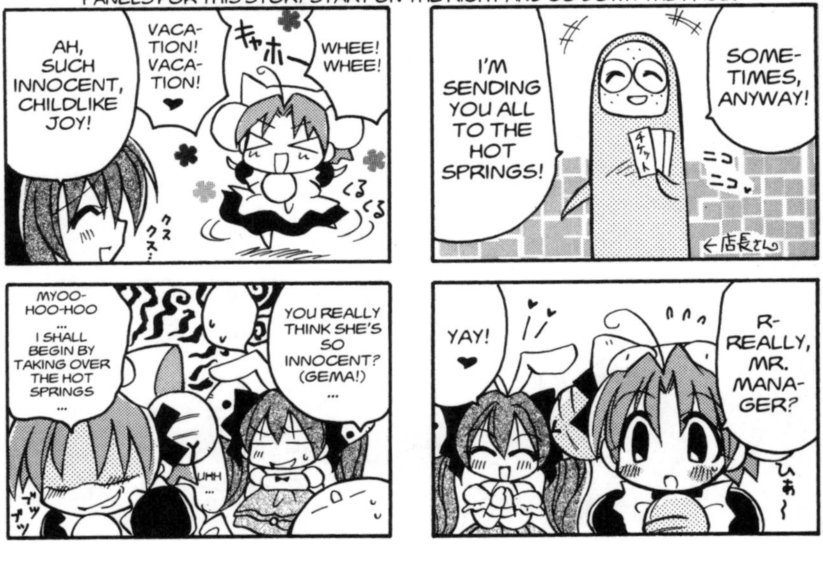
I'M SENDING YOU ALL TO THE HOT SPRINGS!
SOME-TIMES, ANYWAY!
チケット
ニコニコ
←店長さん
R-REALLY, MR. MANAGER?
YAY!
ひあ〜
WHEE! WHEE!
キャホー
VACATION! VACATION!
AH, SUCH INNOCENT, CHILDLIKE JOY!
くるくる
クスクス…
YOU REALLY THINK SHE'S SO INNOCENT? (GEMA!) ...
MYOO-HOO-HOO ... I SHALL BEGIN BY TAKING OVER THE HOT SPRINGS ...
UHH ...
ブツブツ

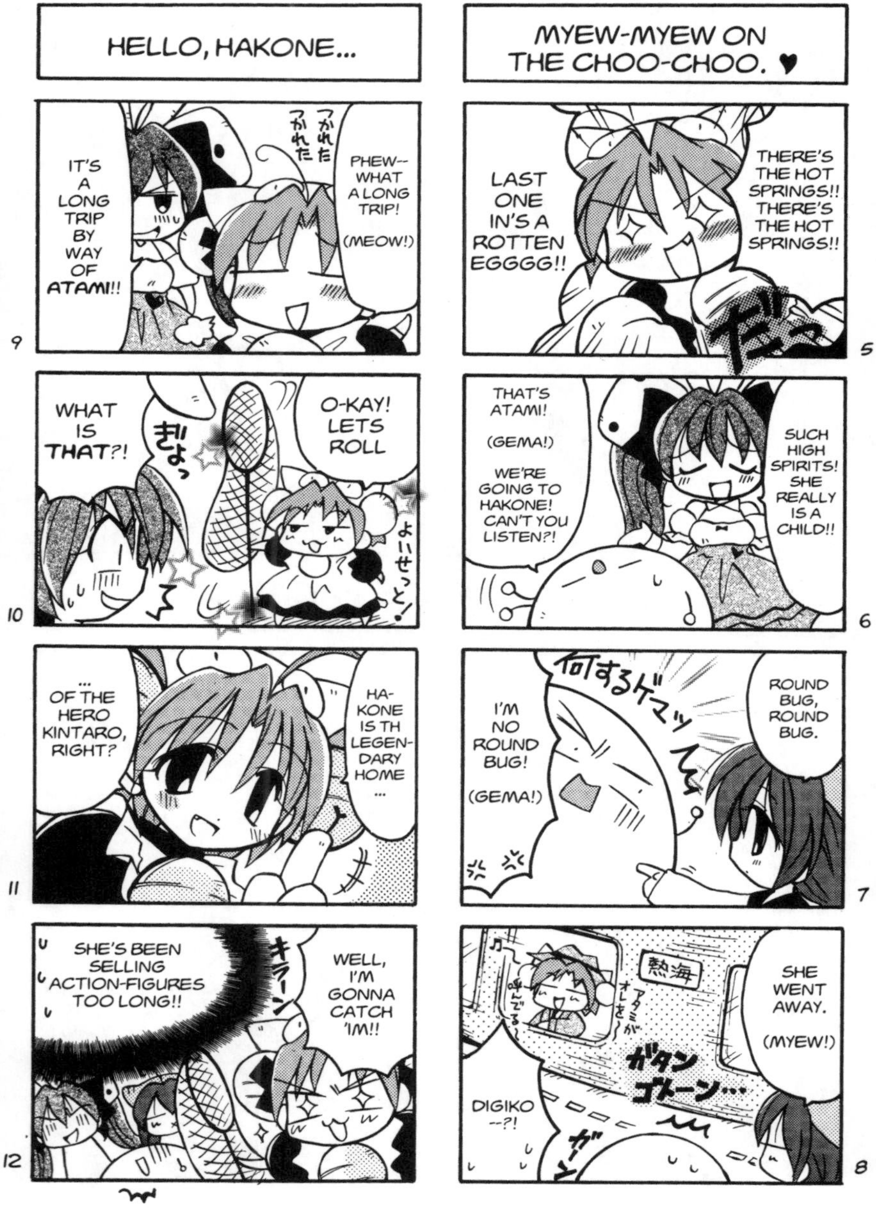
MYEW-MYEW ON THE CHOO-CHOO. ♥
THERE'S THE HOT SPRINGS!! THERE'S THE HOT SPRINGS!!
LAST ONE IN'S A ROTTEN EGGGG!!
5
SUCH HIGH SPIRITS! SHE REALLY IS A CHILD!!
THAT'S ATAMI! (GEMA!) WE'RE GOING TO HAKONE! CAN'T YOU LISTEN?!
6
ROUND BUG, ROUND BUG.
何するゲマッ
I'M NO ROUND BUG! (GEMA!)
7
SHE WENT AWAY. (MYEW!)
熱海
アタミがオレを呼んでる〜
ガタンゴトーン…
DIGIKO--?!
ガーン
8
HELLO, HAKONE...
PHEW-- WHAT A LONG TRIP! (MEOW!)
つかれた つかれた
IT'S A LONG TRIP BY WAY OF ATAMI!!
9
O-KAY! LETS ROLL
よいせっと！
ぎょっ
WHAT IS THAT?!
10
HA-KONE IS TH LEGEN-DARY HOME ...
... OF THE HERO KINTARO, RIGHT?
11
WELL, I'M GONNA CATCH 'IM!!
キラーン
SHE'S BEEN SELLING ACTION-FIGURES TOO LONG!!
12

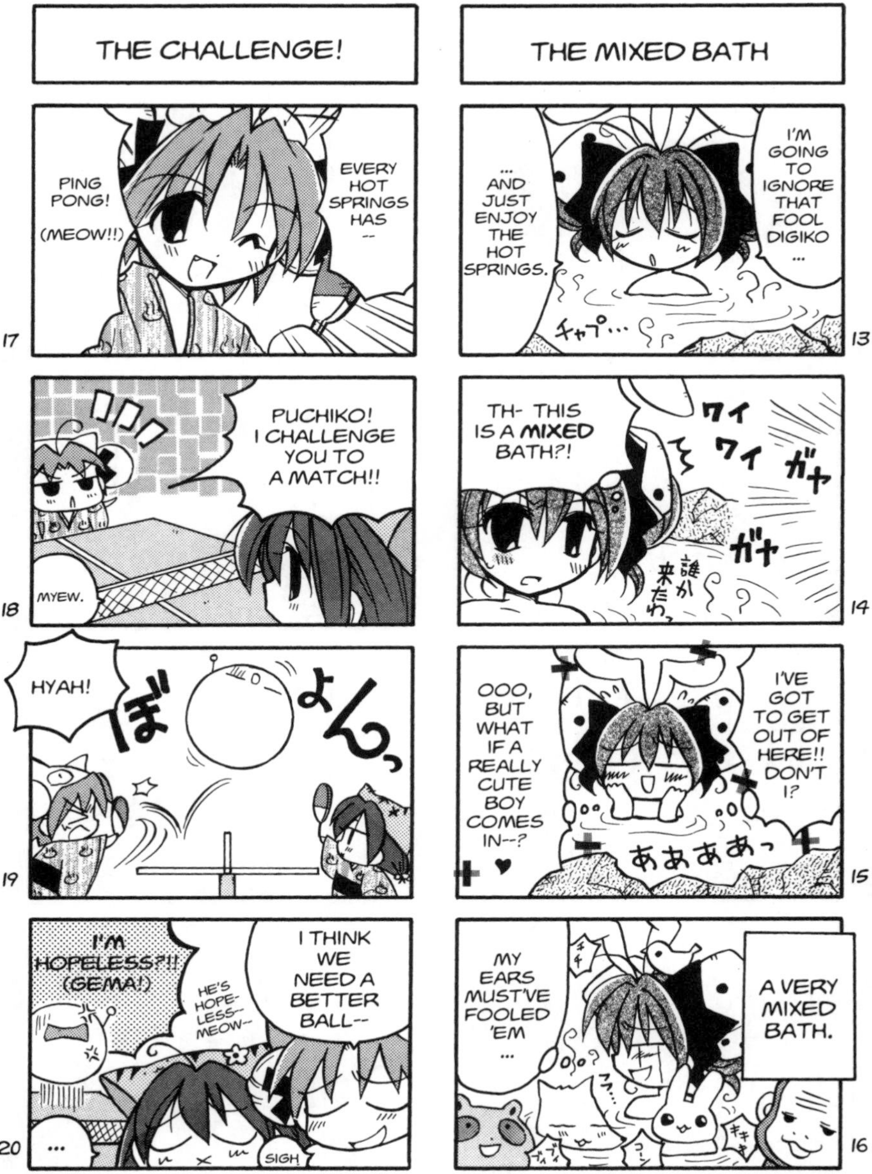
THE MIXED BATH
I'M GOING TO IGNORE THAT FOOL DIGIKO ...
... AND JUST ENJOY THE HOT SPRINGS.
チャプ...
13
TH- THIS IS A **MIXED** BATH?!
ワイワイ
ガヤガヤ
誰か来たわっ
14
I'VE GOT TO GET OUT OF HERE!! DON'T I?
OOO, BUT WHAT IF A REALLY CUTE BOY COMES IN--?
ああああっ
15
A VERY MIXED BATH.
MY EARS MUST'VE FOOLED 'EM ...
16
THE CHALLENGE!
EVERY HOT SPRINGS HAS --
PING PONG!
(MEOW!!)
17
PUCHIKO! I CHALLENGE YOU TO A MATCH!!
MYEW.
18
HYAH!
ぼよんっ
19
I THINK WE NEED A BETTER BALL--
HE'S HOPE-LESS-MEOW--
I'M HOPELESS?!! (GEMA!)
...
SIGH
20

FRESH AIR

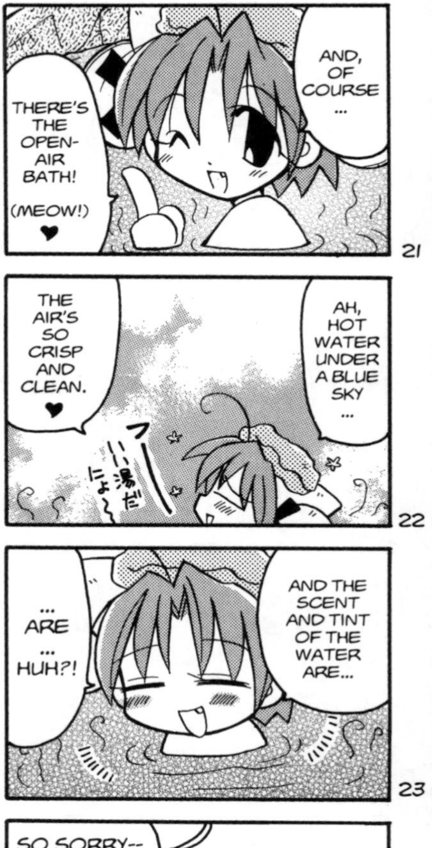
AND, OF COURSE ...
THERE'S THE OPEN-AIR BATH! (MEOW!) ♥
21
AH, HOT WATER UNDER A BLUE SKY ...
THE AIR'S SO CRISP AND CLEAN. ♥
フーー いい湯だにょ～
22
AND THE SCENT AND TINT OF THE WATER ARE...
... ARE ... HUH?!
23
THE SAME AS ME?!
SO SORRY-- THE PIPES BEEN BLOCKED--
OWNER
色も香りも!?
24

THE WATER IS CONTAMINATED!

HOME AGAIN

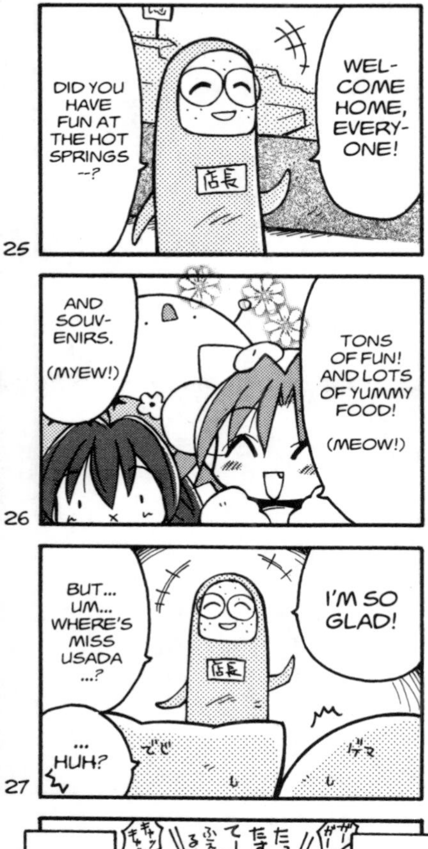
WEL-COME HOME, EVERY-ONE!
DID YOU HAVE FUN AT THE HOT SPRINGS --?
店長
25
TONS OF FUN! AND LOTS OF YUMMY FOOD! (MEOW!)
AND SOUV-ENIRS. (MYEW!)
26
I'M SO GLAD!
BUT... UM... WHERE'S MISS USADA ...?
店長
... HUH?
27
FOR SOME PEO-PLE ...
... VACA-TIONS NEVER END ...
28

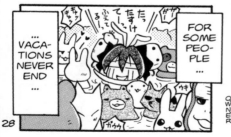

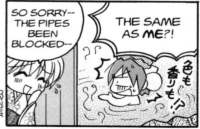

A comment about Di Gi Charat

THANKS
SO
MUCH
FOR
INVITING
ME. ♥

YUKI

I DRAW THE
"DIGIKO »
ADVENTURE"
SERIAL IN THE
MONTHLY
**DRAGON♥
JUNIOR.**
I APPRECIATE
EVERYONE'S
SUPPORT--

YUKI KIRIGA

"THE CAT WHO GOES WALKING CATCHES A PUCHIKO."

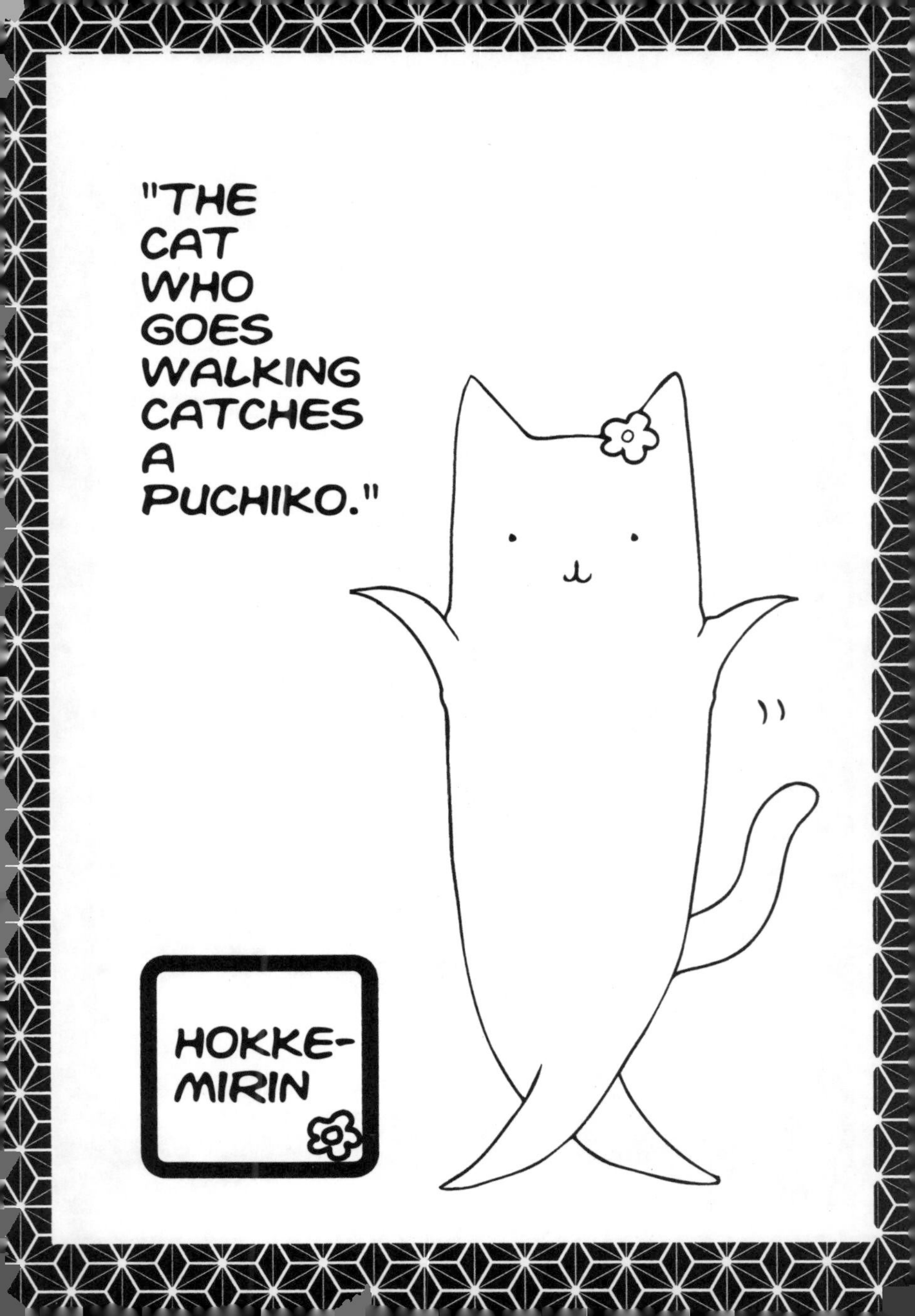

HOKKE-MIRIN

DI GI CHARAT...BONUS STORY

"DIGIKO'S TEA SHOP"

KOGE-DONBO

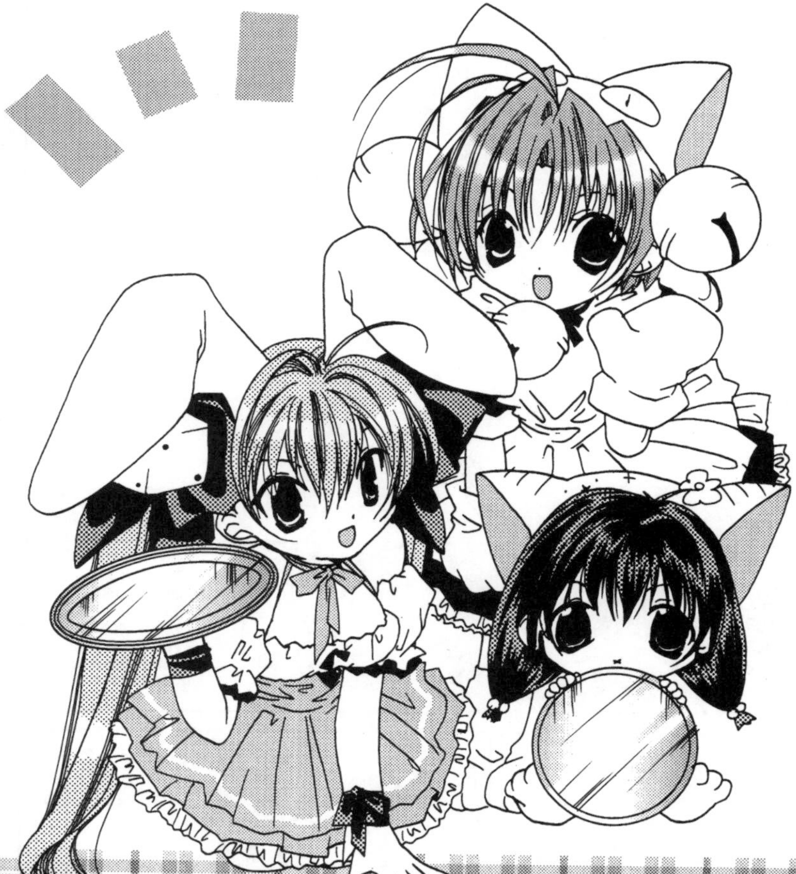

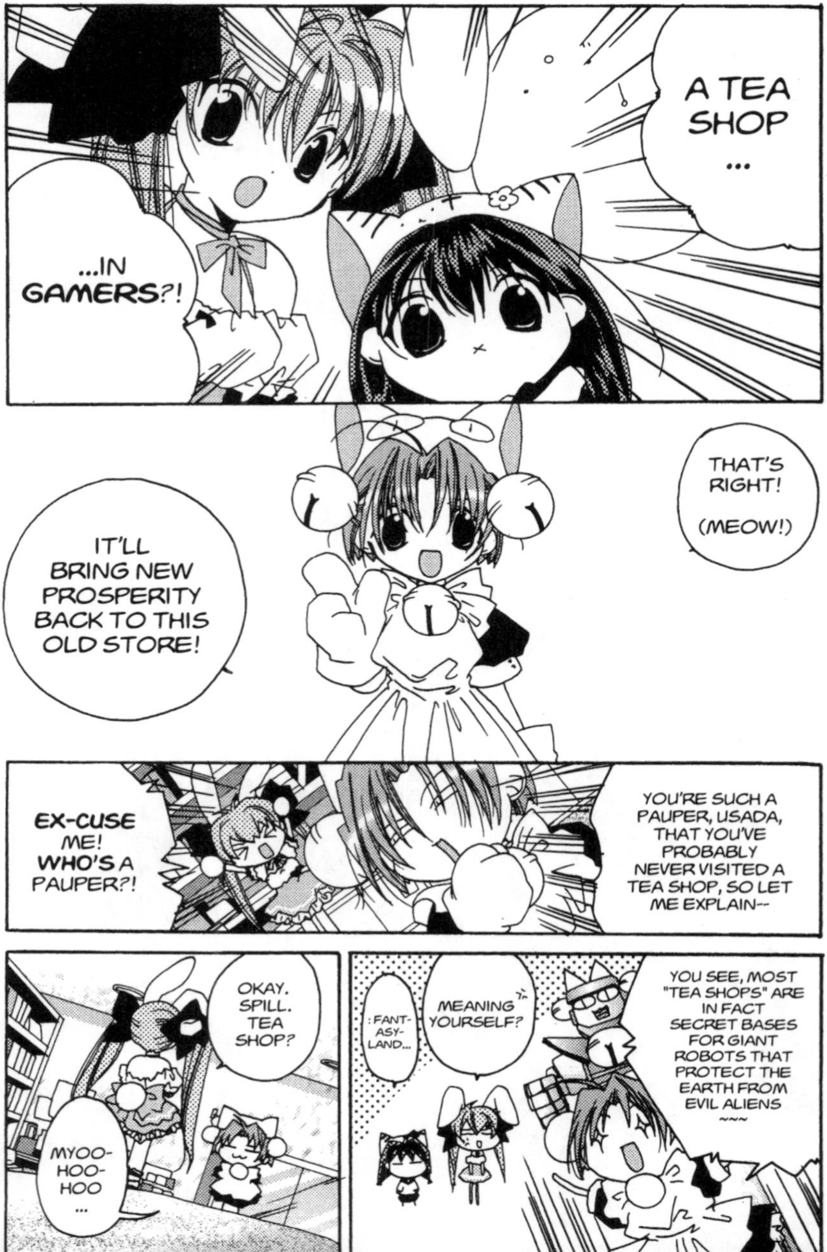
A TEA SHOP ...
...IN GAMERS?!
THAT'S RIGHT! (MEOW!)
IT'LL BRING NEW PROSPERITY BACK TO THIS OLD STORE!
YOU'RE SUCH A PAUPER, USADA, THAT YOU'VE PROBABLY NEVER VISITED A TEA SHOP, SO LET ME EXPLAIN--
EX-CUSE ME! WHO'S A PAUPER?!
YOU SEE, MOST "TEA SHOPS" ARE IN FACT SECRET BASES FOR GIANT ROBOTS THAT PROTECT THE EARTH FROM EVIL ALIENS ~~~
MEANING YOURSELF?
: FANT-ASY-LAND...
OKAY. SPILL. TEA SHOP?
MYOO-HOO-HOO ...

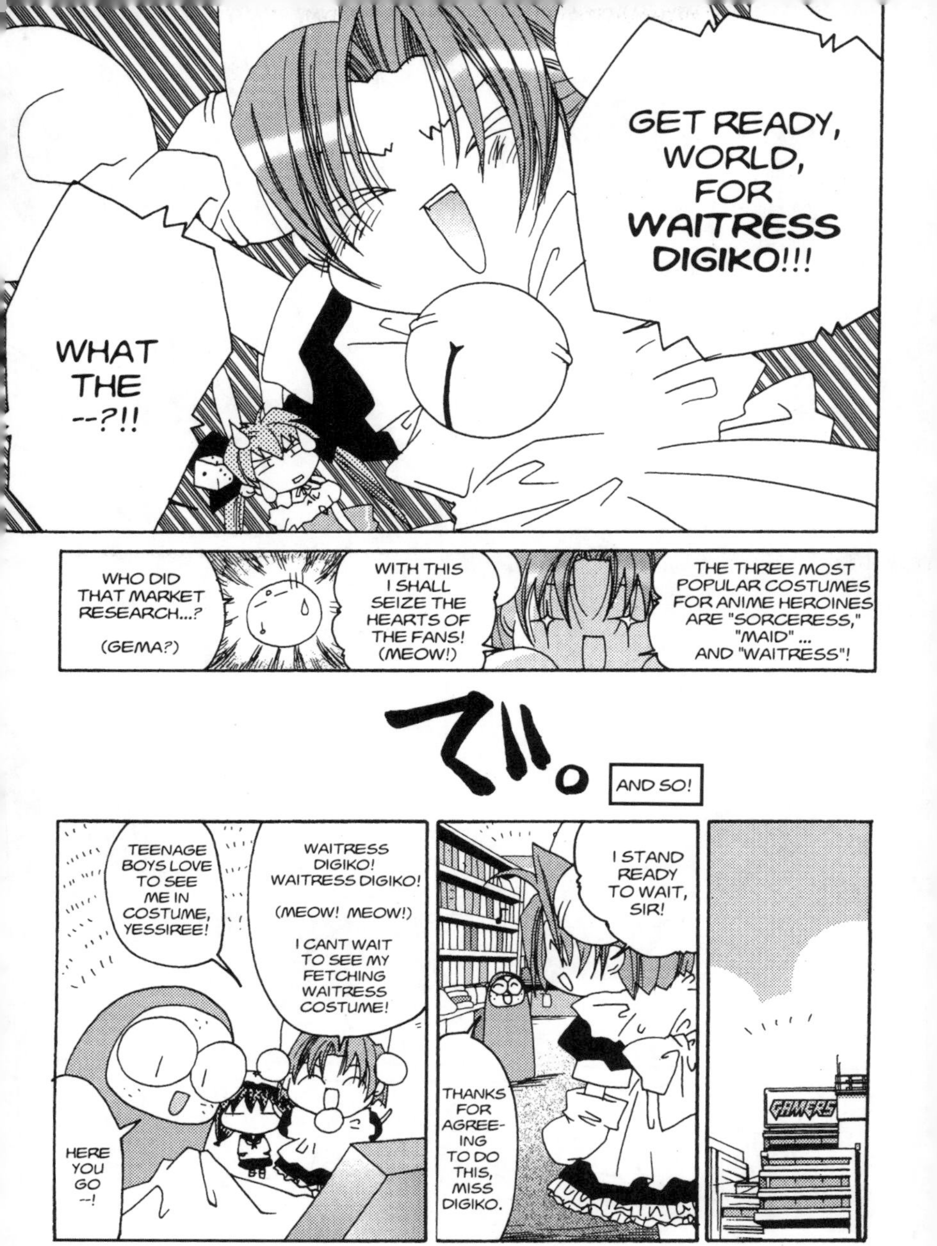
GET READY, WORLD, FOR WAITRESS DIGIKO!!!
WHAT THE --?!!
THE THREE MOST POPULAR COSTUMES FOR ANIME HEROINES ARE "SORCERESS," "MAID" ... AND "WAITRESS"!
WITH THIS I SHALL SEIZE THE HEARTS OF THE FANS! (MEOW!)
WHO DID THAT MARKET RESEARCH...? (GEMA?)
で。
AND SO!
GAMERS
I STAND READY TO WAIT, SIR!
THANKS FOR AGREE-ING TO DO THIS, MISS DIGIKO.
WAITRESS DIGIKO! WAITRESS DIGIKO! (MEOW! MEOW!) I CANT WAIT TO SEE MY FETCHING WAITRESS COSTUME!
TEENAGE BOYS LOVE TO SEE ME IN COSTUME, YESSIREE!
HERE YOU GO --!

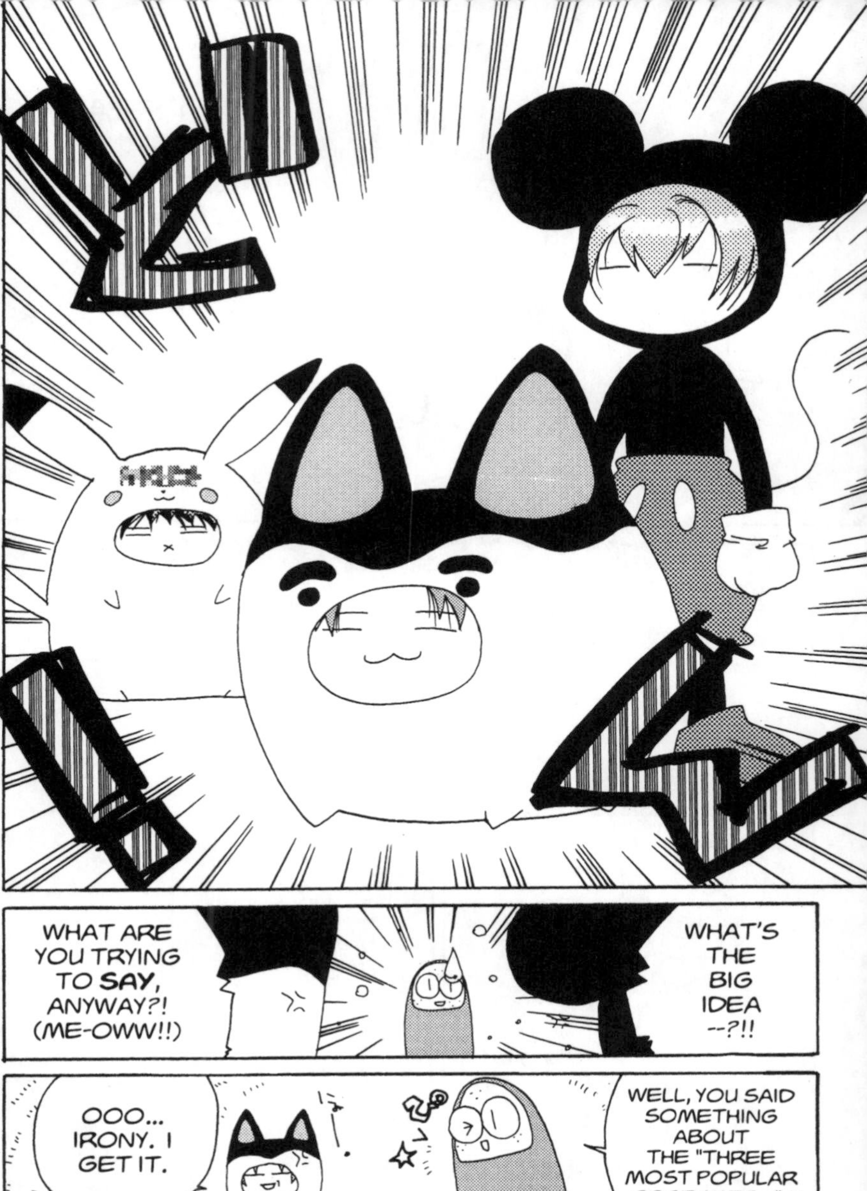
WHAT'S THE BIG IDEA --?!!
WHAT ARE YOU TRYING TO SAY, ANYWAY?! (ME-OWW!!)
WELL, YOU SAID SOMETHING ABOUT THE "THREE MOST POPULAR COSTUMES..." ♥
OOO... IRONY. I GET IT.

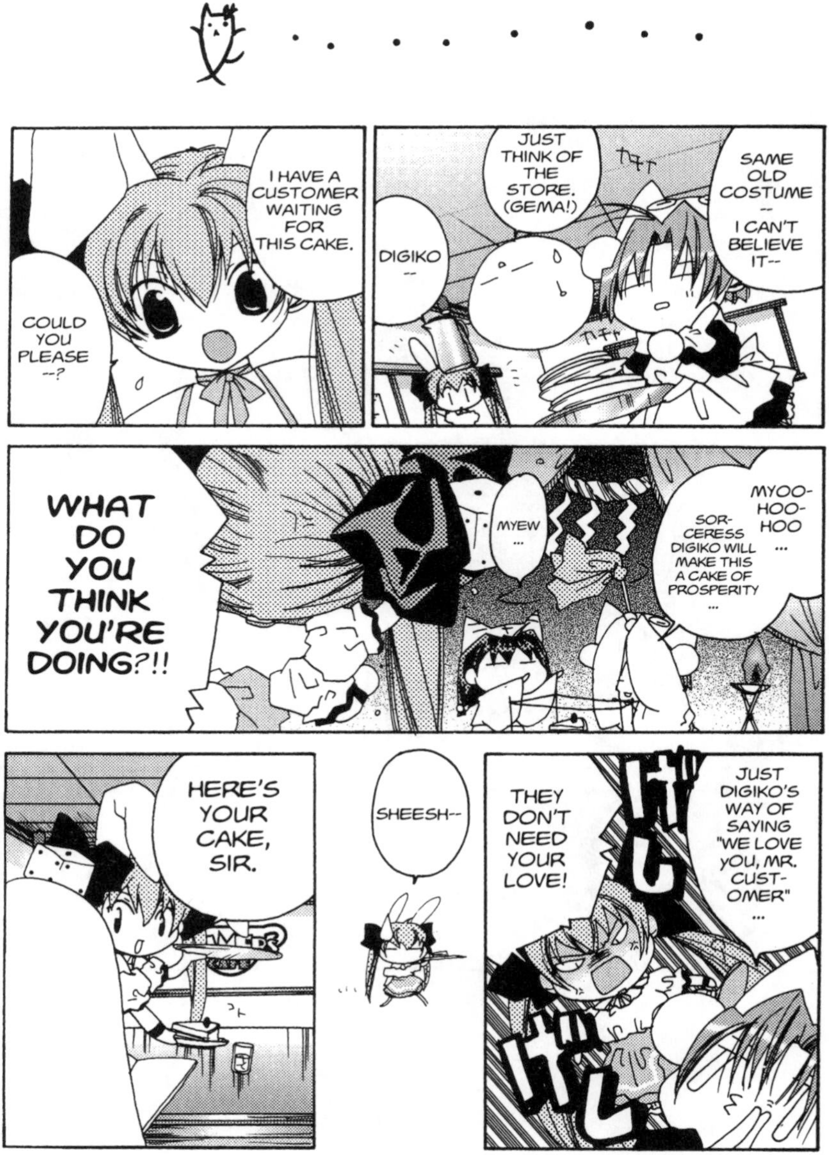
SAME OLD COSTUME -- I CAN'T BELIEVE IT--
JUST THINK OF THE STORE. (GEMA!)
DIGIKO --
I HAVE A CUSTOMER WAITING FOR THIS CAKE.
COULD YOU PLEASE --?
MYOO-HOO-HOO ...
SOR-CERESS DIGIKO WILL MAKE THIS A CAKE OF PROSPERITY ...
MYEW ...
WHAT DO YOU THINK YOU'RE DOING?!!
JUST DIGIKO'S WAY OF SAYING "WE LOVE YOU, MR. CUST-OMER" ...
THEY DON'T NEED YOUR LOVE!
SHEESH--
HERE'S YOUR CAKE, SIR.

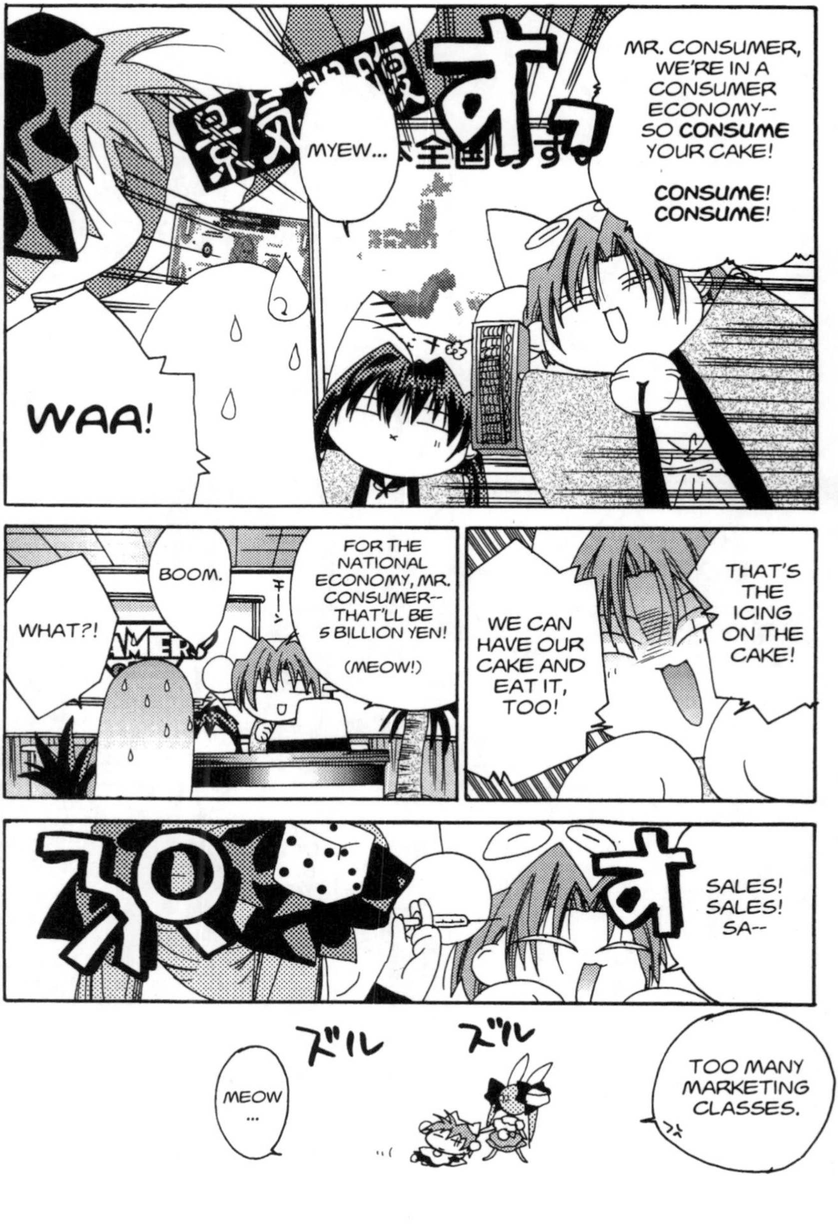

MR. CONSUMER, WE'RE IN A CONSUMER ECONOMY-- SO **CONSUME** YOUR CAKE!
CONSUME! CONSUME!
MYEW...
WAA!
THAT'S THE ICING ON THE CAKE!
WE CAN HAVE OUR CAKE AND EAT IT, TOO!
FOR THE NATIONAL ECONOMY, MR. CONSUMER-- THAT'LL BE 5 BILLION YEN!
(MEOW!)
チーン
BOOM.
WHAT?!
SALES! SALES! SA--
TOO MANY MARKETING CLASSES.
ズル ズル
MEOW ...

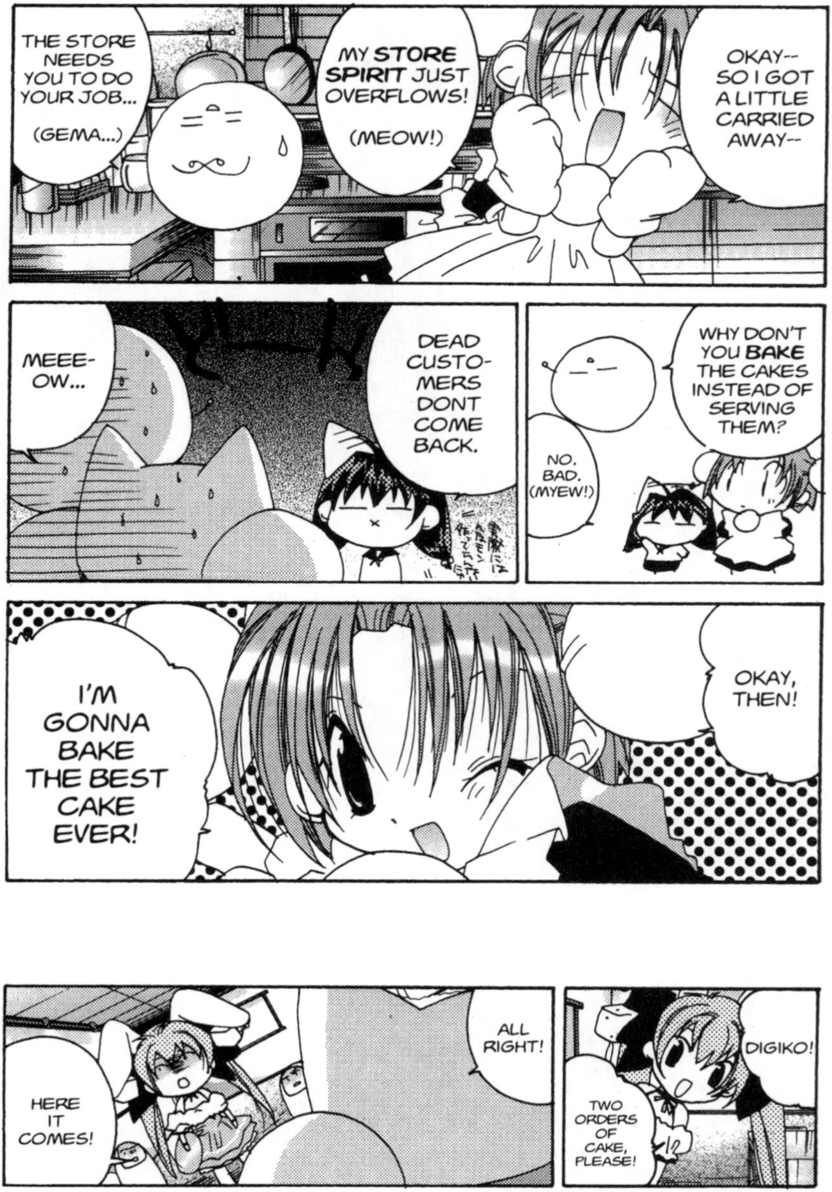
OKAY-- SO I GOT A LITTLE CARRIED AWAY--
MY STORE SPIRIT JUST OVERFLOWS!
(MEOW!)
THE STORE NEEDS YOU TO DO YOUR JOB...
(GEMA...)
WHY DON'T YOU BAKE THE CAKES INSTEAD OF SERVING THEM?
NO. BAD. (MYEW!)
DEAD CUSTO-MERS DONT COME BACK.
MEEE-OW...
OKAY, THEN!
I'M GONNA BAKE THE BEST CAKE EVER!
DIGIKO!
TWO ORDERS OF CAKE, PLEASE!
ALL RIGHT!
HERE IT COMES!

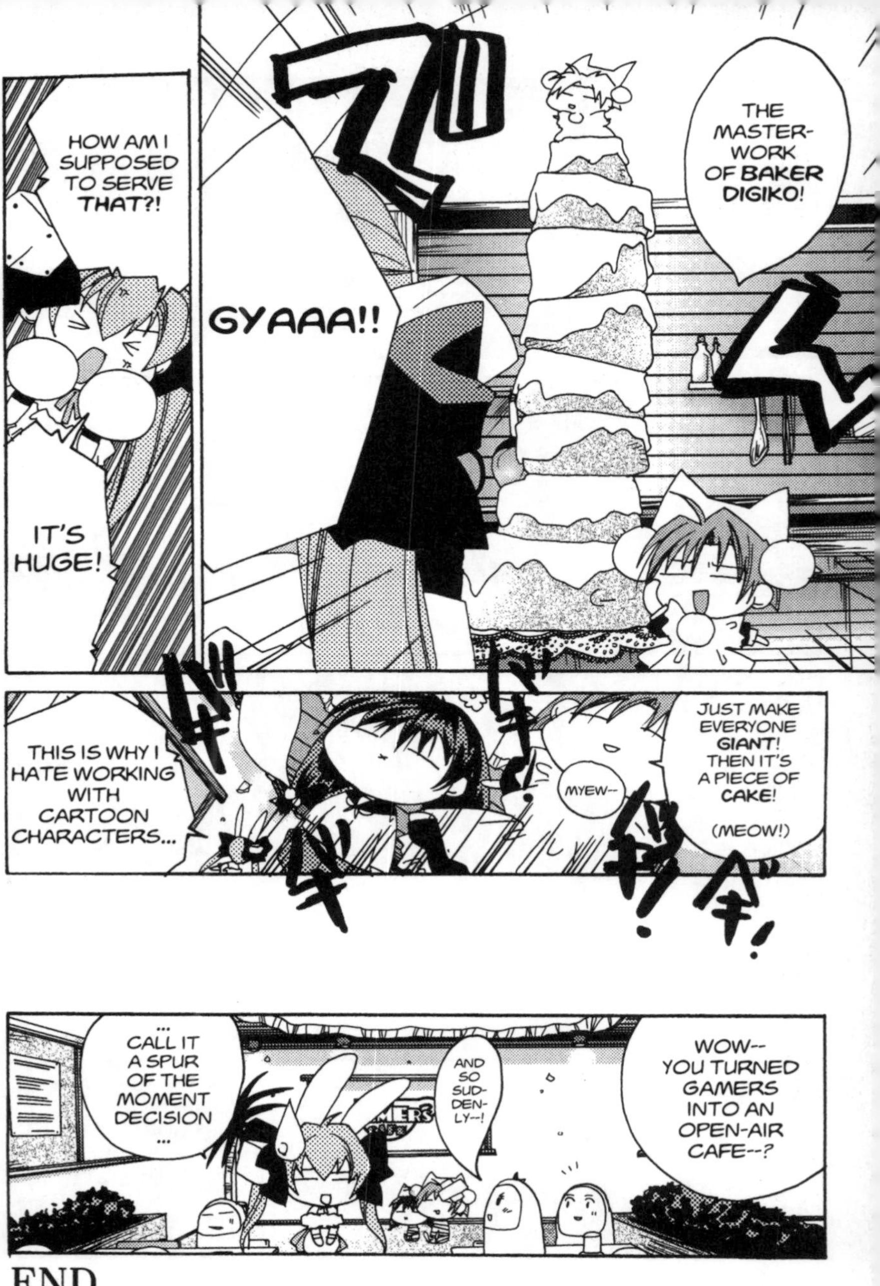
THE MASTERWORK OF BAKER DIGIKO!
GYAAA!!
HOW AM I SUPPOSED TO SERVE THAT?!
IT'S HUGE!
JUST MAKE EVERYONE GIANT! THEN IT'S A PIECE OF CAKE! (MEOW!)
MYEW--
THIS IS WHY I HATE WORKING WITH CARTOON CHARACTERS...
WOW-- YOU TURNED GAMERS INTO AN OPEN-AIR CAFE--?
AND SO SUDDENLY--!
... CALL IT A SPUR OF THE MOMENT DECISION ...

END

Di Gi Charat

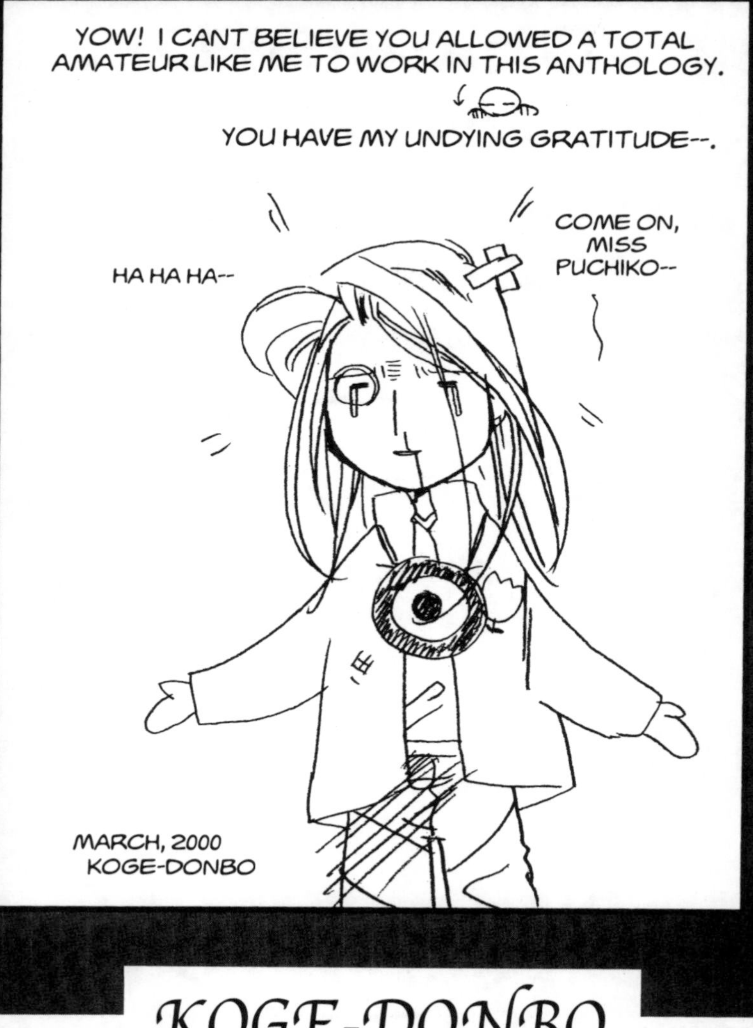
YOW! I CANT BELIEVE YOU ALLOWED A TOTAL AMATEUR LIKE ME TO WORK IN THIS ANTHOLOGY.
YOU HAVE MY UNDYING GRATITUDE--.
COME ON, MISS PUCHIKO--
HA HA HA--
MARCH, 2000
KOGE-DONBO

KOGE-DONBO

"EVEN GEMA
CAN BE
DISGUISED
WITH A
WELL-PLACED
BLOWPIPE."

Di Gi Charat

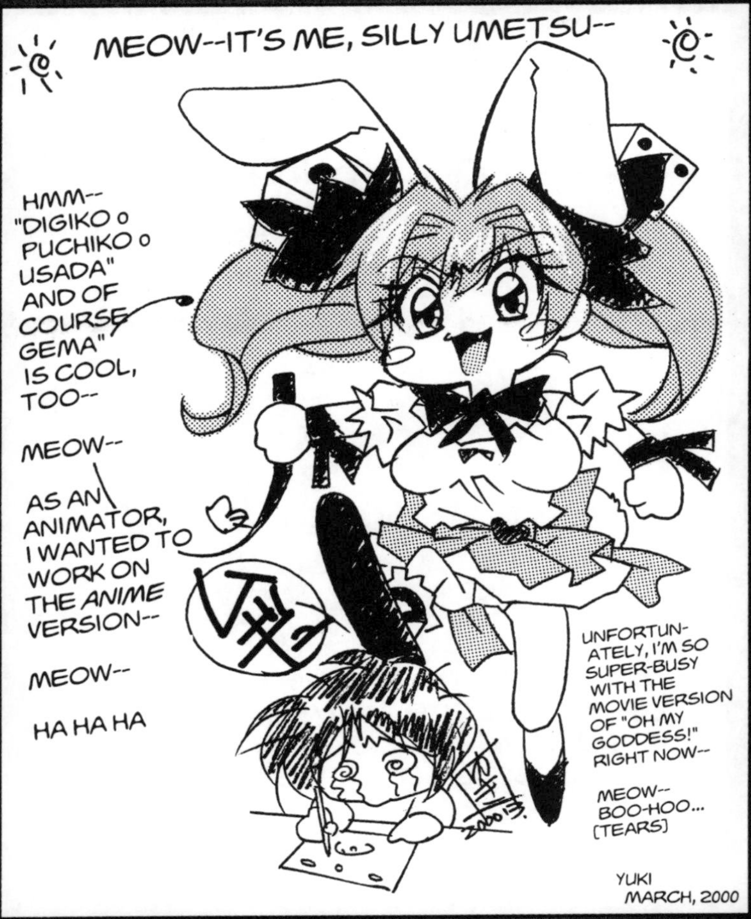

YUKI KIRIGA

A comment about Di Gi Charat

KAPPA:
"I WISH I COULD DRAW USADA AND MURATAKU..."

I'M SORRY. I GUESS I'M REALLY OUT OF PLACE HERE. MAYBE I SHOULDN'T PUSH MY LUCK. SORRY TO HAVE SULLIED YOUR EYES--

KURIMU

KURIMU

The Di Gi Charat Guide to Sound Effects!

As you've undoubtedly noticed, most of the sound effects in ***Di Gi Charat*** are in Japanese. Seeing the various explosions, tantrums and incidental dialogue jump off the page in a foreign language offers a unique experience for readers familiar only with American comics.

Fans of Digiko, Usada and the rest of the gang may applaud our respect for the original source material. Others, however, may be confused by the wildly expressive *koukaon.*

Thus, in an attempt to satisfy everyone, we've compiled this handy glossary. On the following pages you'll find a panel-by-panel account of every Digiko burp and Gema hiccup. In the process, maybe you'll pick up a little bit of Japanese, as well.

4.2	FX: GUI [tug]
5.3	FX: BISHII BISHII BISHII [whack whack whack]
5.11	FX: UFUFUFUFUFU [tee hee hee hee hee]
6.2	FX: GUGUGUGUGU [throttle throttle throttle]
6.4	FX: GAH [yowl]
6.5	FX: KEH [feh]
7.1	FX: BESHI! [slap!]
7.4	POSTER: BIG SALE
8.1	FX: PAA [glow]
8.2	FX: KYA KYA [whee whee]
8.8	FX: BAN [slam]
10.4	FX: KEH [feh]
11.4	FX: ZUN ZUN [stomp stomp]
12.2	T-SHIRT: MEW
13.1.1	FX: DOKA [kick]
13.1.2	FX: BARA BARA [whoosh]
13.6	FX: DOSA! [collide!]
13.7	FX: GATA! [topple!]
14.1	FX: KURU [turn]
14.2	FX: GA-N [d'oh]
14.3	FX: U—[gak!]
14.4	FX: YORO [stagger]
14.5	FX: GASHA-N [crash]
14.7	FX: HAWA HAWAWA HAWA [tremble tremble tremble]
15.2	FX: KYUU [squeek]
16.1	FX DIALOGUE: PIECE OF CAKE, PIECE OF CAKE, MEW—
16.2	FX: PESHI! [slap!]
16.5.1	RECEIPT: FIXED SUM

	POSTAL MONEY ORDER RECEIPT
16.5.2	RECEIPT: FIXED SUM POSTAL MONEY ORDER CERTIFICATE, FIXED SUM POSTAL MONEY ORDER PAYMENT SLIP
16.5.3	ENVELOPE: ENVELOPE
16.6	FX: FUE FUE [uh-huh uh-huh]
16.7	FX: BESHI [whap]
18.3	FX: BOKA BOKA [clobber clobber]
19.2	FX: GA-N! [d'oh!]
20.1.1	FX: GAYA GAYA [chatter chatter]
20.1.2	FX: WAI WA [bustle bustle]
20.4	FX: TATATATA [dash dash dash dash]
20.5	FX: PITA [stop]
20.7	FX: WAI WA [bustle bustle]
20.9	FX: KYORO KYORO [glance glance]
21.2	FX: GACHAA! [ta-daa!]
21.8	SIGN: REMEMBER FIRE SAFETY!
21.10	FX: DIGIKO! DIGIKO!
21.12	FX: DADADADA [stomp stomp stomp]
22.7	FX: NYO—! [mew—!]
23.1	FX: CHI CHI CHI CHI [chirp chirp chirp]
23.3	FX: DOSA [tumble]
23.8	FX: MUKA! [urk!]
24.4	FX: HOW EMBARRASSING
24.5	CAPTION: TOKYO TRANSPORTATION MAP
24.6	FX: GWASSHI! [punch!]
24.10	FX: BUSHU—! [blast!]
24.12	FX: KEH [feh]
24.15	FX: LASER BEAMS FROM THE EYES
25.1.1	SIGN: GAMERS
25.1.2	BANNER: OPEN TODAY
25.4	APRON: MANAGER
26.2	TICKETS: TRIANGLE RAFFLE
27.3	TICKETS: TRIANGLE RAFFLE
28.1	SIGN: PLEASE FEEL FREE TO TAKE ME HOME
29.2	PIECE OF PAPER: DIGIKO
30.2.1	FX: GYU—[push]
30.2.2	FX: MUGYU—[shove]
31.6	FX: U'NYURU U'NYURU [slither slither]
32.3	APRON: MANAGER
33.2.1	POSTER: PETIT-KO
33.2.2	FIRST SIGN: AQUARIAN AGE ACCESSORIES JUST IN!!
33.2.3	SECOND SIGN: CUSTOMERS WHO PURCHASE A BOX OF

63.4.1	FX: UU UU UU [sob sob sob]
63.4.2	FX: CHIRA-N [tinkle]
64.1	FX: PAKAA [pop]
64.2	FX: GYUI-N [voosh]
66	CHARACTER: MA [upside-down wish spell]
69.4	FX: BAFU [bam]
70.1	BLACKBOARD: MINORU HODO ATAMA O TARERU INAHO KANA [the more it ripens, the more the ears of rice will droop]
71.5	FX: BANN [slam]
72.6	FX: SCATTER-BRAINED
73.4	FX: DONN [shove]
73.8	FX: PIJII [twinkle]
74.2	FX: GUII [tug]
74.3	FX: HURURURU [slip]
74.4	FX: BAN [slam]
75.1	FX: BISHII [stomp]
76.2	FX: GYUU [squeeze]
78.1	FX: BON [kaboom]
78.3	ORIGINAL PROVERB: EVEN THE BUDDHA'S FACE WILL LOSE FORM AFTER THE THIRD PROVOCATION
81.1	FX: FUYO [waft]
81.4	FX: PACHIN [sound of snapping fingers]

82.1	FX: PASHII [snatch]
83.1	FX: EYE BEAMS
83.3	FX: MISS DIGIKOOO!
84.1	FX: SHI-N [shhh]
86.1	FX: PONN [poof]
86.3.1	CHARACTER: ABA [short for Abarenbo]
86.3.2	FX: BABAA [zoom]
87.2	FX: PAA-AAAA [literally, the sound of transformation]
88.1	FX: YOBOO [hobble]
89.2	FX: CHAA [click]
89.3	FX: ZUGA-N [kaboom]
89.4	FX: NEKOMA [more]
90	CHARACTERS: MA [upside-down wish spell]
91.1	FX: DON!! [ta-da!!]
91.2.1	FX: BON!! [burn!!]
91.2.2	FX: BI- [zap]
91.4	FX: BII [jab]
91.5	FX: O-!! [yeah!!]
92.3	FX: ORA ORA [wobble wobble]
92.4	FX: GAN [bang]
92.5	FX: GAN [bang]
92.6	FX: PORO PORO [plop plop]
92.7.1	FX: BERI [peel]
92.7.2	FX: BEKO [clop]
92.7.3	FX: GASHA-N [crash]
93.2	FX: GURI GURI GURI [grind grind grind]

93.3 FX: MYEW
93.4.1 FX: GYUMU [squeeze]
93.4.2 FX: BU [hurl]
93.4.3 FX: BU!! [hurl!!]
93.6 FX: BAKO-N!! [kaboom!!]
93.7 FX: TONTEN KANTEN [sound of hammering on metal]

94.1.1 STICKER: SEAL
94.1.2 FIGURE ON RIGHT: POWER SOURCE
94.1.3 FIGURE ON LEFT: FUEL
94.2.1 FX: KAPON [clop]
94.2.2 FX: GABYO-N [tractor beam]
94.3 FX: BOSHUUN!! [boof!!]
94.4 FX: BO-N!! [bong!!]
94.5 FX: MEEOWW
94.6 FX: GASHA-N [crash]
94.7 DIALOGUE FX: SIGH, I'M SO BORED

95.2 FX: GU [growl]
95.3 APRON: MANAGER
95.6.1 FX: GUGYURURURURU [grrrrrowl]
95.6.2 FX: TOBO TOBO [plod plod]

96.1 FX: TATTAKATA [trot trot trot]
96.4 FX: BU [spurt]

97.4 FX: HEH HEH—

98.2 FX: HONWAKA-N [awwww]
98.5 FX: MEOW!
98.6 FX: HO HO HO HO HO

99.1 POSTER: ON SALE IN MAY!!
99.2 FX: HO HO HO
99.3 FX: GASHO-N! [clash!]
99.5.1 FX: FUKABUKA [stern warning]
99.5.2 APRON: MANAGER

100.3 FX: HYO-I [hoist]
100.7.1 FX: BI [zap]
100.7.2 FX: DORON [melt]

101.1 FX: KYAPPIRU-N [ta-daaaaa]

103.1 FX: UHII [heh heh]
103.2 FX: BASHI BASHI BASHI BASHI [slap slap slap slap]
103.3 FX: SHURURU [wrap]

104.2.1 FX: SHUU SHUU SHUU [lash lash lash]
104.2.2 FX: ARA-YOTTO [whoopsie-do]

105.1 T-SHIRTS: DIGIKO
105.2.1 CHART TITLE: SALES
105.2.2 COLUMN ON RIGHT: PUCHIKO
105.2.3 COLUMN IN MIDDLE: RABI EN ROSE WITH USADA CROSSED OUT
105.2.4 COLUMN ON LEFT: DIGIKO
105.3.1 CUSTOMER AT COMPUTER: UHEHE [drooling and laughing]
105.3.2 POSTER: DI GI CHARAT MISSPELLED
105.3.3 CUSTOMER: UHE UHE [more drooling and laughing]
105.3.4 TAG: 1/1 LIFE-SIZE DIGIKO DOLL
105.3.5 PILLOW: DI GI CHARAT MISSPELLED

106.2 FX: PETA PETA [tap tap]
106.3.1 FX: O-HO HO HO HO
106.3.2 FX: TURNED TO STONE

107.2 FX: BE-AM!! [zap!!]

108.2 FX: SHUBIBIBIBIBIBI [zzzaaaappp]

111,1 FX: SHIBIBIBIBI [zzzzap]
111.3.1 FX: ZE-HA [huff pant]
111.3.2 FX: ZE-HA [huff pant]
111.3.3 FX: PUSU... PUSU [sizzle sizzle]

112.1 FX: FUGA—[hiss]
112.2.1 FX: SUKA [swing]
112.2.2 FX: BOKO [clobber]
112.2.3 FX: MUKUU [awaken]
112.3.1 FX: BII [blast]
112.3.2 FX: BIBI BIBI BIBIBI [zzap zzap zzzap]
112.4.1 FX: MUNYAA... [mumble]
112.4.2 FX: PUSU... PUSU [sizzle sizzle]

114.4 FX: PUN PUN [huff puff]

115.1 FX: NYO—HO HO HO [mew—ho ho ho]
115.2 FX: BI [blast]

116.3 FX: WA—[bawl]
116.4 FX: GU—[growl]

117.2.1 FX: JYAA [ta-daa]
117.2.2 POSTER, FROM TOP TO BOTTOM: BREAKFAST, LUNCH, DINNER

118.1.1 FX: BYU [sound of a cold gust of wind]
118.1.2 FX: CHARRI-N [clink]
118.3 FX: BIRO-NN [stretch]

120.2 FX: BII [whirl]
120.4 FX: HAA [gasp]

121.1 FX: AWAWAWA [flail]
121.4 FX: BI [blast]
121.5 FX: CHUN CHUN [chirp chirp]

123.4 FX: GA—[sound of automatic door sliding open]
123.7 APRON: MANAGER

124.4.1 FX: HAH [gasp]
124.4.2 FX: ZANN [stomp]

126.1 FX: JI-N [throb]
126.2 FX: HISHII [hug]

127.2 FX: TOO TOO [trot trot]
127.4 FX: GOSO GOSO [rummage rummage]

128.1 FX: POFU [toss]
128.3 FX: HUH?

130.2 FX: DOKINN [flinch]
130.5 FX: NIYARI [sneer]

135.1 CIRCLE: KIRIGA YUKI
135.2.1 FX: NIKO NIKO [grin grin]
135.2.2 TICKETS: TICKETS
135.2.3 CAPTION: MR. MANAGER
135.3 FX: HYA—[wow—]
135.4.1 FX: KYAHHO [yippee]
135.4.2 FX: KURU KURU [spin spin]
135.4.3 FX: KUSU KUSU [chuckle chuckle]

136.3.1 FX: TSUN TSUN [poke poke]
136.3.2 FX DIALOGUE: WHAT DO YOU THINK YOU'RE DOING? GEMA!

136.4.1 TRAIN: ATAMI
136.4.2 FX: GATAN GOTO-N [clackety-clack]
136.4.3 FX SINGING: ATAMI IS... CALLING TO ME
136.4.4 FX DIALOGUE: GA-N [d'oh]
136.5 FX DIALOGUE: TIRED, SO TIRED
136.6.1 FX DIALOGUE: A-ONE-TWO
136.6.2 FX DIALOGUE: GYOO [d'oh]
136.8 FX: KIRA-N [gleam]

137.1 FX: CHAAPU [splash]
137.2.1 FX: WAI WAI GAYA GAYA [chatter chatter bustle bustle]
137.2.2 FX DIALOGUE: SOMEONE'S COMING
137.3 FX: A—[waaah]
137.4.1 FX DIALOGUE: FUFU [haha]
137.4.2 MONKEY FX: KIKIKI [screech]
137.4.3 FOX FX: KO-N [bark]
137.4.4 BIRD FX: CHICHI [cheep cheep]
137.4.5 RACCOON FX: BUI BUI [grunt grunt]
137.7 FX: BOYONN [bounce]

138.2 FX DIALOGUE: SIGH, WHAT WONDERFUL HOT WATER, MEW—
138.4 FX DIALOGUE: EVEN THE COLOR AND SCENT, TOO
138.5 APRON: MANAGER
138.7 APRON: MANAGER
138.8.1 FX DIALOGUE: HELP! THEY'RE INCREASING IN NUMBER
138.8.2 MONKEY FX: UKI [yap]
138.8.3 ANIMAL FX: GA-GA [roar roar]
138.8.4 ANIMAL FX: KYAA KYAA [screech screech]
138.8.5 FOX FX: GAU—[growl]

144.1 FX: DON! [ta-daa!]
144.3 FX: PI [wink]

145.1 FX: KACHAA KACHAA [clatter clatter]
145.4 FX: GESHI GESHI [stomp stomp]
145.6 FX: KOTO [tap]

146.1 FX: SUU [ta-daa]
146.1 MAP: ECONOMIC MAP OF JAPAN
146.3 FX: CHI-N [ka-ching]
146.4 FX: PUSU [inject]
146.5 FX: ZURU ZURU [drag drag]

147.3 FX: DO-N! [boom!]
147.3 FX DIALOGUE: ACTUALLY, WE DON'T HAVE THE TIME TO BAKE SUCH THINGS, MEW

148.1 FX: DEN [ta-daa]
148.3.1 FX: BEKI! BAKI! [crack! crack!]
148.3.2 FX: BAKI BAKI BAKI [crack crack crack]

151 FX: MUGYUU [squish]

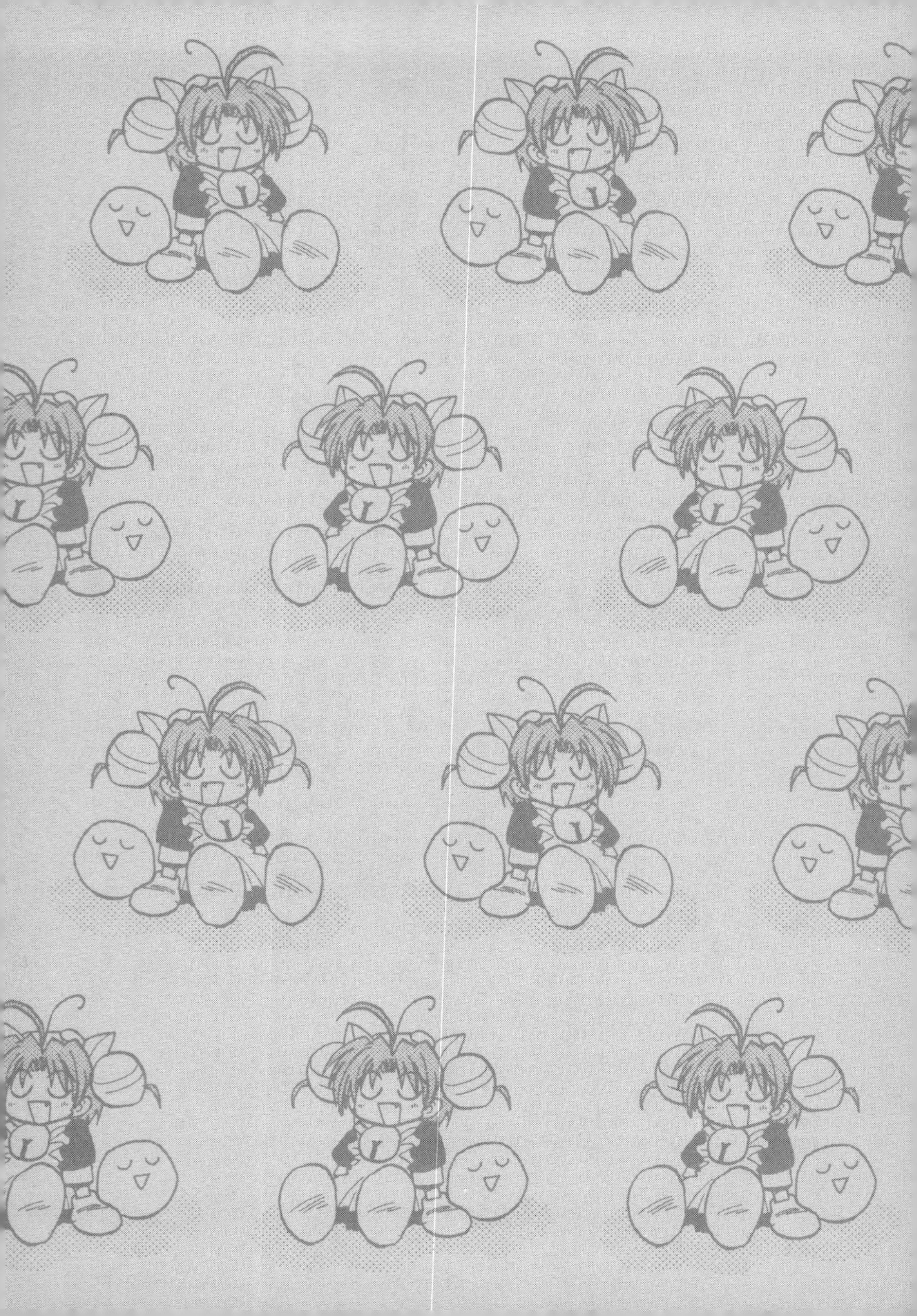